DISCOVER 6

Welcome to Seville and Andalucía..... 8

Reasons to Love Seville
and Andalucía 10

Explore Seville and Andalucía 14

Seville and Andalucía Itineraries.........16

Seville and Andalucía Your Way.........26

A Year in Seville and Andalucía 46

A Brief History..48

EXPERIENCE SEVILLE 54

El Arenal 62

Santa Cruz...72

La Macarena 94

Parque María Luisa 106

Across the River.................................118

EXPERIENCE ANDALUCÍA 126

Huelva and Sevilla...........................132

Córdoba and Jaén.............................148

Cádiz and Málaga 174

Granada and Almería...................210

NEED TO KNOW 236

Before You Go...238

Getting Around.......................................240

Practical Information...........................244

Index...246

Phrase Book...252

Acknowledgments...................................254

Left: One of Seville's ubiquitous orange trees
Previous page: Rowing on the Guadalquivir, with Triana in the background
Cover image: A sunny courtyard in the Generalife, Granada

DISCOVER

Admiring Granada from the Alhambra

Welcome to Seville and Andalucía......8

Reasons to Love
Seville and Andalucía................................10

Explore Seville and Andalucía 14

Seville and Andalucía Itineraries..........16

Seville and Andalucía Your Way..........26

A Year in Seville and Andalucía...........46

A Brief History..48

WELCOME TO
SEVILLE AND
ANDALUCÍA

Staccato handclaps and strumming guitars. Moorish monuments, bejewelled with glinting *azulejos*. Gleaming glasses of sherry savoured beneath heady orange trees on shaded patios. Whatever your dream trip to Seville and Andalucía includes, this DK Eyewitness travel guide is the perfect companion.

1 Picking ripe green olives.

2 A typical street scene in Seville, with a moped parked outside a church.

3 A whitewashed square in Mijas on the Costa del Sol.

4 Córdoba, crowned by the silhouette of La Mezquita.

Think of Andalucía and the high-rise resorts along the Costa del Sol – the sunny coast – may be the first thing that comes to mind. But venture away from here and you'll find empty, windswept Atlantic shores, undulating hills awash with olive trees and rugged mountain ranges clothed with pine forests. This diverse landscape offers a whole host of adventures, from kitesurfing to skiing, golfing to horse riding.

Southern Spain's monumental cities and enchanting *pueblos blancos*, too, are not to be missed. Endlessly romantic Seville – the capital of the *comunidad autónoma* – is a bewitching labyrinth of geranium-filled streets and orange-scented plazas. As the ancestral home of tapas, the city is firmly on the foodie trail. Andalucía's Moorish past is writ large upon the cityscape,

particularly at the Real Alcázar – a stunning fusion of Islamic and Christian architecture. The spirit of al-Andalus is also strong in Córdoba, particularly as you walk beneath the hundreds of striped arches in La Mezquita, its striking mosque-cathedral, and in Granada, where the beguiling Alhambra stands proud above the town below.

So, where to start? We've broken Andalucía down into easily navigable chapters, with detailed itineraries, expert local knowledge and colourful comprehensive maps to help you plan the perfect visit. Whether you're staying for a weekend, a week or longer, this Eyewitness guide will ensure that you see the very best that the region has to offer. Enjoy the book, and enjoy Seville and Andalucía.

REASONS TO LOVE
SEVILLE AND
ANDALUCÍA

Riotous festivals, breathtaking architecture, fiery flamenco, tasty tapas and delectable drinks: there are so many reasons to love Seville and Andalucía. Here, we pick some of our favourites.

1 ORANGES

The heavenly scent of orange blossoms envelops Andalucía's cities in spring. Savour a glass of sherry on a citrus-perfumed square, lined with trees bearing lantern-like fruits.

LA MEZQUITA *2*

Córdoba's mosque is one of the world's finest examples of Islamic architecture *(p154)*. Walk between the 856 columns, in the hypostyle hall, admiring the red-and-white arches.

3 THE TAPEO

As the birthplace of tapas, Andalucía offers a huge variety of these bite-sized dishes, from traditional *jamón ibérico* to sushi-inspired creations *(p32)*. Learn the art of the *tapeo* – tapas bar hopping – in Granada.

FESTIVALS *4*

Did someone say party? Andalucía offers a fiesta for every season, with a packed calendar of festivals celebrating historical events, regional traditions, religious beliefs and more *(p46)*.

PUEBLOS BLANCOS *5*

Charming "white towns", perched on hilltops, invite exploration and are the perfect place to soak up local life *(p208)*. Salobreña is our favourite *(p224)*.

BEACHES *6*

From deserted dunes to bustling beach bars, endless Atlantic stretches to stunning Mediterranean coves, beach lovers are spoilt for choice in Andalucía *(p40)*.

THE ALHAMBRA *7*

Lope de Vega asked, "If what is beneath my feet is paradise, then what is the Alhambra? Heaven?" Decide for yourself whether the Spanish playwright was right on a night tour *(p216)*.

REAL ALCÁZAR *8*

With its intricately carved horseshoe-shaped arches, gilded ceiling beams and jewel-like *azulejos*, this Mudéjar palace will transport you back to al-Andalus *(p78)*.

9 PARQUE NACIONAL DE DOÑANA

Within this national park's varied landscape of marshlands, pine forests and sand dunes, you'll spot pink flamingos, graceful deer and, if you're lucky, the Iberian lynx *(p136)*.

10 FLAMENCO

The soul of Andalucía is encapsulated in flamenco *(p44)*. Seek out an authentic *peña* to feel the *duende* – the soul of flamenco – or take a class to learn how to stomp and clap.

THE RUGGED SIERRAS 11

The region's mountain ranges offer a plethora of outdoor activities *(p42)*. Hike through pine forests, look out for golden eagles or try your hand at chestnut foraging.

SAVOURING SHERRY 12

From dry and crisp finos to fragrant olorosos, discover the subtleties of this fortified wine in the "Sherry Triangle" *(p35)*. Head to a *bodega* for a tour and tasting.

EXPLORE
SEVILLE AND
ANDALUCÍA

This guide divides Seville and Andalucía into five colour-coded sightseeing areas, as shown on this map. Find out more about Seville on page 58 and Andalucía on page 128.

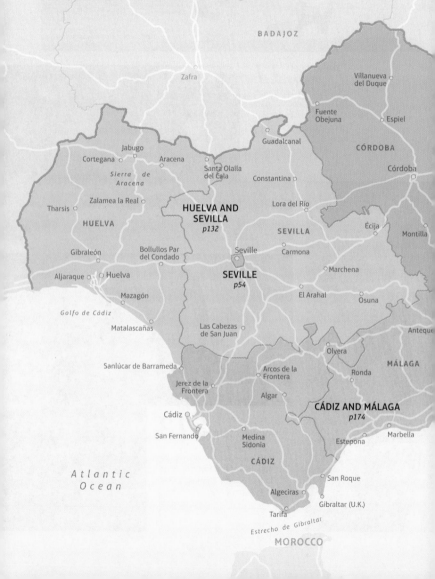

BADAJOZ

Zafra

Villanueva
del Duque

Fuente
Obejuna

Espiel

Guadalcanal

CÓRDOBA

Jabugo

Cortegana

Aracena

Santa Olalla
del Cala

Constantina

Córdoba

Sierra de
Aracena

Tharsis

Zalamea la Real

**HUELVA AND
SEVILLA**
p132

Lora del Río

HUELVA

SEVILLA

Écija

Montilla

Gibraleón

Bollullos Par
del Condado

Seville

Carmona

Aljaraque

Huelva

SEVILLE
p54

Marchena

Mazagón

El Arahal

Osuna

Golfo de Cádiz

Matalascañas

Las Cabezas
de San Juan

Antequer

Olvera

MÁLAGA

Sanlúcar de Barrameda

Arcos de la
Frontera

Ronda

Jerez de la
Frontera

Algar

CÁDIZ AND MÁLAGA
p174

Cádiz

San Fernando

Medina
Sidonia

Estepona

Marbella

CÁDIZ

*Atlantic
Ocean*

San Roque

Algeciras

Gibraltar (U.K.)

Tarifa

Estrecho de Gibraltar

MOROCCO

Aranjuez

Toledo

CIUDAD REAL

Consuegra

Malagón

Ciudad Real

Manzanares

Puertollano

IRELAND UNITED KINGDOM NETHER-LANDS GERMANY

BELGIUM

Atlantic Ocean

FRANCE SWITZ.

ITALY

PORTUGAL

Madrid

SPAIN

Barcelona

Seville

ANDALUCÍA

MOROCCO ALGERIA TUNISIA

SOUTHWEST EUROPE

Sierra Morena

La Carolina

Puerto de Génave

Bailén

Andújar

Baeza

Villacarrillo

Úbeda

Púsble de Don Fabrique

MURCIA

Bujalance

CÓRDOBA AND JAÉN
p148

Huéscar

María

JAÉN

Baena

Jaén

Baza

Cúllar

Alcaudete

Albox

Diezma

Guadix

GRANADA AND ALMERÍA
p210

ALMERÍA

Los Lobos

Archidona

Granada

Sierra Nevada

Gérgal

Carboneras

Sierra de Loja

GRANADA

Ugíjar

Tabernas

álaga

Lanjarón

Berja

Almería

Nerja

Motril

Adra

San José

Costa del Sol

Mediterranean Sea

0 kilometres   50

0 miles   50

N

←

1 Climbing up to the top of the Metropol Parasol.

2 La Giralda, towering above the cathedral.

3 Real Alcázar's gardens.

4 Mariatrifulca restaurant.

Andalucía offers endless options for exploration, from weekends in Seville to longer tours taking in the region's other cities and the surrounding countryside. Wherever you choose to go, our hand-picked itineraries will help you plan the perfect trip.

24 HOURS
in Seville

▌ *Morning*

Fuel up with a traditional breakfast of *jamón ibérico* on toast with freshly squeezed orange juice at Crème de la Crème *(Calle Regina 1; www.lacremedela creme.es)*. Then, head for the waffle-like structure soaring above the plaza in front of you – the Metropol Parasol *(p103)*. Wander through the market on the ground floor, before marvelling at the Roman remains housed in the Antiquarium Museum. Next, jet up to the Observation Deck for amazing views of the cityscape. Your ticket entitles you to a free drink at the café-bar, so sip a coffee while you soak up the panorama. Back at street level, window-shop along Calle Sierpes *(p81)* and admire the Ayuntamiento *(p80)* as you pass through the Plaza de San Francisco on your way to Seville Cathedral and La Giralda *(p76)*. There's often a queue to get in so it's best to buy your ticket online in advance. Explore the world's largest Gothic cathedral with an audio guide, admiring its soaring central nave and 80 side chapels. After taking in the interior, climb to the top of La Giralda and look down on the rows of orange trees in the Patio de los Naranjos below.

▌ *Afternoon*

Donaire Azabache is a good choice for a traditional *Sevilliano* lunch *(p86)*. Order a selection of tapas – note that you can only sit at the outdoor tables if you order from the à la carte menu. Next, make for the Real Alcázar, a stunning example of Mudéjar craftsmanship *(p78)*. Again, it's best to have booked your ticket in advance. After appreciating the intricate plasterwork, ornate tiles and interlaced wood-beamed ceilings – the Salón de Embajadores is particularly arresting – make for the lush gardens. On leaving the palace, pass through the sandy Patio de Banderas and into the heart of Santa Cruz, stopping off in Plaza Venerables for a glass of cold, crisp sherry at Casa Roman *(casaroman sevilla.com)*, before heading back to your hotel to freshen up before dinner.

▌ *Evening*

Stroll along the Río Guadalquivir, crossing over the Puente de Isabel II to Triana *(p120)*. Mariatrifulca is perched right at the end of the bridge, and you can feast on succulent seafood on the rooftop terrace here, while looking out at the illuminated cathedral *(p123)*. Triana is known for its flamenco so why not take in a show after dinner? Casa Anselma is one of the city's most authentic spots, where the crowd sits inches from the impassioned performers *(Calle Pagés del Corro 49; 606 16 25 02)*. Doors don't open until 11:45pm and it can be quite difficult to find – look for the two traditional tiled panels reading "Cafe Refrescos Vinos" above the arched entrance – but this all adds to the clandestine atmosphere.

←

1 The city's skyline at dusk, bathed in golden light.

2 Patio de las Doncellas in the Real Alcázar.

3 Young women dancing the flamenco on the Plaza de España.

4 Café culture on the bustling Calle Sierpes.

2 DAYS
in Seville

Day 1

Morning Arrive early to beat the queue for one of Seville's most recognizable landmarks, La Giralda, the minaret-cum-bell tower next to the vast cathedral *(p76)*. The tomb of Christopher Columbus can be found inside the cathedral, along with a wealth of lavish artworks, but the highlight is the extraordinary view from the top of the tower. Nearby, Donaire Azabache makes an excellent tapas stop – try the succulent *jamón ibérico*, an Andalucían speciality *(p86)*.

Afternoon Walk off your lunch with a gentle stroll through the Jardines de Murillo *(p87)* and the charming Parque María Luisa *(p110)*, pausing on one of its colourful benches to listen to the tinkling fountains. Close by is the former Real Fábrica de Tabacos, the former Royal Tobacco Factory and workplace of Carmen in the opera of the same name. It is now part of the Universidad *(p114)*. Seville features in many operas, and one way to learn more is to take a tour with a soprano, who – with musical accompaniment – will show you the sights that inspired composers *(p114)*.

Evening Round off your journey through Seville's musical heritage at intimate Tablao El Arenal *(tablaoelarenal.com)*. Sip on rioja and savour the delicate dishes as you watch the swirling skirts, stamping feet and strumming fingers of the guitarists. Flamenco is the city's heart and soul.

Day 2

Morning Start your day admiring the superb art collection in the Museo de Bellas Artes *(p66)*. Seek out *La Servilleta*, an image of the Virgin and Child, which is said to have been painted on a napkin *(servilleta)*. Next, window-shop along Calle Sierpes, admiring the flamenco dresses and *mantilla* shawls *(p81)*. Cross over the river to soulful Triana – the city's working-class heart *(p120)*. Head straight for the neighbourhood's bustling market and discover its best-loved tapas bars on a culinary walking tour, starting at 12:30pm *(www.azahar-sevilla.com)*.

Afternoon While away the remainder of the afternoon in the Barrio Santa Cruz *(p72)*, an enchanting warren of narrow lanes lined with whitewashed houses sporting geranium-filled balconies. Wrought-iron gates give tempting glimpses of the leafy patios and gardens so typical of this neighbourhood. Don't miss out on visiting the grand courtyard and garden of the Casa de Pilatos *(p89)*, a breathtaking mansion that is still home to the Dukes of Medinaceli.

Evening For an unforgettable experience, book a night visit to the sumptuous Real Alcázar *(p78)*, where actors posing as Fernando III, Isabel la Católica or Lope de Vega will act as your guide. After exploring this must-see Mudéjar sight, join the locals for a late dinner at Vinería San Telmo, famous for its creative tapas *(p86)*.

←

1 Cycling along the river bank, opposite Triana.

2 The Puente Nuevo, linking the two sides of Ronda.

3 A decorated house in the Albaicín, Granada.

4 An art installation in Málaga's city centre.

5 DAYS
in Andalucía

Day 1

The spirit of old al-Andalus is strongest in Granada (p214). Start your day in the old Moorish neighbourhood of the Albaicín (p220), whose narrow lanes are lined with craft shops, bathhouses and cafés. Stop for lunch at Mirador de Morayma (p214), which has fabulous views, then head up to explore the Alhambra's honeycomb-like rooms and arcaded patios (p216), as well as the Generalife gardens (p218). In the evening, take in a clandestine flamenco show in one of the caves in Sacromonte, where the art form originated. We love Zambra Maria la Canastera, where the eponymous dancer performed (www.marialacanastera.com).

Day 2

A two-hour drive west of Granada is Córdoba (p152). When you reach the city, head straight for the Mercado Victoria – a gourmet food hall (p153). At Córdoba's heart is the Mezquita (p154), where you can easily spend a couple of hours walking beneath the hallowed arches. Next, wander the narrow lanes of the former Jewish Quarter to the Sinagoga (p152). Take in the beautiful interior before seeking out the statue of Maimonides, the philosopher. Finish your day with supper at Bodegas Campos (www.bodegascampos.com), where you can dine in the library, office or the Sala los Célebres (Room of Celebrities).

Day 3

Wake up early to allow yourself plenty of time to explore your next stop, Seville (p54). After the 90-minute drive there, potter around the evocative Barrio Santa Cruz (p72) and climb La Giralda (p76). When you're peckish, nibble on tapas at time-warped Casa Plácido (www.casaplacido.es). Allow a couple of hours to visit the Real Alcázar, one of Spain's most dazzling buildings (p78). In the evening, cross the river to Triana for some flamenco (p120).

Day 4

It's best to arrive early in Ronda (p184), so that you beat the coach-trippers. It's a beautiful city in its own right, perched astride a gorge, but its bullring steals the show. With its colonnaded stands curving around the vast sandy stage, it seems straight out of Ancient Rome. Then, stroll across the vertigo-inducing Puente Nuevo for lunch at Bardal (www.restaurantebardal.com) in the Old Town. It's a 90-minute drive from Ronda to Málaga (p186). Once you reach the city, make for the Museo Picasso Málaga (p188), before seeking out an old-school seafood bar. Our favourite is El Tintero II, where the waiters carry around dishes for diners to peruse (Avenida Salvador Allende 340; 952 20 68 26).

Day 5

Begin your final day with a visit to the imposing Alcazaba (p189), and perhaps a little window-shopping along the nearby Calle Marqués de Larios. Then, it's time to head for the beach at El Pedregalejo for a long lunch at one of the seafood restaurants, before you sleep it off in the shade. The Centre Pompidou Málaga is open until 8pm so explore this collection of contemporary art once the sun has gone down (p188). Round off your tour with a tasty traditional meal of crispy-skinned lamb at Restaurante Miguel (www.restaurantemiguel.es).

→

1 Horses grazing in El Rocío.

2 The Gruta de las Maravillas.

3 Cycling along a Vía Verde, a railway turned cycle path.

4 Entering the Mezquita in Córdoba.

On this driving tour of Andalucía's wild countryside, you'll get the chance to try a variety of outdoor activities. All of the suggested pursuits are suitable for those with no prior experience and can be adapted for children.

10 DAYS
in Andalucía

Day 1

After setting off from Seville, relish a hearty breakfast at La Mundana in Camas, just outside the city *(lamundana-cafe. negocio.site)*. Next, drive 70 km (43 miles) west to El Rocío *(p144)*. This village, with its sandy streets, is situated at the edge of the Parque Nacional de Doñana *(p136)*, so check out the flamingos on the marshlands before having lunch at Aires de Doñana *(p147)*. The menu celebrates local ingredients, including white prawns. Spend the afternoon on a four-wheel drive tour of the national park, keeping your eyes peeled for the ever elusive lynx. Then, hit the sack in one of Complejo Pequeño Rocío's cottages *(p141)*.

Day 2

Follow the coast towards Huelva, taking a break in Mazagón, a 45-minute drive away, to feel the sand between your toes *(p140)*. After some beach time, journey north to Aracena, the main town in the Sierra de Aracena *(p138)*. Here, you can fill up on *jamón iberico* and other regional specialities at the Restaurante Tapas Jesús Carrión *(p138)*. Allow an hour to visit the stunning Gruta de las Maravillas caves and the nearby laundry station, with its old stone tubs, then wander around the pretty town centre, enveloped by chestnut trees. Spend the night at the Hotel Convento Aracena & Spa, a 17th-century convent *(www.hotelconventoaracena.es)*.

Day 3

Snake your way through mountain villages to Cazalla de la Sierra in the Sierra Norte *(p145)*, stopping off for picnic supplies at Embutidos y Quesos Corral *(p145)*. Hire bikes from Bicicletas Verde Vía *(www. bicicletasverdevia.com)* and then follow the 19.5-km (12-mile) route to Cerro de Hierro alongside the bubbling cascades of the Hueznar river. Find a nice spot to picnic along the way. Before heading back to Cazalla de la Sierra to return your bike, order some tapas at Bar La Plaza *(Plaza de España s/n, San Nicolás del Puerto)*. The Sierra Norte is a UNESCO Starlight Reserve, so be sure to gaze up at the spectacularly starry sky before going to bed at family-run hotel Las Navezuelas *(www.lasnavezuelas.com)*.

Day 4

Hit the road to Córdoba *(p152)*, which is just two hours away. Take a stroll along the river before lunch at Casa Pepe de la Judería, located right in the heart of the city's historic quarter *(p153)*. Afterwards, indulge with a "Water Journey" in the spa Hammam Al Ándalus *(www.cordoba. hammamalandalus.com)*. Relax, you've earned it! Round off the evening with sundowners and an innovative meal on the terrace at painfully cool Horno San Luís *(www.hornosanluis.com)*. Historic Hospedería del Atalia is a great hotel choice *(www.hospederiadelatalia.com)*.

→

1

2

3

Day 5

What better way to experience Córdoba's market than taking a tour? Foodie & Experiences will guide you around the stalls, helping you to select the freshest ingredients, before teaching you how to create traditional Spanish dishes *(foodie andexperiences.com)*. It's all rounded off with a decadent four-course lunch, accompanied by Andalucían white wine. While away the afternoon roaming the quaint cobblestone streets of the city centre, stumbling upon lovely patios overflowing with colourful flowers, before setting off for Benameji. Savour the dining experience of Mesón Puerta del Convento, which sometimes features live entertainment *(mesonpuertadelconvento. com)* and then settle down for the night at Posada de Momo *(laposadademomo.es)*.

Day 6

A day full of adventure is in store so have a big breakfast at Bar Puerta del Sol before setting off *(puerta-del-sol-bar-and-grill.negocio.site)*. Report to OcioAventura Cerro Gordo in Cuevas Bajas for your

adrenaline-fuelled itinerary *(www.ocio aventuracerrogordo.co.uk)*. Go abseiling through precipitous gorges to the river bank below, enjoy a barbecue lunch and then conquer the rapids while whitewater rafting. After drying off, head to Antequera, a 30-minute drive away *(p200)*. Jamonería Fuentes is the perfect place to stock up on tomorrow's picnic provisions *(Calle San Agustín 8)*. After such a full-on day, you'll probably fall asleep as soon as your head hits the pillow at Hotel Infante Antequera *(www.hotelinfanteantequera.com)*.

Day 7

Be sure to book your ticket for today's challenge – the Caminito del Rey – well in advance *(p197)*. After the hour-long drive there, you'll skirt the edge of steep chasms over 100 m (330 ft) above the Guadalhorce river on this skyscraping boardwalk. Next, rent a kayak to explore the nearby Embalse Conde de Guadalhorce, an astonishingly blue reservoir *(www. zonarecreativalaisla.com)*. When it's time for dinner, Casa Abilio in Álora *(p200)* serves up sustainable seasonal dishes

① Foodie & Experiences in Córdoba.
② Whitewater rafting in Cuevas Bajas.
③ Embalse Conde de Guadalhorce.
④ Puerto Deportivo El Candado.
⑤ The Playa Burriana in Nerja.
⑥ Mountain biking in Las Alpujarras.

(www.restaurantecasaabilio.com). Stay at nearby B&B Casa Arroyo de la Montaña *(Partido de Sabinal 5; 952 11 21 72)*.

Day 8

After a hearty breakfast at the B&B, it's time to hit the road. The Real Golf Club el Candado is just an hour's drive away and gives golfers the opportunity to perfect their swing while taking in some gorgeous views of the Mediterranean *(www.clubelcandado.com)*. Sink nine holes before ordering lunch at the club's restaurant. After admiring it from afar, it's time to explore the Med at close quarters on a four-hour boat tour from Puerto Deportivo El Candado, on the outskirts of Málaga *(p186)*. You'll take in the coastline before heading out onto the high seas for a dip and, if you're lucky, dolphin sightings *(www.malagacharter.com)*. For dinner, try the innovative takes on traditional fare at Mulse Bar & Restaurante in Rincón de la Victoria *(mulse.es)*. Then, rest your head at Balcón de La Cala in La Cala del Moral, which overlooks the beach *(Calle Salvador Dalí 45; 674 73 77 75)*.

Day 9

After a well-deserved lie-in, drive east to Nerja *(p202)* and make your way down to Playa Burriana, where you can rent kayaks to paddle around the local coves *(nerja diving.com)*. Sample some *espetos* (grilled sardines) at Merendero Moreno *(p202)*. In the evening, watch the sunset from El Balcón de Europa, before splashing out on a top-notch meal at Restaurante Jacky *(Calle el Chaparil 7; 952 52 11 38)*. Boutique Hotel Carabeo continues the luxury vibe *(www.hotelcarabeo.com)*.

Day 10

Bubión, at the heart of Las Alpujarras, is a 75-minute drive away *(p234)*. This verdant mountain range is the perfect place to go horse riding. Canter over ancient bridle paths, surrounded by diverse flora and fauna. Sierra Trails will pack a lunch for you to enjoy at a picturesque spot *(www. spain-horse-riding.com)*. Out of the saddle, head into Bubión for regional cuisine at Teide *(Calle Carretera 1; 958 76 30 37)*. Round off your holiday at Hotel Villa de Bubión *(www.villasdeandalucia.com)*.

Golden Age Galleries

Known as the *Siglo de Oro* (Golden Century), the 1600s saw groundbreaking artists, known as the Seville School *(p50)*, operating in the city. The Museo de Bellas Artes *(p66)* houses an extraordinary collection of their works. For the best experience, visit on a Sunday morning when an art market is held in the square and the old and new Seville School sit side by side.

→

Admiring artworks in a light-filled gallery in the Museo de Bellas Artes

SEVILLE AND ANDALUCÍA FOR
ART FANS

With its intense light, diverse landscapes and vibrant traditions, Andalucía has inspired countless artists over the centuries, from Diego Velázquez to Pablo Picasso. Yes, there are plenty of glittering galleries, but there are also more off-beat ways to experience the region's art and crafts scene.

TOP 4 ANDALUCÍAN ARTISTS

Diego Velázquez (1599-1660)
Considered the star of 17th-century painting.

Bartolomé Esteban Murillo (1617-1682)
Master of the Spanish Baroque, Murillo is renowned for his religious artwork.

Luisa Roldan (1652-1706)
"La Roldana" is Spain's first documented female sculptor.

Pablo Picasso (1881-1973)
The most influential modern artist of the 20th century.

Open-air Art

From sombre religious icons to gravity-defying graffiti, you'll find it all in Andalucia's public spaces. Check out the Romantic statuary in Seville's Glorieta de Bécquer arbour *(p110)*. Málaga is known for its funky street art *(p186)*. Seek out OBEY's 25-m- (80-ft-) tall *Paz y Libertad* mural (2013).

→

Glorieta de Bécquer arbour (1911), a tribute to the poet

INSIDER TIP
Pick Up Your Paintbrush

Why not try your hand at creating your own masterpiece on a painting holiday? Paint Andalucía *(paint-andalucia.com)* in the little village of Torrox will show you the ropes.

Modern Málaga

Andalucía's art scene had a second "golden age" in the 20th century, with artists such as Pablo Picasso on the scene. The Museo Casa Natal de Picasso *(p188)* explores the artist's early life, while the Museo Picasso Málaga *(p188)* shows his transition from Realism to Cubism. If you love contemporary art, make for the Centre Pompidou nearby.

↑ The exterior of the Museo Picasso Málaga, dedicated to the artist

Seize the Clay

Andalucía is renowned for its ceramics and Triana is a potter's paradise. The Centro Cerámica Triana displays ceramics dating back to the Moorish occupation *(p120)*. Looking for the perfect souvenir? Why not pick up something from Ceramica Ruíz *(www.ceramicaruiz.es)* or, better yet, paint your own ceramic tile at Barro Azul *(p120)*.

←

Decorating ceramic tiles with colourful patterns at Barro Azul in Triana

Super Markets

Arts and crafts markets pop up every day throughout the region, from Córdoba to Cádiz. You'll find paintings, pottery and everything in between at the Mercado Paseo de Arte, held on weekends in Triana. We Love Granada Market erects stalls along Paseo de las Tristes once a month.

→

An artisan jewellery stall at the We Love Granada Market

Glitzy Gothic

Vaulted ceilings, stained-glass windows and twisted spires were the height of fashion in the 15th century. The finest expression of the Gothic style in Andalucía is also the largest Gothic church in the world: Seville Cathedral *(p76)*. Discover the secrets of its construction on a walking tour of its terraced rooftops.

←

An ornamented stone balustrade on the roof of Seville Cathedral

SEVILLE AND ANDALUCÍA FOR
ARCHITECTURE

Soaring Gothic cathedrals, a wealth of Moorish treasures *(p30)* and divisive contemporary constructions: the region's monuments represent the whole spectrum of architectural styles. Marvel at the façades, scale the towers and walk the rooftops to get under the skin of Andalucía.

TOP 3 ANDALUCÍAN ARCHITECTS

Hernán Ruiz the Younger (1514-1569)
Along with his father and son (all of the same name), Ruiz designed part of Cordoba's mighty Mezquita *(p154)*.

Eufrasio López de Rojas (1628-1684)
The Baroque architect who masterminded the 17th-century additions to Jaén Cathedral *(p158)*.

Aníbal González (1876-1929)
His flamboyant works include the photogenic Plaza de España *(p112)*.

The Regal Renaissance

In the 16th century, buildings were graced with a harmonious balance of fine detail and good taste. Seville's great monument to the Age of Discovery, the Archivo de Indias *(p86)*, is a prime example of this style. Climb the impressive marble stairs to pore over ancient maps in the elegant vaulted reading rooms. With its soaring twin towers and ornate façade, Jaén's cathedral is another Renaissance masterpiece *(p158)*. Don't miss the sacristy, with its religious paintings, sculptures and silverwork.

→

The main organ beneath the soaring vaulting in Jaén's cathedral

↑ The sun setting over Seville, seen from the Metropol Parasol

Modern Andalucían Architecture

Although Seville and Andalucía are home to an embarrassment of historical riches, many of the region's most striking buildings are looking firmly towards the future. When you first set eyes on the Metropol Parasol *(p103)* it won't be hard to understand why the locals call it *Las Setas* – "The Mushrooms". Designed by Jürgen Mayer, it's formed of six toadstool-shaped wooden pavilions sheltering a market, museum, restaurant and a sweeping walkway. Book a ticket for one of the last entry slots so that you can enjoy a drink at the rooftop bar as the sun sets over the city below.

⛰ GREAT VIEW
Torre de Force

The highest point in Seville is the modern Torre Sevilla *(p124)*, which reaches 180 m (590 ft) into the sky. For the best view of the tower itself, head to the top of the adjacent shopping centre.

Something Old, Something New

Andalucía's long history as a cultural crossroads led to the creation of entirely new styles of architecture. The 19th century saw a Mudéjar revival – the fusion of Moorish and European tastes and techniques. Head for Seville's Parque María Luisa and rent a rowing boat to take in the Neo-Mudéjar Plaza de España *(p112)*, admiring its curving colonnades, bubbling fountains and beautiful *azulejo* ceramics.

A rowing boat on the water, and *(inset)* the curving Plaza de España ↑

Fearsome Fortresses

Nowhere is the might of the Moors more evident than in their impenetrable fortresses. One of the most dramatic examples is Málaga's Alcazaba, which was built on a tree-covered mountainside over the ruins of a Roman town. Book a ticket to a drama or music performance in the amphitheatre below the fortress to soak up the evocative surroundings (p189). Another picturesque example is Almería's Alcazaba. Here, hulking walls conceal landscaped gardens bursting with fragrant plants (p222). It's the perfect spot for an afternoon stroll.

SEVILLE AND ANDALUCÍA FOR
MOORISH MARVELS

For all the myriad architectural styles that can be enjoyed in Seville and Andalucía, there's one associated with the region more than any other: that of the Moors. Explore any one of Andalucía's many Moorish buildings to be transported back to the age of al-Andalus.

🔍 HIDDEN GEM
The Medina Azahara

Most of Andalucía's great Moorish buildings still stand proud at the heart of modern cities, but some have been left to the sands of time. The ghostly ruins of Medina Azahara, west of Córdoba, are all that remain of a mosque, gardens and royal palaces (p164).

Places of Worship

Many mosques became churches after the reconquista. Nowhere exhibits this religious syncretism quite like the Mezquita (p154). Here, a 16th-century cathedral sits beside a Moorish prayer hall, lined with row upon row of candy-cane-like arches.

→

The red-and-white striped Caliphal arches in the Mezquita, Córdoba

GREAT VIEW
A View with Some Welly

The most iconic viewpoint in Granada is undoubtedly the Mirador de San Nicolás. Here, the Alhambra is seen rising from the dark forest of elms planted by (of all people) the Duke of Wellington in 1812. It's particularly gorgeous at sunset.

←

Málaga's Alcazaba, towering above Roman ruins

Impressive Towers

Whether in the soaring minarets of their mosques or the looming towers which stood guard over their fortresses, Moorish architects reached for the heavens. Keeping watch over Seville's old city walls, on the banks of the Guadalquivir river, is the Torre del Oro *(p69)*. Venture inside the 12-sided tower for a great view of Triana over the battlements.

Seville's Torre del Oro, surrounded by palm trees ↑

Opulent Palaces

The architects of the Alhambra set out to create paradise on Earth, and it seems that they succeeded *(p216)*. Take a tour of the Nasrid Palaces, at the heart of the complex, to learn about the design. Visiting at night, when the patios are atmospherically lit, is an unforgettable experience.

↑ Stucco framing a window in the Nasrid Palaces, the Alhambra

Take a Tapeo

Sevillanos will tell you that their city invented tapas, but you'll have the opportunity to enjoy these delightful mouthfuls all over Andalucía. Córdoba *(p152)*, for example, is famed for its sheep's milk cheese, while *tortillitas de camarones* (prawn fritters) are a speciality of Cádiz *(p180)*. The *tapeo* (tapas bar hopping) is the classic way to spend an Andalucían evening, and in Granada, where they still do things the old-fashioned way, you get a free *tapa* with every drink *(p214)*.

→

An inviting tapas bar serving traditional dishes in central Granada

SEVILLE AND ANDALUCÍA FOR
FOODIES

Many of Spain's most beloved culinary traditions reach their crowning glory in Andalucía. Most famously of all, this is the home – if you believe the locals, at least – of tapas, those tiny appetizers offering the perfect opportunity to experience a little bit of everything.

Vitamin Sea

As you would expect from a region with both an Atlantic and Mediterranean coastline, Andalucía has an impressive daily catch. Savour fried *choco* (cuttlefish), *coquinas* (clams) simmered in garlic and white wine, and tuna, particularly in Barbate *(p193)*. We suspect that you'll enjoy Andalucía's seafood so much that you'll want to recreate it at home. Learn to whip up a paella with Cooking Olé *(www.cooking ole.com)*, or create fishy tapas with Spain Food Sherpas in Málaga *(www.spainfood sherpas.com)*.

←

A hearty portion of paella, served at a restaurant in Seville

The Great Outdoors

The beautiful Andalucían countryside is responsible for some of the region's tastiest dishes. You'll see black Iberian pigs roaming the region's hillsides and fields. Reared on a special acorn diet, these pigs are to thank for *jamón ibérico*, the tasty cured ham that locals feast on both at breakfast and on the *tapeo*. Cheese also features heavily in Andalucían cuisine, with many different varieties produced across the region. Visit Finca Los Robledos, an organic farm in the Sierra de Aracena *(p138)*, to learn all about the strong, hard cheese made here from goat's milk *(Carretera Castanuelos s/n; 658 52 88 00)*.

INSIDER TIP
Cooking Up A Storm

A cookery course is the perfect way to take some of the unique flavours of Andalucían cuisine home with you. Seville's Taller Andaluz de Cocina will see you shop for ingredients at a local market before getting to grips with gazpacho, *carillada* (pork cheek) and other Andalucían classics *(www.tallerandaluz decocina.com)*.

← Creamy goat's cheese, from animals grazing in Málaga province

↑ Sitting beneath orange trees at a street-side café in Seville

EAT

With such a wealth of culinary heritage, it'll come as no surprise that Andalucía boasts so many Michelin-starred restaurants. These are our favourites.

Aponiente
🅰B4 🚇Calle Francesco Cossi Ochoa, El Puerto de Santa Maria
🌐aponiente.com

€€€

Noor
🅰D3 🚇Calle Pablo Ruiz Picasso 8, Córdoba
🌐noorrestaurant.es

€€€

Overflowing With Oranges

Perhaps no food is more evocative of Seville than oranges, but think twice before plucking one off a tree – these bitter fruits are only good for marmalade. Sweet oranges are grown elsewhere in Andalucía and Coín hosts an annual festival each May to celebrate the harvest *(www.turismocoin.com)*.

Get Crafty

When the mercury begins to rise, many Andalucíans forgo *fino* in favour of a refreshing beer. Many towns and cities have breweries, including Seville. Sip the city's best brews at Cervezas Río Azul (*www.cervezasrioazul.com*) or Maquila (*Calle Delgado 4; 955 18 23 20*). A Córdoba hotspot is Cervezas Califa, where you can sample everything from stouts to wheat beers (*www.cervezas califa.com*).

→

Gleaming fermentation tanks used to make beer at Cervezas Río Azul

SEVILLE AND ANDALUCÍA
RAISE A GLASS

Andalucía's searing summer heat makes seeing the sights thirsty work. Fortunately the range of local tipples is as varied as the myriad tapas dishes which invariably accompany them. Whether your preference is for wine, beer, spirits or all three, there's no end of ways to quench your thirst here.

The Spirits of Andalucía

If you like the strong stuff, Andalucía has got you covered. Gin is popular and Málaga, in particular, is the source of some interesting infusions – Simbuya, for instance, produces a gin flavoured with purple carrot (*www.simbuyagin.com*). Brandy is big business in Jerez de la Frontera, with *bodegas* like González Byass offering distillery tours (*p179*). Learn about the sweet, aniseed-flavoured liqueur Anisette at the Anis Museum in Rute (*www.museodelanis.com*) or try Miura, a cherry liqueur made to a centuries-old recipe from a Cazalla de la Sierra convent (*p145*).

←

Old-fashioned barrels in the Anis Museum in Rute, near Lucena

Lighten Up

Sometimes the hot weather calls for something a little lighter, and Andalucíans are experts when it comes to converting their favourite beers and wines into something less heavy. The most famous example is sangria, a red wine, fruit and juice punch, which is drunk only during fiestas by Andalucíans but is served all year round at touristy bars. Less sweet, and more popular among locals, is *tinto de verano*, a chilled spritzer that's equal parts red wine and soda. If the idea of red wine on a hot afternoon doesn't sound appealing, order a *clara* – the Andalucían version of shandy. Fresh lemon juice is sometimes added to give it a refreshing citrusy kick.

← Glasses of *tinto de verano*, garnished with mint and slices of fresh orange

DRINK

When the weather gets hot, city-dwelling Andalucíans head up to rooftop terraces for a refreshing drink.

El Balcón de Las Setas
🅐 B3 🅐 Plaza de la Encarnación, Seville
🅦 elbalcondelassetas.es

La Terraza de San Juan
🅐 D4 🅐 Calle San Juan 11, Málaga 🅦 hotel malagapremium.com

Hotel Alhambra Palace
🅐 E4 🅐 Plaza Arquitecto García de Paredes 1, Granada
🅦 h-alhambrapalace.es

Eat, Drink and Be Sherry

Hundreds of vineyards across Andalucía produce different varieties of reds, whites and fortified wines. Most famous of them all is sherry (or *fino*, as it's known locally), which, by law, must come from the "Sherry Triangle" – the area between Jerez de la Frontera *(p178)*, Sanlúcar de Barrameda *(p190)* and El Puerto de Santa María *(p191)*. Founded in 1730, Bodegas Fundador has a vast store, known as "La Mezquita" (the Mosque) because of its Moorish arches, which houses more than 40,000 barrels of sherry *(p179)*. Book a tour and tasting to learn about how the fortified wine is made or indulge in a paired lunch, where every dish is complemented by a different sherry or brandy.

→ Sampling different varieties of sherry at an Andalucían fiesta

Cocktail Hour

Evenings kick off at *la hora del aperitivo* - the traditional tapas time - between 8:30pm and 10pm. Join the locals on a traditional *tapeo (p32)* before heading to a *bar de copas* (cocktail bar). In Seville, our favourites include Bar Gigante, where fruity cocktails can be sipped al fresco *(p98)*, and the jazzy, Art-Deco-style Bar Americano at the Hotel Alfonso XIII *(p114)*.

SEVILLE AND ANDALUCÍA
AFTER DARK

The fact that there's a specific Spanish word – *madrugada* – for the hours between midnight and dawn says everything about Andalucía's nightlife. From traditional tapas bars to pumping nightclubs, swanky rooftops to dingy flamenco *tablaos (p44)*, there's something for everyone.

Club Life

Andalucía's big cities offer something for nightclubbers of all stripes. Marbella's glitzy "Golden Mile" is lined with megaclubs. Not your scene? Indie and rock fans should seek out Seville's Fun Club, which hosts up-and-coming bands *(www. funclubsevilla. com)*. For a similar vibe, make for Granada's underground spots, such as Planta Baja *(plantabaja.net)*.

←

A band rocking out on stage at Planta Baja in Granada, a popular student spot

↑ The view from the rooftop bar at EME Catedral Mercer

Al Fresco Fun

Seville is not a sky-scraping city, but it does have its fair share of terraces. As the name suggests, the bar at the EME Catedral Mercer hotel is *the* place to go to admire the cathedral *(www.emecatedralmercer.com)*, while El Balcón de Las Setas at the top of the Metropol Parasol is another quiet spot to take in the view *(p34)*. If this all sounds far too sedate, dance the night away at Terraza Bilindo in the Parque María Luisa *(p112)*.

↑ A street in Santa Cruz, Seville, lined with tapas and cocktail bars

🔍 HIDDEN GEM
Alcázar Dark

The Real Alcázar's gardens host a variety of musical performances during the summer months. Can you think of a better setting than these paradisal gardens? Check the Noches en los Jardines del Real Alcázar website for the programme *(www.actidea.es)*.

↑ Festival de Flamenco de Jerez, and *(inset)* a poster for the event

Fiesta Time

Andalucía's calendar is jam-packed with festivals. July sees jazz musicians come together in Almuñécar for Jazz en la Costa *(www.jazzgranada.es)*, while the blues and soul world congregate for the BluesCazorla Festival *(p47)*. For something more traditional, visit Jerez for the Flamenco Festival *(p47)* or check out the Certamen Internacional de Guitarra Clásica Andrés Segovia *(ww.certamenandressegovia.com)*.

Park Life

Thrill-seekers will love Andalucía's theme parks. Seville's Isla Mágica takes kids on a voyage of exploration, with hair-raising roller coasters and imaginative reconstructions of the Americas in the 16th century *(p122)*. Step inside the world of the movies and embrace your inner cowboy in the arid Tabernas Desert *(p231)*. Dress up in costume, watch a staged shoot-out and explore the surprising set for scores of 1960s and 1970s spaghetti westerns at Oasys – Parque Temático del Desierto de Tabernas *(www.oasysparquetematico.com)* and Fort Bravo Texas Hollywood *(www.fortbravo.es)*.

→

A traditional swing ride, and *(inset)* roller coaster, at Seville's Isla Mágica

SEVILLE AND ANDALUCÍA FOR
FAMILIES

Home to expansive beaches, adrenaline-inducing theme parks and endless outdoor activities, Andalucía is the ultimate family-friendly destination. In the cities, most attractions are kid-friendly and there's always a green space nearby to let off some steam.

Active Fun

Andalucía really is a land of adventure. Scour the Strait of Gibraltar for dolphins with Dolphin Safari *(www.dolphin safari.gi)*. Fancy playing captain? Row a boat in the Parque María Luisa *(p110)* or kayak on the mirror-still waters of the Embalse Conde de Guadalhorce *(www.indian sport.es)*. Back on dry land, take the Peque Safari in the Parque Natural del Torcal *(p200)* to discover fossils and flowers as you hike through massive boulders *(www. torcaldeantequera.com)*.

←

Hiking between dramatic rock formations in the Parque Natural del Torcal

TOP 3 FAMILY-FRIENDLY FESTIVALS

Día de los Reyes
The Three Kings parade through Andalucía's towns on the night of 5 January. They ride in small carriages and throw sweets to the excited children.

Carnival
Kids all over Spain wear fancy dress to school over these two weeks in February and there are colourful processions everywhere. Some say that Cádiz's festivities rival those of Río de Janeiro in Brazil.

Fiesta de San Juan
The feast of St John the Baptist is celebrated on 23 June with fireworks.

A lemur hanging out at the Parque de las Ciencias, Granada ↑

Rainy Day Activities
If rain stops play, the obvious place to head is a museum. Granada's Parque de las Ciencias makes science fun *(www.parqueciencias.com)* while Seville's CaixaForum hosts family events, including concerts, painting workshops and film screenings *(p123)*. For a change of pace, bounce about on the huge trampolines at Costajump *(www.costajump.com)*. Another good indoor option is taking a cooking class. Try A Taste of Spain *(www.atasteofspain.com)*.

Family Fun

Andalucía has plenty of kid-friendly coastal spots. Wannabe pirates should explore the Castillo de San Ramon above the Playa El Playazo in the Parque Natural de Cabo de Gata (p230), which once guarded the coast against buccaneers. For active teens, Málaga's city beaches have a lot to offer, with mini outdoor gyms, volleyball courts, and electric bikes available for cruising along the promenade (p186). Similarly, the resorts at Benalmádena (p203) and Fuengirola (p204) teem with activities on and off the sand.

Resting on the beach ↑
at Fuengirola on the
Costa del Sol

SEVILLE AND ANDALUCÍA FOR
BEACHES

With over 900 km (600 miles) of sun-drenched coastline, beach lovers are spoiled for choice in Andalucía. Take your pick from Marbella's glamorous sands, the wild windsurfing waters off Tarifa and everything in between.

Sporty Sands

Tarifa is world renowned for its windy waves (p192). Learn how to master the swell with Surf Center Tarifa (www.surfcentertarifa.com). For kinder conditions, Cabopino, 14 km (9 miles) from Marbella, is a great spot for beginners. Nalusur runs classes (nalusur.com).

←

Kitesurfing on the turquoise
waters off Tarifa

Glitz and Glamour

Marbella's beaches have long been the destination of choice for the international jet set, with 23 beaches to choose from (p204). Nikki beach is the most famous (marbella.nikkibeach.com). A less well-known choice of the well-heeled is Poblado de Sancti Petri, 35 km (22 miles) from Cádiz. This resort has high-end restaurants, luxury hotels and Real Novo Sancti Petri, a course designed by Spanish golfer Seve Ballesteros, where you play alongside the sand (www. clubgolfreal novosancti petri.com).

← Straw umbrellas shading deckchairs on one of Marbella's golden beaches

TOP 5 CITY BEACHES

Matalascañas
This golden beach is a 70-minute drive from Seville (p147).

Mazagón
The seemingly endless stretch of sand at Mazagón (p140) is only a 25-minute drive from the city of Huelva.

Punta Umbría
This historic beach resort is only 20 km (12 miles) from central Huelva (p138).

Playa de Caleta
Cádiz's beach is easily reached by public transport from the centre (p180).

Playa la Barrosa
This 6-km- (4-mile-) long stretch of sand is only a 40-minute drive from Cádiz.

HIDDEN GEM
Deserted Sands

The Parque Natural de Cabo de Gata has wild, dune-backed sands that you'll often have all to yourself (p230). These virgin beaches aren't easy to get to and have very few - if any - facilities, but they're well worth the effort. Our favourite is Playa San Pedro.

Party Time

Chiringuitos (beach bars) are a quintessential element of summer in Spain. Tarifa's surf culture attracts partygoers, as well as boarders, and the *chiringuitos* host some of the world's top DJs (p192). Check out Waves Beach Bar to dance with the sand between your toes (beachbartarifa.com). Elsewhere, laid-back Mosquito Club (www.mosquitoclub.es) is right on the beach at Punta Umbría (p138).

The sun setting over a ↑ laid-back bar on the beach at Tarifa

Take a Hike

The Sierra Nevada mountain range is perfect for walkers *(p226)*. For a challenging but extremely rewarding hike, scale Trevenque, known locally as "The King" due to the difficult ascent *(p226)*. If that sounds far too strenuous, try the Cañada Sereno, a family-friendly trail in the Sierra de Huétor Natural Park, northeast of Granada. See the Trek Nevada website for maps *(treksierranevada.com)*.

←

Walking towards the Puente Nuevo, soaring above the gorge in Ronda

SEVILLE AND ANDALUCÍA FOR
OUTDOOR ACTIVITIES

Blessed with a glorious climate and a varied landscape, ranging from marshlands to mountains, Andalucía's great outdoors invites exploration. Surf on the Strait of Gibraltar, ski in the Sierra Nevada or cycle along reclaimed railway lines: the choice is yours.

Water You Waiting For?

Teeming with a colourful cast of fish, the headlands at La Herradura and the Parque Natural de Cabo de Gato *(p230)* are known for their scuba diving. The Federación Española de Actividades Subacuáticas will direct you to the nearest dive school *(fedas.es)*.

→

Preparing to snorkel at Punta de la Mona, a cove on La Herradura bay

Hit the Slopes

Snow may not be the first thing that comes to mind when you think of sun-drenched Andalucía, but the frosty peaks of the Sierra Nevada are perfect for winter sports *(p226)*. As well as skiing and snowboarding, you can try out sledding, snowmobiling and snow-shoeing. The beauty of skiing in the Sierra Nevada is that you can hit the slops in the morning and then warm up with a dip in the Med in the afternoon. The après-ski, based in the resort village of Pradollano, is pretty cool, too, with many students flocking here from nearby Granada.

→

A group of skiers taking a selfie on the slopes of the Sierra Nevada

Wild Things

The vast wilderness areas of Andalucía are home to a wide variety of creatures great and small. The Parque Nacional de Doñana *(p136)* is home to the elusive Iberian lynx; red deer and wild boar roam in the Parque Natural de Cazorla, Segura y Las Villas *(p170)*; and Fuente de Piedra attracts thousands of birds from near and far *(p201)*.

←

A fox in the Parque Natural de Cazorla, Segura y Las Villas

Ride On

If you prefer life on two wheels, then you're in luck. Mountain biking, naturally, is popular in the sierras – take a tour with Cycle Sierra Nevada *(www.sierranevada.cc)*. For something gentler, try one of Andalucía's flat trails known as *vías verdes* ("greenways"). Check out the routes online *(www.viasverdes.com)*.

→

Cycling towards a village in the foothills of the Sierra Nevada

The Great Fiesta

Unquestionably, the best place to appreciate all things flamenco is the Bienal da Flamenco (*www.labienal.com*). In September and October on even years, the flamenco world gathers in Seville and atmospheric venues such as the Teatro Lope de Vega *(p115)* and the Plaza de Toros de la Maestranza *(p69)* host swirling skirts, clapping hands and stamping feet. Other flamenco festivals include Concurso Nacional de Flamenco *(nacionaldearteflamenco. webnode.es),* held every third May in Córdoba, and the Jerez Annual Flamenco Festival *(p47).*

→
Dancing by the Río Guadalquivir during the opening ceremony of the Bienal da Flamenco, Seville

SEVILLE AND ANDALUCÍA FOR
FLAMENCO

No art form is more closely associated with Andalucía than flamenco *(p85)*. The yearning songs, expressive guitar playing and exuberant hand claps beat the rhythm of the soul of southern Spain. Listen to the music, catch a performance or try your hand at dancing flamenco for yourself.

TOP 4 FLAMENCO ARTISTS

Camarón de la Isla (1950-92)
One of the greatest singers of all time.

Paco de Lucía (1947-2014)
This genre-bending guitarist injected flamenco with jazz.

Carmen Linares (b 1951)
One of the first flamenco singers to perform with the New York Philharmonic Orchestra.

Nina Pastori (b 1978)
Pastori has won four Latin Grammys.

Go Flamenco

There's no better way to feel the *duende* (spirit) than to give it a go for yourself. In Seville, join a dance or *cajón* workshop at the Museo del Baile Flamenco *(p84)*. For a more intensive experience, Taller Flamenco offers day- or month-long courses in guitar, singing, percussion and dance (*www.tallerflamenco.com*).

→
Taking a dance class at a flamenco school in Triana, Seville

Tablaos v Peñas

The historic venues in which flamenco is performed are just as cherished as the art form itself. Most towns are home to at least one *peña* – a gritty flamenco club where you're sure to feel the *duende*. In Jerez de la Frontera, for example, you'll find Peña La Bulería *(Calle Empedrada 20; 856 05 37 72)*. The most visible flamenco venues, however, are *tablaos*, which can be a great place to get a taste of the art form. Unlike *peñas, tablaos* often charge an entrance fee, but this may include drinks or dinner. Find a list of our favourite *tablaos* in Seville on p85. If you really want to get under the skin of the art form, follow one of the Flamenco Routes on Andalucía's tourism website to discover the region's best *tablaos* and *peñas (www.andalucia.org)*.

HIDDEN GEM
Flamenco Caves

Granada's Sacromonte neighbourhood is the traditional home of the city's Romani community, who settled here in the late 15th century. People would travel to the caves honeycombing the hillside here to enjoy spontaneous outbursts of flamenco. Visit Venta El Gallo to be transported back in time *(www.venta elgallo.com)*.

← A flamenco show at the Tablao El Cardenal, a *tablao* in Córdoba

↑ Rodrigo y Gabriela playing their *nuevo flamenco* music on stage

Flamenco Fusion

Flamenco developed from various traditions from Europe, Asia and the Middle East, so it's not surprising that it continues to blend with other forms of music to create new genres. Flamenco rock emerged in the 1960s and 1970s with bands like Triana, while legendary guitarist Paco de Lucía incorporated Cuban rumba into his flamenco style in the 1970s. Popular folk duo Rodrigo y Gabriela combine flamenco with classical and rock music to create a unique *nuevo flamenco* style.

A YEAR IN
SEVILLE AND ANDALUCÍA

JANUARY

△ **Día de los Reyes** *(5 Jan)*. The Three Kings throw sweets to children.

Fiesta de San Anton *(16–17 Jan)*. To celebrate the patron saint of animals, many Andalucían towns host bonfires, fireworks and feasts.

FEBRUARY

△ **Los Carnavales** *(Feb/Mar)*. Every town erupts in colourful celebrations. Cádiz's offering is the best.

Festival de Música Antigua *(Feb/Mar)*. Seville hosts three weeks of classical music in various venues throughout the city.

MAY

△ **Festival de los Patios** *(second week in May)*. Neighbours in Córdoba get competitive as they deck their patios in colourful flowers.

Romería del Rocío *(late May/early Jun)*. Pilgrims from all over Andalucía make for El Rocío in ox-drawn wagons.

JUNE

Festival Internacional de Música y Danza *(mid-Jun–early Jul)*. Classical music and ballet are staged at the Alhambra and the Generalife.

△ **Noche de San Juan** *(23 Jun)*. Street parties, fireworks and bonfires are found everywhere to celebrate John the Baptist. In Cádiz, elaborate *Juanillos* (effigies) are burned.

SEPTEMBER

△ **Fiesta de la Vendimia de Jeréz** *(first 2 weeks of Sep)*. Jerez de la Frontera's harvest is celebrated with grape stomping, wine tasting and other activities.

Bienal de Arte Flamenco *(Sep/Oct, even years only)*. Top flamenco artists fight it out with their footwork in Seville.

OCTOBER

△ **Festival Iberoamericano de Teatro** *(last 2 weeks of Oct)*. This performing arts festival brings together Spanish and Latin American theatre companies in Cádiz.

Fería de San Lucas *(mid-Oct)*. Jaén's annual fair is a week-long celebration of regional dancing, food, drink and sport.

MARCH

△ **Jerez Annual Flamenco Festival** *(Feb/Mar)*. Jerez de la Frontera feels the *duende*.

Semana Santa *(Mar/Apr)*. Solemn processions by hooded devotees are held throughout the region. Head to Seville to experience it.

APRIL

△ **Feria de Abril** (2 weeks after Easter). Seville's exuberant Andalucían fiesta features over 1,000 tents buoyed up on free-flowing sherry, fairground rides and crowds dancing *sevillanas* (a genre of folk music and dance that is unique to the city). Hands down, this is the most elaborate festival in the region's calendar.

JULY

Guitar Festival *(early Jul)*. Córdoba celebrates the stringed instrument in performances ranging from classical to flamenco.

△ **Blues Festival** *(mid-Jul)*. International artists convene in Cazorla for the biggest blues festival in Spain.

Fiesta de la Virgen del Carmen *(15 Jul)*. The Virgin is honoured in coastal villages.

AUGUST

△ **Fiestas Colombinas** *(3 Aug)*. Watersport competitions, concerts and other activities are held in homage to Christopher Columbus and the other navigators who set sail from Huelva.

Fiestas de la Exaltación del Río Guadalquivir *(third week in Aug)*. As the sun sets on the Atlantic, horses race along the beach at Sanlúcar de Barrameda, accompanied by music and festivities.

NOVEMBER

Festival Internacional de Jazz *(early Nov)*. Granada and Seville host the best musicians.

△ **Jornadas Micologicas** *(mid-Nov)*. Forage and cook *setas* (wild mushrooms) in Aracena, Huelva and Constantina.

National Flamenco Competition *(mid-Nov)*. Córdoba hosts music and dance contests.

DECEMBER

Nochebuena *(24 Dec)*. The family gathers for a feast on Christmas Eve, before heading to Midnight Mass.

△ **Fiesta de los Verdiales** *(28 Dec)*. Musical groups called *pandas*, dressed in colourful costumes and lavish headdresses, compete in performances of *verdiales* – a type of folk music – in Málaga.

HISPANIA

1

A BRIEF
HISTORY

Andalucía has been shaped by the different cultures that made this land their home over the centuries. It was in Andalucía that the Moors launched their first attack on Iberia and here that they lingered longest. The unique cultural identity resulting from this past makes this a truly beguiling region.

Early Andalucía

Early humans first settled on the Iberian Peninsula in around 800,000 BC. In 5000 BC, these hunter-gatherers were usurped by Neolithic farmers. Next, merchants arrived from across the Mediterranean, starting with the Phoenicians in around 1100 BC. They established a trading centre in Cádiz, founding what would become one of Europe's oldest cities. The Greeks followed in about 600 BC. During this time, Celts assimilated with the native tribes, resulting in the Celtiberians. These cultures coexisted until the Carthaginians invaded in 500 BC.

1 A map showing how Roman Hispania was divided into provinces.

2 Paintings in the Cueva de los Letreros, Almería.

3 An intricate Roman mosaic found at Itálica.

4 Ornate plasterwork at the Alhambra in Granada.

Timeline of events

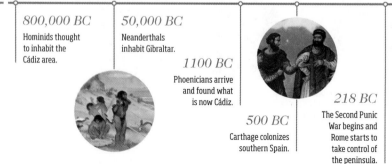

800,000 BC
Hominids thought to inhabit the Cádiz area.

50,000 BC
Neanderthals inhabit Gibraltar.

1100 BC
Phoenicians arrive and found what is now Cádiz.

500 BC
Carthage colonizes southern Spain.

218 BC
The Second Punic War begins and Rome starts to take control of the peninsula.

Baetica

Carthage's old enemy, Rome, was intent on halting its expansion and, after the Second Punic War, the Carthaginians ceded Iberia to the Romans. The new conquerors named the land Hispania and divided it into three provinces: Tarraconensis, Lusitania and Baetica. Andalucía corresponds roundly to Baetica, which quickly became one of Rome's wealthiest provinces due to its olive oil and wheat production. After centuries of prosperity, the fall of the Western Roman Empire in AD 476 left Hispania in the hands of the Visigoths, a nomadic Germanic tribe.

Did You Know?

The Roman name Hispania means "Nearer Iberia".

Al-Andalus

North African Arabs and Berbers known as the Moors took advantage of the Visigoths' lack of political organization in 711 and conquered the peninsula. At its height, al-Andalus – as they called their new territory – included part of southern France. During the subsequent 700 years, the Moors made great strides in the fields of mathematics, science, art and architecture. A rich and powerful caliphate was established in Córdoba in 929 and the city became the epicentre of these al-Andalusian advances.

201 BC
Carthage cedes its Spanish possessions to the Romans.

AD 415
Visigoths arrive in Spain from northern Europe; 61 years later they control the whole of Spain.

476
Western Roman Empire falls, leaving Hispania under the control of the Visigoths.

711
The Moors take control of the peninsula from the Visigoths.

716
First recorded use of "al-Andalus" on coinage.

The Reconquista

In northern Spain, Christian kingdoms reclaimed the lands taken by the Moors almost as soon as they were taken, in an effort that became known as the *reconquista* (reconquest). By the 11th century, the peninsula was split into the Christian north and the Muslim south. Córdoba and Seville fell to the Christians in 1236 and 1248, leaving the Nasrid kingdom of Granada as the last remaining Moorish enclave in the area.

Isabel I of Castile and Fernando II of Aragón, known as the "Catholic Monarchs", finally took Granada in 1492. It was from their court in the Alhambra that they granted the explorer Christopher Columbus patronage for his first expedition.

The Age of Discovery

During the ensuing years, *conquistadors* travelled to Central and South America, establishing colonies for the Spanish Crown and returning with vast wealth at the cost of the indigenous population. In 1503, the Casa de Contratación (House of Trade) was established in Seville, handing the city a monopoly on trade with the Americas. Seville flourished as a result. Exquisite

THE SEVILLE SCHOOL
Known as the Seville School because they were taught at the city's Academia de Bellas Artes (Academy of Fine Arts), artists such as Velázquez, Murillo and Zurbarán became famed throughout Europe in the 17th century for their religious masterpieces. They used chiaroscuro (simulating light and shadow) to bathe their subjects in a holy glow.

Timeline of events

1212
The first Christian victory in Andalucía is won, at Las Navas de Tolosa.

1252–84
Alfonso X reconquers much of Andalucía from Moorish rule.

1492
Granada falls to the Catholic Monarchs, completing the *reconquista*; Columbus sails to the Americas.

1236
Fernando III conquers Córdoba, taking Seville 12 years later.

4

buildings were constructed and people flocked to this new cultural hub. When Carlos I, Spain's Habsburg king, was elected Holy Roman Emperor in 1516, the country cemented its position as Europe's powerhouse. But this brilliance occurred against a backdrop of ruinous wars with the Low Countries and France. As the country's principal port, Seville suffered greatly from these misfortunes and, when the Río Guadalquivir silted up in the 18th century, the trading monopoly passed to Cádiz.

Bourbon Kings

When Carlos II died without an heir, the Habsburgs and Bourbons fought over the Spanish Crown. The latter were victorious and Bourbon ties with France dragged Spain into the Napoleonic Wars. Following the Battle of Trafalgar in 1805, the Spanish King Carlos IV abdicated in 1808 and Napoleon Bonaparte placed his brother on the Spanish throne. The Peninsular War ensued and, with British help, the French were driven out of Spain. But the country had been weakened and Andalucía, whose economy had come to rely almost entirely on the Americas, suffered from the loss of its colonies at the end of the 19th century.

① Muslims being forced to convert to Christianity during the *reconquista*. ↑

② A painting showing Seville's bustling port in the 17th century.

③ The interior patio of Seville's Casa de Contratación.

④ Portrait of King Carlos IV of Spain, who abdicated in 1808.

1580
Seville becomes the largest city in Spain.

1605
Cervantes, active in Madrid and Seville, publishes *Don Quixote*.

1898
Spanish American War; Spain loses the last of its colonial possessions, including Cuba and the Philippines.

1717
Trade monopoly moves from Seville to Cádiz.

DISCOVER A Brief History

Civil War

Andalucía continued to decline, remaining so deeply feudal that by the turn of the 20th century social protest was rife. Spain's increasing instability was briefly checked by Primo de Rivera, who seized power in 1923, but he lost the support of the king and army in 1930 and resigned. Following a public vote, Alfonso XIII was also forced to abdicate and the Second Republic was declared in 1931.

The Second Republic implemented liberal measures but the Confederación Española de Derechas Autónomas – a conservative party – won the 1933 elections. In response, anarchists and socialists rose up the following year. Another election in 1936 saw the liberal Popular Front narrowly defeat the right-wing National Front. Political tensions came to a head and Civil War broke out. The Nationalists, led by General Franco, invaded from a Moroccan-based garrison, declaring war on the Republic. Andalucía soon fell to Nationalist forces, providing Franco with a base to push north. Franco declared victory in 1939, installing himself as a dictator. Under Franco, Spain was a fascist state, ruled by a single party. The Andalucían people suffered brutally under the regime; it is estimated that over 50,000 people were executed in the province.

1 A Spanish Civil War poster, presenting Nationalist propaganda.

2 Felipe González, leader of the Spanish Socialist Workers' Party (PSOE) and the third prime minister of Spain, speaks to parliament after Adolfo Suárez resigned as prime minister in 1981.

3 People dancing flamenco, a traditional art form that is still part of Spain today.

Timeline of events

1923
General Primo de Rivera seizes power.

1931
The Second Republic is declared, with a coalition between Socialists and Republicans.

1936
Nationalists rise up and the Spanish Civil War begins.

1939
Franco declares victory and installs himself as a military dictator.

1975
Death of Franco; Juan Carlos is proclaimed king.

52

Seville and Andalucía Today

Franco named Juan Carlos, Alfonso XIII's grandson, as his heir. He inherited Franco's absolute power, but chose not to exercise it, instead installing himself as a constitutional monarch. Sevillian Felipe González became the third prime minister of the newly democratic Spain in 1982. In reaction to decades of brutally enforced centralized power, Spain's regions clamoured for devolution, and in the same year Andalucía became one of Spain's 17 autonomous regions. Spain joined the EEC – the precursor of the EU – in 1986 and, benefiting from European investment, the 1990s saw economic growth. Seville evolved into a modern city, hosting the Expo '92 world fair.

The Spanish parliament approved Andalucía's second Statute of Autonomy in 2007, recognizing the region as a "historic nationality" with a distinct identity. But, just a year later, the 2008 global financial crisis hit Spain hard, and Andalucía was not spared. Despite a thriving tourist industry, the economy is still recovering slowly, resulting in factionalism. The far-right Vox party was bolstered in the 2019 Spanish election, but the socialist Partido Socialista Obrero Español proved victorious.

FEDERICO GARCÍA LORCA

Born in Granada in 1898, Lorca is perhaps Andalucía's most celebrated writer. He became famous for his modernist and symbolist poetry and plays, which showed a distinct Andalucían flavour. He was executed by Nationalist forces in 1936, early on in the Spanish Civil War, and his works were subsequently censored by the Franco regime.

1992
Seville hosts Expo '92, and some 41 million people visit the exhibition.

2009
Andalucía's first subway system opens in Seville.

2014
King Juan Carlos abdicates in favour of his son, Felipe VI.

2018
Marta Bosquet is elected President of Andalucía.

EXPERIENCE
SEVILLE

El Arenal 62

Santa Cruz 72

La Macarena 94

Parque María Luisa 106

Across the River 118

EXPLORE
SEVILLE

This section divides Seville into four colour-coded sightseeing areas, as shown on this map, plus an area across the river.

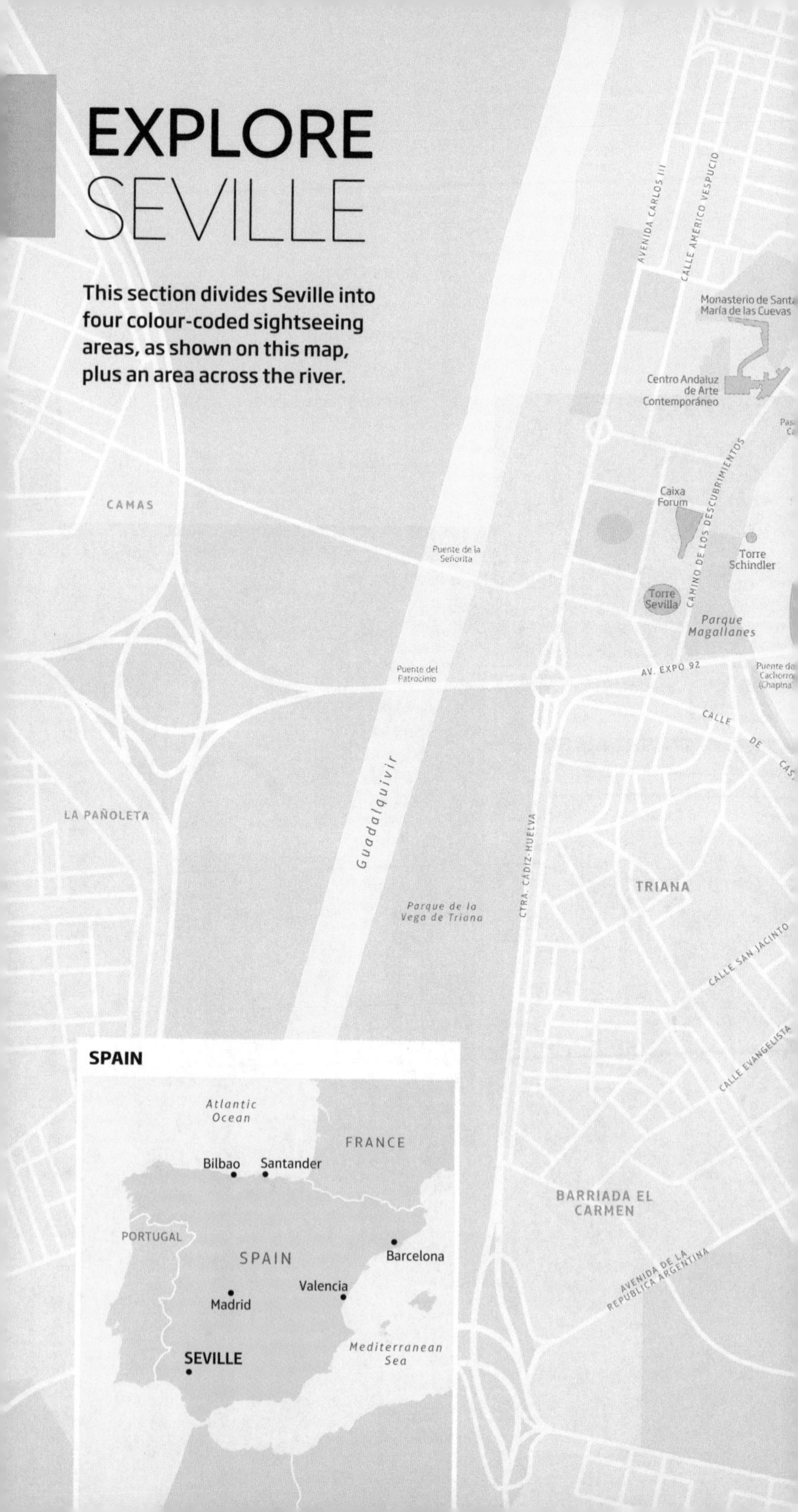

AVENIDA CARLOS III

CALLE AMERICO VESPUCIO

Monasterio de Santa María de las Cuevas

Centro Andaluz de Arte Contemporáneo

CAMAS

Caixa Forum

Puente de la Señorita

CAMINO DE LOS DESCUBRIMIENTOS

Torre Schindler

Torre Sevilla

Parque Magallanes

Puente del Patrocinio

AV. EXPO 92

Puente del Cachorro (Chapina)

CALLE

DE

CAS

Guadalquivir

LA PAÑOLETA

CTRA. CÁDIZ-HUELVA

TRIANA

CALLE SAN JACINTO

Parque de la Vega de Triana

CALLE EVANGELISTA

SPAIN

Atlantic Ocean

FRANCE

Bilbao   Santander

PORTUGAL

BARRIADA EL CARMEN

SPAIN

Barcelona

Valencia

AVENIDA DE LA REPÚBLICA ARGENTINA

Madrid

SEVILLE

Mediterranean Sea

Parque Jardín del Guadalquivir

Puente de la Barqueta

Torre de los Perdigones

Parlamento de Andalucía

LA MACARENA

RESOLANA ANDUEZA

Basílica de la Macarena

CALLE MUÑOZ LEON

Monasterio de San Clemente

CALATRAVA

LUMBRERAS

SAN GIL

Convento de Santa Clara

CALLE DE RELATOR

Jardín Capuchinos

CALLE DEL TORNEO

CALLE DE SAN VICENTE

SANTA ANA

CALLE JESUS DEL GRAN PODER

CALLE SAN LUIS

FERIA

Convento de Santa Paula

CALLE DE LA ENLADRILLADA

SAN VICENTE

CALLE GOLES

CALLE DE BAÑOS

AMOR DE DIOS

LA MACARENA
p94

CALLE CASTELLAR

BUSTOS TAVERA

CALLE GERONA

CALLE DE LA

CALLE MARIA AUXILIADORA

CALLE DEL SOL

EL FONTANAL

Museo de Bellas Artes

ALFONSO XII

MUSEO

LARAÑA

IMAGEN

Palacio de Lebrija

C. VELAZQUEZ TETUAN

CENTRO

MEJIAS

Casa de Pilatos

SAN ESTEBAN

CALLE DE RECAREDO

EL ARENAL
p62

Iglesia de la Magdalena

REYES CATOLICOS

EL ARENAL

SANTA CRUZ
p72

VIRGENES SAN JOSE

SANTA CRUZ

CALLE DE ARJONA

PASEO DE CRISTOBAL COLON

PASEO CALLE DE ADRIANO

Seville Cathedral

Plaza de Toros de la Maestranza

CALLE DE MENENDEZ PELATO

LA FLORIDA

Guadalquivir

CALLE BETIS

Iglesia de Santa Ana

Torre del Oro

Real Alcázar

Jardines de Murillo

Jardines del Alcázar

CALLE SAN FERNANDO

NERVIÓN

PLAZA DE CUBA

Puente de San Telmo

Universidad

AVENIDA DE CARLOS V

AVENIDA DE LA REPÚBLICA ARGENTINA

Palacio de San Telmo

PASEO DE LAS DELICIAS

AVENIDA DE MARIA LUISA

Jardines del Prado

AVENIDA DE PORTUGAL

CALLE DE ASUNCION

Teatro Lope de Vega

Capitanía General

LOS REMEDIOS

PARQUE MARÍA LUISA
p106

Parque María Luisa

DISTRITO SUR

0 metres   300
0 yards   300

N

GETTING TO KNOW
SEVILLE

One of the world's most romantic cities, Seville is made up of diverse, but equally beguiling, neighbourhoods. The heart of the city lies to the east of the Río Guadalquivir and it's here that you'll find the city's big-name sights, but the area to the west of the river is just as rewarding.

PAGE 62

EL ARENAL

Once the city's port, the area between the Avenida de la Constitución and the Río Guadalquivir wears its seafaring past on its sleeve. It'll come as no surprise then that El Arenal has some fine *freidurias* (fried fish takeaways), where everything from cod to cuttlefish comes in a paper cone for you to savour while watching the boats on the river. Back on the cobbled streets, old-fashioned tapas bars and *abacerias* (grocery stores), selling jars of jam and hulking legs of marbled Iberian ham, stand side by side with slick, modern gastropubs.

Best for
Old-fashioned bars and restaurants

Home to
Museo de Bellas Artes

Experience
A bike ride along the riverfront

PAGE 72

SANTA CRUZ

Many of Seville's best-known sights are grouped here in the oldest part of the city, including the cathedral and royal palace. Spreading northeast from these great monuments is an enchanting maze of cobblestone streets. Narrow walkways meander into hidden court-yards, where window boxes are ablaze with flowers and the strains of flamenco and scent of jasmine waft through the air. Further north, busy Calle Sierpes is the city's favourite shopping street, lined with traditional stores selling hats, fans and *mantillas* (lace headdresses).

Best for
Iconic monuments

Home to
Seville Cathedral and La Giralda, Real Alcázar

Experience
A guided tour of the cathedral to admire the stained-glass windows up close

$\rightarrow$

PAGE 94

LA MACARENA

Often overlooked by visitors, the north of Seville is perhaps the most off-beat corner of the city. Artsy bookshops, independent boutiques, Moroccan tea-houses, micro-theatres and vintage stores are found alongside magnificent churches, palatial residences and modest apartments. Bisecting the area is the wide promenade of Alameda de Hércules. Lined with trendy bars and restaurants, it's always buzzing, and street markets, live music and dance, and all kinds of entertainment only add to the atmosphere.

Best for
Experiencing local life

Home to
Historic churches and contemporary constructions

Experience
Rifling through the bizarre selection of goods for sale at the Thursday-morning flea market on Calle de la Feria

PAGE 106

PARQUE MARÍA LUISA

This lush area is the ideal place to take a break from the bustling city, with its sparkling arabesque fountains, peaceful lagoons, bougainvillea-covered pergolas and sprawling grassy lawns. Take a stroll, enjoy a picnic or hire a boat to explore the mini-canal encircling the majestic Plaza de España, with its colourful ceramics. And there's more – the *pabellóns* (pavilions) built for the 1929 exhibition now house museums, atmospheric Moroccan teahouses and, after dark, neon-lit, open-air nightclubs.

Best for
Leafy strolls

Home to
Parque María Luisa

Experience
Rowing a boat along the Plaza de España's canal, passing under the fairy-tale bridges

ACROSS THE RIVER

The other side of the Río Guadalquivir seems a world away from central Seville. Triana's quiet cobbled streets are home to historic potteries and intimate flamenco *peñas*, resounding with the clacking of castanets and stomping of feet. To the north is La Cartuja, which was once best known for its monastery but now draws visitors for the Torre Sevilla. Disparagingly christened "The Lipstick" by locals due to its incongruous form on the city's skyline, the tower's observation deck has amazing views of Seville – although Triana's riverfront cafés and bars afford equally inspiring vistas.

Best for
Authentic flamenco

Home to
Triana

Experience
Using a kiln to make your own ceramic tile in Triana

EL ARENAL

Bounded by the Río Guadalquivir and guarded by the mighty 13th-century Torre del Oro, El Arenal used to be a district of munitions stores and shipyards. Positioned at the last point where ships can sail upstream, Seville was perfectly placed to take advantage of Columbus's landing in the Americas. In 1503, the city was awarded the Puerto de Indias trade monopoly and El Arenal flourished due to the wealth sailing into the port from the Americas.

Along with the rest of the city, the area's fortunes saw an about-face in the 18th century after the city's trade monopoly was transferred to Cádiz. Once central to the city's life, the influence of the Guadalquivir declined during this period and it was left to silt up. By the end of the 18th century, El Arenal had become a notorious underworld haunt clinging to the city walls. After being converted into a canal in the early 20th century, the river was restored to its former navigable glory just in time for Expo '92. The east riverfront was transformed into a tree-lined, shady promenade with excellent views of Triana and La Cartuja across the river.

5

6

8

EL ARENAL

Must See
① Museo de Bellas Artes

Experience More
② Hospital de la Caridad
③ Iglesia de la Magdalena
④ Torre del Oro
⑤ Teatro de la Maestranza
⑥ Plaza de Toros de la Maestranza

Eat
① La Casapuerta

Stay
② Hotel Mercer Sevilla

1 ✍

MUSEO DE BELLAS ARTES

📍 E5 🏠 Plaza del Museo 9 🚌 3, 6, 43, C3, C4, C5 🕐 Mid-Sep-mid-Jun: 9am-8pm Tue-Sat, 9am-3pm Sun; mid-Jun-mid-Sep: 9am-3pm Tue-Sun 🌐 museosdeandalucia.es

The former Convento de la Merced Calzada is now one of the finest art museums in Spain. The museum's impressive collection of Spanish art and sculpture extends from the medieval to the modern, focusing on the work of the Seville School (p50), including Bartolomé Esteban Murillo, Juan de Valdés Leal and Francisco de Zurbarán.

Completed in 1612 by Juan de Oviedo, the Convento de la Merced Calzada is built around three patios, adorned with *azulejos*. The Claustro Mayor is the largest of these, and the Claustro de los Bojes is enclosed by Tuscan-style arches. Starting in the Claustro del Aljibe, signs lead you on a self-guided chronological tour through the museum's 14 galleries. Works on the ground floor progress from the 14th century through to Baroque; those upstairs from the Baroque to the early 20th century. Among the star attractions is Murillo's *La Servilleta, a Virgin and Child*, which is said to be painted on a napkin *(servilleta)*. It now hangs in the restored convent church, which is noteworthy for its Baroque domed ceiling, painted by Domingo Martínez. Elsewhere, you'll find several fine works by Zurbarán and a gallery devoted to Juan de Valdés Leal's forceful religious paintings.

> 💬 INSIDER TIP
> **Sunday Art Day**
>
> An art market takes place in the Plaza del Museo every Sunday morning. More than 40 artists exhibit their works here and you can pick up everything from prints to photos, sculptures to paintings. Browse the stalls for the next big name.

↑ One of the light and airy galleries of the Museo de Bellas Artes

TOP 5 COLLECTION HIGHLIGHTS

La Servilleta, a Virgin and Child (1665-8)
One of Murillo's most popular works.

San Hugo en el Refectorio (1655)
Created by Zurbarán for the Monasterio de Santa María de las Cuevas *(p124)*, it depicts the monks renouncing meat.

San Jerónimo (1528)
Sculpted by the Florentine Torrigiano.

La Inmaculada (1672)
This work hangs in Sala 8, the gallery devoted to Valdés Leal.

Apoteosis de Santo Tomás de Aquino (1631)
Zurbarán's vivid use of colour brings the scene to life.

1 The Claustro del Aljibe, where the route begins, centres on a well.

2 The elaborate interior of the former convent, with its painted domed ceilings, acts as a dramatic backdrop to the museum's collection.

3 The main entrance was built in the Baroque style, with twisted columns and elaborate statuary.

The glittering Baroque interior of the Iglesia de la Magdalena

EXPERIENCE MORE

2 Hospital de la Caridad

F8 Calle Temprado 3 M Puerta de Jerez 3, 21, 40, 41, C4, C5 954 22 32 32 10am-7:30pm Mon-Sat, 12:30-2pm Sun

Founded in 1674, this charity hospital is still used today as a sanctuary for the elderly and the infirm. In the gardens opposite the entrance stands a statue of its benefactor, Miguel de Mañara, who led a dissolute life before joining a Christian brotherhood.

The hospital centres around two square patios adorned with plants, 18th-century Dutch *azulejos (p88)*, and fountains with Italian statues depicting Charity and Mercy. At their northern end a passage to the right leads to another patio, containing a 13th-century arch, which survives from the city's shipyards, and a bust of Mañara.

The façade of the hospital church, with its whitewashed walls, reddish stonework and framed *azulejos*, provides a glorious example of Sevillian Baroque. Inside the church are a number of original canvases. Directly above the entrance is the ghoulish *Finis Gloriae Mundi* (The End of the World's Glories) by Juan de Valdés Leal, and opposite hangs his morbid *In Ictu Oculi* (In the Blink of an Eye). Works by Murillo include *St John of God Carrying a Sick Man, St John the Baptist as a Boy* and *St Isabel of Hungary Curing the Lepers*.

Looking south from the hospital's entrance you can see the octagonal Torre de Plata (Tower of Silver) rising above Calle Santander. Like the Torre del Oro, it dates from Moorish times and was built as part of the city defences.

Did You Know?

Miguel de Mañara is said to have been the inspiration for the character of Don Juan.

3 Iglesia de la Magdalena

F6 Calle San Pablo 10 Plaza Nueva 40, 41, 43, C5 11am-1:30pm Tue-Thu (and for services daily) W rpmagdalena.org

This immense Baroque church by Spanish architect Leonardo de Figueroa, completed in 1709, has been restored to its former glory. In its southwest corner is a Mudéjar chapel with three cupolas, which survived from an earlier church where the great Spanish painter Bartolomé Murillo, the creator of *La Servilleta (p66)*, was baptized in 1618. You can see the font in the baptistry.

A painting by Francisco de Zurbarán, *St Dominic in Soria*, adorns the Capilla Sacramental (to the right of the south door), while frescoes by Lucas Valdés above the sanctuary depict *The Allegory of the Triumph of Faith*. On the north transept is a cautionary fresco, which depicts a medieval *auto-da-fé* (trial of faith).

> The gold in the tower's name may refer to gilded *azulejos* that once clad its walls, or to treasures from the Americas unloaded at the Torre del Oro.

④ 🏛

Torre del Oro

📍 F8 **🏠 Paseo de Colón s/n** **Ⓜ🚎 Puerta de Jerez** **🚌 3, 6, 21, 40, 41, C3, C4, C5** **☎ 954 22 24 19** **🕐 9:30am-6:45pm Mon-Fri, 10:30am-6:45pm Sat & Sun** **🚫 Public hols**

In Moorish times the Tower of Gold formed part of the walled defences, linking up with the Real Alcázar (p78) and the rest of the city walls. It was built in 1220, when Seville was under the rule of the Almohads (a Berber group) and had a companion tower on the opposite river bank. A mighty chain would be stretched between the two to prevent ships from sailing upriver. In 1760 the turret was added.

The gold in the tower's name may refer to gilded *azulejos* that once clad its walls, or to treasures from the Americas unloaded at the Torre del Oro. The tower has had many uses, including acting as a chapel and a prison, but it is now the Museo Marítimo, exhibiting maritime maps and antiques.

⑤

Teatro de la Maestranza

📍 F8 **🏠 Paseo de Colón 22** **Ⓜ🚎 Puerta de Jerez** **🚌 3, 21, 40, 41, C4, C5** **🕐 For performances** **🌐 teatrodela maestranza.es**

Seville's 1,800-seat opera house and theatre opened in 1991 and many international opera companies perform here. Like many of the edifices built in the run-up to Expo '92 (p53), it was designed in a rather austere style by architects Luis Marín de Terán and Aurelio del Pozo. Ironwork

remnants of the 19th-century ammunition works that first occupied the site decorate the river façade. Tickets are sold from the box office in the adjacent Jardín de la Caridad.

⑥ 🏛 Ⓜ

Plaza de Toros de la Maestranza

📍 F7 **🏠 Paseo de Colón 12** **Ⓜ Puerta de Jerez** **🚇 Archivo de Indias** **🚌 3, 21, 40, 41, C3, C4, C5** **🕐 Apr-Oct: 9:30am-9pm daily (to 3pm on bullfight days); Nov-Mar: 9:30am-7pm daily** **🌐 real maestranza.com**

Seville's famous bullring is arguably the finest in all of Spain and hosts *corridas* (bullfights) from Easter Sunday until October, usually on Sunday evenings. Whatever your opinion is of bullfighting, this magnificent arcaded arena, with its whitewashed walls, red fences and merciless circle of sand, remains an integral element of the city's psyche. Constructed between 1761

and 1881, this immense building can hold a mind-boggling 12,500 spectators.

Guided tours start from the main entrance on Paseo de Colón. On the west side is the Puerta del Príncipe (Prince's Gate), through which the very best matadors are carried triumphant on the shoulders of admirers from the crowd.

Passing the *enfermería* (emergency hospital), visitors reach a museum which details the history of the bullfight in Seville, with a large collection of costumes, portraits and posters. The tour also takes in the chapel where matadors pray for success, and the stables where the horses of the *picadores* (lance-carrying horsemen) are kept.

← Statue of Seville-born matador Curro Romero outside the Plaza de Toros de la Maestranza

A SHORT WALK
EL ARENAL

Distance 1.5 km (1 mile) **Nearest metro**
Puerta de Jerez **Time** 25 minutes

Once the bustling home of Seville's port, ammunition works and artillery headquarters, El Arenal is now best known for its bullring, the majestic Plaza de Toros de la Maestranza. El Arenal is a popular nightlife hub year-round, but during the bullfighting season the area's bars and restaurants are especially packed. The riverfront is dominated by one of Seville's best-known monuments, the Moorish Torre del Oro, while the long, tree-lined promenade beside the Paseo de Cristóbal Colón is perfect for a slow, romantic walk along the Guadalquivir.

Locator Map
For more detail see p64

The **Plaza de Toros de la Maestranza**, *Seville's 18th-century bullring, has a Baroque façade in white and ochre (p69).*

CALLE DE ADRIANO

CALLE ANTONIA DÍAZ

PASEO DE CRISTÓBAL COLÓN

A bronze sculpture of **Carmen**, *the character from the opera, stands opposite the bullring.*

Paseo Alcalde Marqués de Contadero

The **Teatro de la Maestranza**, *a showpiece theatre and opera house, was opened in 1991. It is home to the Orquesta Sinfónica de Sevilla (p69).*

← Cycling by the Torre del Oro, a Moorish tower on the bank of the Guadalquivir

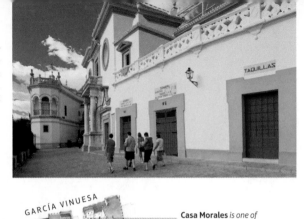

The striking exterior of the Plaza de Toros de la Maestranza, Seville's bullring

El Postigo is an arts and crafts market.

GARCÍA VINUESA

ARFE

DOS DE MAYO

TEMPRADO

TOMÁS DE IBARRA

AVENIDA DE LA CONSTITUCIÓN

CALLE SANTANDER

START

Casa Morales is one of many traditional tapas bars in El Arenal.

In the secluded Plaza de Cabildo, **El Torno** sells sweets made in a convent.

Did You Know?

El Arenal gets its name from *arena*, the Spanish word for sand, as this area was once sandy river banks.

FINISH

The walls of the **Hospital de la Caridad**'s church are hung with fine paintings by Bartolomé Esteban Murillo and Juan de Valdés Leal (p68).

Maestranza de Artillería

Built in the 13th century to protect the port, the **Torre del Oro** now houses a small maritime museum (p69).

| 0 metres | | 75 |
| 0 yards | | 75 |

N

SANTA CRUZ

The Barrio de Santa Cruz, Seville's old Jewish quarter, is a warren of white alleys and patios that has long been the most picturesque corner of the city. When Fernando III of Castile took the city from the Moors in 1248, he consigned Seville's Jewish population to this corner of the city until they were expelled from Spain in 1492. The neighbourhood saw a period of decline after this until the 16th century when, like the rest of the city, wealth flooded into the area from the New World. The Archivo de Indias testifies to this time of exploration and conquest.

To the north, the charming Plaza del Salvador acted as a backdrop for some of Cervantes' stories, including *Rinconete y Cortadillo*. Here, the Spanish writer exposes the criminal underworld that operated during this 16th-century "Golden Age". Other famous Spaniards have also been inspired by the *barrio*'s enchanting maze of whitewashed streets. The artist Bartolomé Esteban Murillo lived here in the 17th century while his contemporary Juan de Valdés Leal decorated the Hospital de los Venerables with fine Baroque frescoes.

In the 18th century, Santa Cruz underwent a process of urban renewal and since then it has been at the top of visitors' lists due to it being home to some of the city's best-known sights: the cavernous Gothic cathedral with its landmark Giralda, and the splendid Alcázar with its royal palaces and lush Jardines del Alcázar.

SANTA CRUZ

Must Sees
1. Seville Cathedral and La Giralda
2. Real Alcázar

Experience More
3. Palacio de Lebrija
4. Ayuntamiento
5. Iglesia del Salvador
6. Calle Sierpes
7. Museo del Baile Flamenco
8. Plaza Virgen de los Reyes
9. Archivo de Indias
10. Hospital de los Venerables
11. Jardines de Murillo
12. Plaza del Triunfo
13. Casa de Pilatos

Eat
1. Vinería San Telmo
2. Donaire Azabache
3. La Quinta Braseria

Stay
4. Un Patio en Santa Cruz
5. Hotel Inglaterra
6. Palacio Villapanés

0 metres   200
0 yards   200

N ↑

SEVILLE CATHEDRAL AND LA GIRALDA

📍E7 🏛Avenida de la Constitución s/n Ⓜ Puerta de Jerez 🚇Archivo de Indias 🚌C1, C2, C3, C4, 5, 41, 42 ⏰Summer: 10:30am-4pm Mon, 10:30am-6pm Tue-Sat, 2-7pm Sun; winter: 11am-3:30pm Mon, 11am-5pm Tue-Sat, 2:30-6pm Sun 🚫1 & 6 Jan, 25 Dec 🌐catedraldesevilla.es

Seville's cathedral is an arresting sight not only for its size (it's the world's largest Gothic cathedral) but also for its mighty Moorish bell tower – La Giralda. A visit here is a great introduction to Seville's Muslim and Christian heritage.

Officially named Santa María de la Sede, Seville's cathedral occupies the site of a great mosque built by the Almohads in the late 12th century, which had been based on the Koutoubia Mosque of Marrakesh. Eclipsed by the Christian construction, La Giralda and the Patio de los Naranjos are the only lasting legacy of the original Moorish structure. Work on the cathedral, the second largest in Europe, began in 1401 and took just over a century to complete. As well as enjoying the cathedral's Gothic immensity and the works of art in its chapels and sacristy, visitors flock here to ascend the ramped La Giralda for stunning city views.

Did You Know?

The bronze weathervane (giraldillo) crowning the tower gave La Giralda its name.

La Giralda

Group entrance

THE RISE OF LA GIRALDA

The tower was built as a minaret for the mosque in 1198. But, in the 14th century, after Fernando III had successfully taken the city from the Moors in 1248, the bronze spheres at its top were replaced by Christian symbols. A new belfry was planned in 1557, but built to a more ornate design by Hernán Ruiz in 1568.

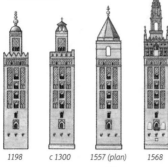

| 1198 | c 1300 | 1557 (plan) | 1568 |

Puerta del Perdón (exit)

In Moorish times worshippers would wash their hands and feet in the Patio de los Naranjos's fountain.

Roman pillars from Itálica (p144) surround the steps.

The tree- and café-lined Calle Mateos Gago, leading to La Giralda

Santa María de la Sede, the cathedral's patron saint, sits at the high altar below a waterfall of gold.

The Sacristía Mayor houses many works of art, including paintings by Murillo.

↑ The decorated dome of the Sacristía Mayor, lit by stained glass

Monumental iron grilles, forged in 1518–32, enclose the Capilla Mayor, which is dominated by the overwhelming Retablo Mayor.

Main entrance

The Tomb of Columbus dates from the 1890s. His coffin is carried by bearers representing the kingdoms of Castile, León, Aragón and Navarra.

←

Seville Cathedral and La Giralda

The Puerta de la Asunción is Gothic in style, though the portal was not completed until 1833.

Puerta del Bautismo

Iglesia del Sagrario, a large 17th-century chapel

 INSIDER TIP
Step Out of Line

As one of Seville's biggest sights, the cathedral attracts hordes of visitors. To skip the queue at the ticket office, buy a combined ticket at the church of El Salvador, in the nearby plaza of the same name.

② 🗺️ 🗺️

REAL ALCÁZAR

📍 F8 🏛️ Patio de Banderas Ⓜ️ Puerta de Jerez 🚃 Archivo de Indias 🚌 C5
🕐 9:30am–7pm daily (to 5pm Oct–Mar); for night visits with theatre, check
website (book in advance) 🗓️ 1 & 6 Jan, Good Fri, 25 Dec 🌐 alcazarsevilla.org

Home to Spanish kings for almost seven centuries,
the Real Alcázar is one of the most beautiful buildings
in the world. Set in a huge paradise garden, it is a
celebration of Mudéjar architecture.

In 1364 Pedro I ordered the construction of a
royal residence within the palaces which had
been built by the city's Almohad rulers in the
12th century. Craftsmen from Granada and
Toledo created a jewel box of Mudéjar patios
and halls, the Palacio Pedro I, now at the heart
of Seville's Real Alcázar. Later monarchs added
their own distinguishing marks: Isabel I
dispatched navigators to the
New World from her Casa de
Contratación, while Carlos I had
grandiose apartments built.
More recently, in 2014, the
Alcázar was used as a location for
the hit TV series *Game of Thrones*.

The Salón de
Embajadores'
dome is made
of carved and
gilded wood.

Azulejos and
complex plasterwork
decorate the Salón
de Embajadores.

Jardín de
Troya

The Patio de las
Doncellas (Patio of
the Maidens) boasts
plasterwork by the top
craftsmen of Granada.

The gardens are laid out
with terraces, fountains
and pavilions.

Tapestries and 16th-century azulejos
decorate the vaulted halls of the
apartments and chapel of Carlos I.

💬 INSIDER TIP
Open the Dorne

With its paradise garden
and glinting *azulejos*,
the Real Alcázar is a
ready-made set for a
fantasy epic. Step into
the world of the Water
Gardens of Dorne on a
Game of Thrones tour of
the palace with Sevilla
Walking Tours *(sevilla
walkingtours.com)*.

The Patio del
Crucero lies above
the old baths.

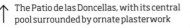

↑ The Patio de las Doncellas, with its central pool surrounded by ornate plasterwork

The Patio de las Muñecas (Patio of the Dolls) is named after the two tiny faces on one of its arches.

Casa de Contratación

The façade of the Palacio Pedro I is a prime example of Mudéjar style.

↑ A room decorated with geometric *azulejos* in the Palacio Pedro I

Craftsmen from Granada and Toledo created a jewel box of Mudéjar patios and halls, the Palacio Pedro I.

The Patio de la Montería was where the court met before hunting expeditions.

Puerta del León (entrance)

The Patio del Yeso (Patio of Plaster), a garden featuring flowerbeds and a water channel, retains features of the earlier, 12th-century Almohad Alcázar.

↑ Illustration showing the Palacio Pedro I, only part of the vast Real Alcázar

←
Roman mosaic floor in the main courtyard of the Palacio de Lebrija

EXPERIENCE MORE

③

Palacio de Lebrija

📍 E6 🏠 Calle Cuna 8
🚌 27, 32 🕙 10:30am–7:30pm daily 🌐 palacio delebrija.com

The home of the family of the Countess Lebrija since 1901, this mansion illustrates palatial life in Seville. The ground floor houses Roman and medieval exhibits, while the first floor features a library and a world-class art collection, including Moorish-inspired *azulejos (p88)*.

The house itself dates from the 15th century and has some beautiful Mudéjar features, including the arches around the main patio. Many of its Roman treasures were taken from the ruins at Itálica *(p144)*, including the mosaic floor in the main patio. The geometric ceiling above the staircase came from the palace of the Dukes of Arcos in Marchena, near Seville.

Ancient Roman glassware, coins and later examples of marble from Medina Azahara *(p164)* are displayed in rooms off the main patio.

④

Ayuntamiento

📍 E6 🏠 Plaza Nueva 1
🚇 Plaza Nueva 📞 955 01 00 10 🕙 By guided tour only at 7pm Mon–Thu (and 8pm Tue–Thu in summer), 10am Sat

Seville's city hall stands between the historic Plaza de San Francisco and the modern expanse of Plaza Nueva.

In the 15th–18th centuries, Plaza de San Francisco was the venue for *autos-da-fé*, public trials of heretics held by the Inquisition. These days, it is the focus of activities during Semana Santa and Corpus Christi. Plaza Nueva was once the site of the Convento de San Francisco. In its centre is an equestrian statue of Fernando III, who liberated Seville from the Moors.

The Ayuntamiento was built between 1527 and 1534. The east side of the city hall, looking on to Plaza de San Francisco, is a fine example of the ornate Plateresque style favoured by the architect Diego de Riaño. The west front is part of a Neo-Classical extension built in 1891. This later addition virtually envelops the original building, but richly sculpted ceilings survive in the vestibule and in the lower Casa Consistorial (Council Meeting Room). This room contains Velázquez's *Imposition of the Chasuble on St Ildefonso*, one of many artworks in the building. The upper Casa Consistorial has a dazzling gold coffered ceiling.

⑤

Iglesia del Salvador

📍 E6 🏠 Plaza del Salvador 🚇 Plaza Nueva 📞 954 21 16 79 🕙 Sep–Jun: 11am–6pm Mon–Sat, 3–7:30pm Sun; Jul & Aug: 10am–5pm Mon–Sat, 3–7pm Sun

The cathedral-like proportions of this church result in part

THE SIGN OF SEVILLE

You'll see the curious abbreviation "no8do" emblazoned everywhere in Seville, from the venerable walls of the Ayuntamiento to the sides of the municipal buses. It is traditionally said to stand for "*No me ha dejado*" ("She has not deserted me"). These words were reputedly uttered by Alfonso the Wise, after the city remained loyal to him in the course of a dispute with his son Sancho during the *reconquista (p50)*. The double-loop symbol in the middle represents a skein of wool, the Spanish word for which is *madeja*, thus *no (madeja) do*.

> **Long-established stores selling the Sevillian archetypes – *mantillas (lace headdresses)*, hats and fans – stand alongside boutiques.**

from the desire of Seville's Christian conquerors to outdo the Moors' architectural splendours. A mosque first occupied the site and part of the Moorish patio survives beside Calle Córdoba. As you exit onto this street, you'll see that the bell tower rests on part of the original minaret. The current Baroque structure, designed by Esteban García, was completed in 1712 by Leonardo de Figueroa. The nave is by José Granados, architect of Granada's cathedral (p214). In the Capilla Sacramental there is a fine statue, *Jesus of the Passion* by Juan Martínez Montañés (1568–1649).

On the east side of the church, in the Plaza Jesús de la Pasión, you'll see bridal shops – the Iglesia del Salvador is a favourite wedding venue among *sevillanos*.

6

Calle Sierpes

📍 E6 🚉 Plaza Nueva

The city's main shopping promenade, the "Street of the Snakes" runs north from the Plaza de San Francisco. Long-established stores selling the Sevillian archetypes – *mantillas* (lace headdresses), hats and fans – stand alongside boutiques, selling clothes and souvenirs. The parallel streets of Cuna and Tetuán on either side also offer enjoyable window-shopping.

At the southern end of Calle Sierpes, on the wall of the Banco Central Hispano, a plaque marks the site of the Cárcel Real (Royal Prison), where the famous Spanish writer Miguel de Cervantes (1547–1616) was incarcerated. Walking north from here, at the junction with Calle Pedro Caravaca, you'll see the grand exterior of the Real Círculo de Labradores, a private men's club founded in 1856. Only members can see the anachronistic interior. Right at the end of the street is Seville's best-known *pastelería* (cake shop), La Campana.

Calle Sierpes, popular for shopping and for the *paseo* – a leisurely evening stroll ↑

The beautiful skyline of Santa Cruz, with the cathedral in the background

Museo del Baile Flamenco

📍F6 🏠 Calle Manuel Rojas Marcos 3 🚉 Plaza Nueva ⏰10am–7pm daily 🌐museoflamenco.com

Although flamenco was supposedly born across the river, in Triana, the Barrio de Santa Cruz has become its de facto home in Seville. This museum of flamenco dance, occupying a restored 18th-century house on a small street between the Plaza del Alfalfa and the cathedral, is intended as an introduction to the art form for the visitor. As well as a space for exhibits in the traditional sense, it is also a venue for live performances of flamenco and a school offering regular classes in flamenco music and dance. Performances start at 5pm, 7pm, 8:45pm and 10:15pm, in either the courtyard or the more intimate surroundings of the museum cellars.

Plaza Virgen de los Reyes

📍F7 Ⓜ Puerta de Jerez

The perfect place to pause for a while and admire the Giralda (p76), this historic plaza presents an archetypal Sevillian tableau: horse-drawn carriages, orange trees, flower-sellers and imposing religious buildings. At its centre is an early 20th-century monumental lamppost and fountain by sculptor José Lafita, with grotesque heads copied from the Roman originals in the Casa de Pilatos (p89).

At the north of the square is the Palacio Arzobispal – the Archbishop's Palace – begun in the 16th century, finished in the 18th and commandeered by Marshal Soult, the commander of the French troops, during the Napoleonic occupation of 1810 (p51). A fine Baroque palace, it has a jasper staircase and paintings by Zurbarán and Murillo, but as a current episcopal residence it is not open to the public.

INSIDER TIP
Beat It

The *cajón* used in flamenco – the box-shaped drum that you sit on and slap with your hands – has become popular in many genres, including blues, folk, jazz and indie pop. You can take part in a *cajón* workshop at the Museo del Baile Flamenco.

On the opposite side of the square is the whitewashed Convento de la Encarnación (closed to the public), which was founded in 1591. The convent stands on grounds that have also been the site of a mosque and of a hospital.

The Plaza Virgen de los Reyes was once home to the Corral de los Olmos (Courtyard of the Elms), an infamous inn which features in the writings of Spain's greatest writers, Miguel de Cervantes. Look for the plaque bearing an inscription testifying to this literary connection on one of the convent's walls.

↑ Plaza Virgen de los Reyes, with its unusual fountain-and-lamppost combination

FLAMENCO, THE SOUL OF ANDALUCÍA

More than just a dance, flamenco is a rousing artistic expression of the joys and sorrows of life. There is no strict choreography – dancers improvise from basic movements. Although there are interpretations all over Spain, it is a uniquely Andalucían art form. Head to one of Seville's *tablaos* to experience it.

A decorative flower

A fan is a typical prop

THE BAILAORA AND THE BAILAOR

The *bailaora* (female dancer) is renowned for amazing footwork as well as intense dance moments. Eva Yerbabuena and Sara Baras are both famous for their personal styles. Both lead their own acclaimed flamenco companies. Another flamenco star is Juana Amaya. The *bailaor* (male dancer) plays a less important role than the *bailaora*. However, many have achieved fame, including Antonio Canales. He has introduced a new beat through his original foot movements.

The proud yet graceful posture of the *bailaora* is suggestive of a restrained passion.

Traditional dress

THE MUSIC AND RHYTHM

Although the dancer often steals the show, it is through the music that they feel the *duende* ("magic spirit"). The guitar has a major role in flamenco, traditionally accompanying the singer. Flamenco guitars have a lighter, shallower construction than the modern classical guitar and a thickened plate below the sound hole, used to tap rhythms. Although the unmistakable rhythm of flamenco is created by the guitar, the beat created by hand-clapping and by the dancer's feet in heeled shoes is just as important. The *bailaoras* may also beat a rhythm with castanets. Graceful hand movements, accompanying the castanets, are used to express the dancer's feelings of the moment – whether pain, sorrow or happiness.

Swirling skirt

↑ A *bailaora*, wearing a traditional red dress and holding a fan

TOP 3 SEVILLE TABLAOS

La Carbonería
Catch a performance in this covered courtyard *(Calle de los Céspedes 21; 954 22 99 45)*.

Casa de la Memoria
A small theatre set in a gorgeous patio, with performances most nights *(www.casa delamemoria.es)*.

Los Gallos
A little more formal, but authentic nonetheless *(www.tablao losgallos.com)*.

↑ A troupe of dancers and musicians performing flamenco in the early 20th century

9

Archivo de Indias

Q E7 **A** Avenida de la Constitución **M** Puerta de Jerez **⬚** Archivo de Indias **C** 954 50 05 28 **⊙** 9:30am–5pm Tue–Sat, 10am–2pm Sun

The Archive of the Indies illustrates Seville's pre-eminent role in the colonization and exploitation of the Americas.

EAT

Vinería San Telmo
A favourite with locals and tourists alike, Vinería San Telmo serves up mouthwatering, innovative tapas, with a global twist, and homemade desserts to die for.

Q G7 **A** Paseo de Catalina de Ribera 4 **w** vineriasantelmo.com

€€€

Donaire Azabache
Feast on traditional favourites here. There's also a good selection of wines on offer.

Q E8 **A** Calle Santo Tomás 11 **w** donaire azabache.com

€€€

La Quinta Braseria
A palatial 20th-century residence now hosting exquisite dining. Expect modern takes on regional cuisine, including savoury rice dishes, juicy chargrilled meat and succulent fish. Book in advance.

Q G5 **A** Plaza Padre Jeronimo de Córdoba 11 **w** grupopanot.com

€€€

Built between 1584 and 1598 to designs by Juan de Herrera, co-architect of El Escorial near Madrid, it was originally a *lonja* (exchange), where merchants traded. In 1785, Carlos III had all Spanish documents relating to the "Indies" collected under one roof, creating a fascinating archive of the Spanish presence in the Americas and the Philippines. It contains letters from Columbus, Cortés, Cervantes and George Washington, the first American president, as well as the correspondence of Felipe II. The vast collection amounts to some 86 million handwritten pages and 8,000 maps and drawings, housed on an estimated 9 km (5.5 miles) of shelving. An extensive programme of document digitization is ongoing.

Visitors to the Archivo de Indias climb marble stairs to library rooms where drawings and maps are exhibited in a reverential atmosphere. Displays change on a regular basis, but might include a watercolour map from the days when the city of Acapulco was little more than a castle, drawings recording a royal *corrida* (bullfight) held in Panama City in 1748 or designs and plans for a town hall in Guatemala.

10

Hospital de los Venerables

Q F7 **A** Plaza de los Venerables 8 **⬚** Archivo de Indias **C** 954 56 26 96 **⊙** 10am–2pm Thu–Sun

Located in the heart of the Barrio de Santa Cruz, the Hospital of the Venerables was founded as a home for elderly priests. It was begun in 1675 and completed around 20 years later by Leonardo de Figueroa. FOCUS (Fundación Fondo de Cultura) has restored it as a cultural centre.

The building is designed around a central, sunken patio. The upper floors, along with the infirmary and the cellar, are used as galleries for exhibitions. A separate guided tour visits the hospital church, a showcase of Baroque splendours, with frescoes by local painter Juan de Valdés Leal and his son Lucas Valdés. Other highlights include the

↑ The Baroque interior of the barrel-vaulted church of the Hospital de los Venerables

↑ Colourful monument to Catalina de Ribera in the Jardines de Murillo

sculptures of St Peter and St Ferdinand by Pedro Roldán, flanking the east door; and *The Apotheosis of St Ferdinand* by Lucas Valdés, top centre in the *retablo* of the main altar. Its frieze (inscribed in Greek) advises visitors to "Fear God and Honour the Priest". In the sacristy, the ceiling has an effective *trompe l'oeil* depicting *The Triumph of the Cross* by Juan de Valdés Leal.

⑪ Jardines de Murillo

◉ F8 Ⓜ🚊 Prado de San Sebastián

These formal gardens at the southern end of the Barrio de Santa Cruz once used to be orchards and vegetable plots in the grounds of the Real Alcázar. They were donated to the city in 1911. Their name commemorates Seville's best-known painter, Bartolomé Murillo (1617–82), who lived in nearby Calle Santa Teresa.

> **Rising above the garden's palm trees is a monument to Columbus, incorporating a bronze of the *Santa María*, the caravel that bore him to the Americas in 1492.**

A long promenade, Paseo de Catalina de Ribera, pays tribute to the founder of the Hospital de las Cinco Llagas, which is now the seat of the Parlamento de Andalucía. Rising above the garden's palm trees is a monument to Columbus, incorporating a bronze of the *Santa María*, the caravel that bore him to the Americas in 1492 (p139).

⑫ Plaza del Triunfo

**◉ E7 Ⓜ Puerta de Jerez
🚊 Archivo de Indias**

The beautiful Plaza del Triunfo lies at the centre of a group of UNESCO World Heritage buildings – Seville cathedral (p76), the Archivo de Indias and the Real Alcázar (p78). The square was built to celebrate the triumph of the city over an earthquake in 1755. The earthquake devastated Lisbon, over the border in Portugal, but caused comparatively little

📷 PICTURE PERFECT
Venerable Trees

Pose against the huge, ancient ficus trees in the Jardines de Murillo. Some of these tropical giants are more than a century old, and their contorted trunks are wide enough for several people to stand against.

damage in Seville – a salvation attributed to the city's great devotion to the Virgin Mary. She is honoured by an impressive Baroque column beside the Archivo de Indias. In the centre of the Plaza del Triunfo, a monument commemorates Seville's belief in the Immaculate Conception.

In Calle Santo Tomás, off the southwestern corner of the Plaza del Triunfo, lies a building used by the Archivo de Indias. Formerly the Museo de Arte Contemporáneo – now in the Monasterio de Santa Mariá de las Cuevas (p124) – the building is no longer open to the public. Dating from 1770, it was once a barn where tithes collected by the Church were stored. Parts of the Moorish city walls were uncovered during building renovations.

THE ART OF AZULEJOS

Durable and colourful, glazed ceramic tiles, known as *azulejos*, have been a striking feature of Andalucían façades and interiors for centuries. The techniques for making them were first introduced by the Moors – the word *azulejo* derives from the Arabic *az-zulayj* or "little stone".

Moorish *azulejos* are elaborate mosaics made of unicoloured stones. In Seville the craft flourished and evolved in the potteries of Triana *(p120)*. A later process, developed in 16th-century Italy, allowed tiles to be painted in new designs and colours. Then, the Industrial Revolution enabled *azulejos* to be mass-produced in ceramics factories including the famous "Pickman y Cia" at the Monasterio de Santa María de las Cuevas *(p124)*.

↑ Glazed *azulejos* in the Alhambra *(p216)*, Granada

MUDEJAR-STYLE AZULEJOS

The Moors created fantastic mosaics of tiles in sophisticated geometric patterns as decoration for their palace walls. The colours used were blue, green, black, white and ochre.

AZULEJOS FOR COMMERCIAL USE

As techniques for making and colouring *azulejos* improved, their use was extended from interior decor to decorative signs and shop façades. Even billboards were produced in multicoloured tiles. The eye-catching results can still be seen all over Andalucía.

↑ Advertisements made out of *azulejos* on display in the Centro Cerámica Triana *(p120)*

↑ A bridge decorated in blue and yellow tiles, in the Plaza de España *(p112)*

13 🚫 Ⓜ️

Casa de Pilatos

📍 G6 🏛 Plaza de Pilatos 1
🚌 C5 🕐 Apr-Oct: 9am-7pm
daily; Nov-Mar: 9am-6pm
daily 🌐 fundacion
medinaceli.org

In 1518 the first Marquess of Tarifa departed on a Grand Tour of Europe and the Holy Land. He returned two years later, enraptured by the architectural and decorative wonders of High Renaissance Italy. He spent the rest of his life creating a new aesthetic, which was very influential. His palace in Seville, called the House of Pilate because the Marquess discovered that it was the same distance from a temple at Cruz del Campo as Pontius Pilate's home was from Calvary, became a luxurious showcase for the new style. Over the centuries, subsequent owners added their own embellishments. Today, the Casa de Pilatos is the residence of the Dukes of Medinaceli and is still one of the finest palaces in Seville.

Visitors enter through a marble portal, commissioned by the Marquess in 1529 from Genoan craftsmen. Across the arcaded carriage yard is the Patio Principal. This courtyard is Mudéjar in style with *azulejos* and intricate plasterwork. It is surrounded by irregularly spaced arches capped with delicate Gothic balustrades. In its corners stand three Roman statues, Minerva, a dancing muse and Ceres, and a fourth statue, a 5th-century BC original of the Greek goddess Athena. In its centre is a

↑ Casa de Pilatos' Patio Principal, a filming location for David Lean's *Lawrence of Arabia* (1962)

fountain imported from Genoa. To the right, through the Salón del Pretorio with its coffered ceiling and marquetry, is the Corredor de Zaquizamí. Among the antiquities in adjacent rooms are a bas-relief of *Leda and the Swan* and two Roman reliefs commemorating the Battle of Actium in 31 BC. Further along, in the Jardín Chico, there is a pool with a bronze of Bacchus.

Coming back to the Patio Principal, you turn right into the Salón de Descanso de los Jueces. Beyond this is a rib-vaulted chapel, which has a copy of a 4th-century sculpture in the Vatican, *The Good Shepherd*. Left through the Gabinete de Pilatos, with its small fountain, is the Jardín Grande. The Italian architect Benvenuto Tortello created the loggias in the 1560s.

> **Today, the Casa de Pilatos is the residence of the Dukes of Medinaceli and is still one of the finest palaces in Seville.**

Returning once more to the main patio, behind the statue of Ceres, a tiled staircase leads to the apartments on the upper floor. It is roofed with a wonderful *media naranja* (half orange) cupola built in 1537. There are Mudéjar ceilings in some rooms, which are filled with family portraits, antiques and furniture. Plasterwork by Juan de Oviedo and frescoes by Francisco de Pacheco still survive in the rooms bearing these artists' names.

Did You Know?

Casa de Pilatos was the first private residence in Seville to have a staircase.

A SHORT WALK
SANTA CRUZ

Distance 1 km (0.5 miles) **Nearest metro** Puerta de Jerez **Time** 15 minutes

The compact maze of narrow streets to the east of Seville Cathedral and the Real Alcázar represents Seville at its most romantic. As well as the expected souvenir shops, tapas bars and strolling guitarists, there are plenty of picturesque alleys, hidden plazas and flower-decked patios to reward the casual wanderer. Once a Jewish ghetto, its restored buildings, with characteristic window grilles, are now a harmonious mix of upmarket residences and tourist accommodation. Good bars and restaurants make the area well worth an evening visit.

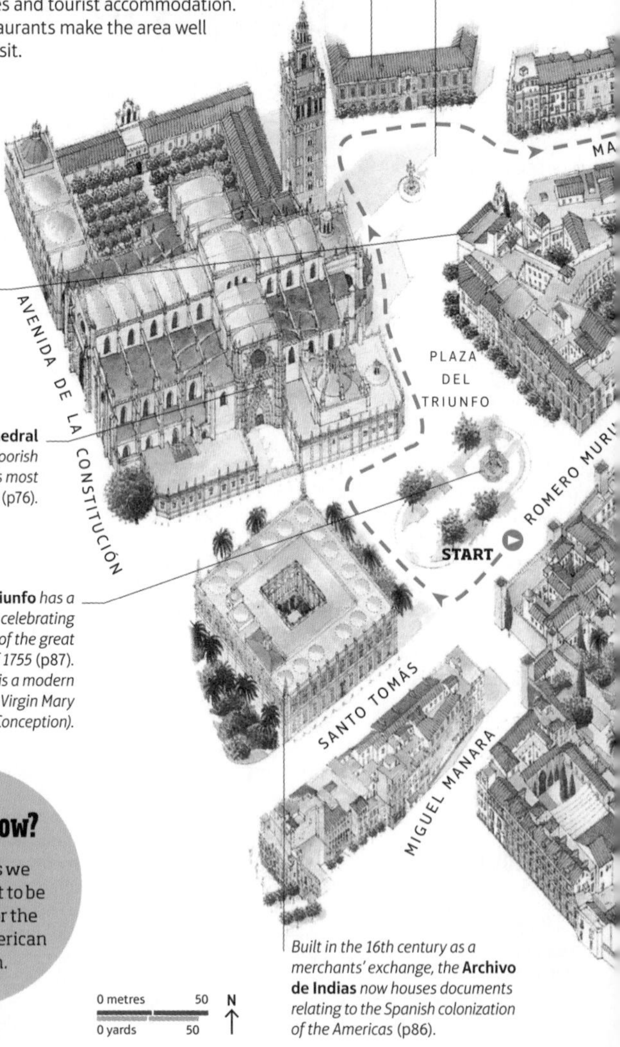

Calle Mateos Gago is shaded by orange trees and filled with souvenir shops, cafés and tapas bars.

The 18th-century **Palacio Arzobispal** *is still used by Seville's clergy (p84).*

In the centre of the **Plaza Virgen de los Reyes** *is a 20th-century fountain by José Lafita (p84).*

Convento de la Encarnación (p84)

The huge Gothic **Cathedral** *and* **La Giralda***, its Moorish bell tower, are Seville's most popular sights (p76).*

PLAZA DEL TRIUNFO

The **Plaza del Triunfo** *has a Baroque column celebrating the city's survival of the great earthquake of 1755 (p87). In the centre is a modern statue of the Virgin Mary (Immaculate Conception).*

START

Did You Know?

Santa Cruz as we know it was set to be demolished for the 1929 Ibero-American Exposition.

Built in the 16th century as a merchants' exchange, the **Archivo de Indias** *now houses documents relating to the Spanish colonization of the Americas (p86).*

0 metres 50 N
0 yards 50 ↑

↑ Outdoor café tables in the pretty Plaza Santa Cruz

Locator Map
For more detail see p74

Plaza Santa Cruz *is adorned by an ornate iron cross from 1692.*

MESÓN DEL

RODRIGO

XIMÉNEZ ENCISO

SANTA TERESA

JAMERDANA

REINOSO

LOPE DE RUEDA

STA CRUZ

GLORIA

PL DOÑA ELVIRA

SUSONA

PIMIENTA

CALLEJÓN DEL AGUA

VIDA

FINISH

The **Hospital de los Venerables** *was a home for elderly priests in the 17th century (p86).*

Callejón del Agua *(Water Street) is a whitewashed alleyway offering glimpses into enchanting plant-filled patios.*

The **Real Alcázar** *is a rewarding combination of exquisite Mudéjar craftsmanship, regal grandeur and land-scaped gardens (p78).*

→

A beautiful tree-shaded building on picturesque Callejón del Agua

A LONG WALK
SEVILLE

Distance 3.5 km (2 miles) **Walking time** 90 minutes **Difficulty** Easy **Nearest metro** Puerta de Jerez

This walk begins in one of the city's most elegant parks and explores one of its oldest *barrios*: the medieval Jewish quarter of Santa Cruz. The tiny alleys and squares of Santa Cruz conceal the birthplace of one of the city's great painters, Murillo, as well as a host of churches and many craft galleries and restaurants. The walk then takes you through Seville's grandest square before heading for the Guadalquivir river, a historic bridge and the Triana area, famous for its ceramics district and as the cradle of Seville's flamenco culture.

Locator Map
For more detail see p64, p74 and p119

Turn into Calle San Eloy; at its end is the **Iglesia de la Magdalena** (p68), *which was built on the remains of a mosque.*

Calle San Pablo, which becomes Reyes Catolicos, leads straight to **Puente de Isabel II**, *which was built on the foundations of a 12th-century Arab bridge.*

The barrio of **Triana** (p120) *will forever be associated with azulejos. For ceramics workshops and shops, bear right into Calles San Jorge and then left into Calle Callao.*

Turn left into Calle Victoria and right into Pelay Correa to reach Seville's oldest church, the 13th-century **Iglesia de Santa Ana** (p124).

Head for Triana's bar-lined riverfront, Calle Betis, which offers amazing views across to the **Torre del Oro** (p69).

Puente de Isabel II (Puente de Triana)

Plaza de Toros de la Maestranza

Iglesia de Santa Ana

↑ Eduardo Chillida's peace monument, *La Tolerancia*, seen from Calle Betis

0 metres	300
0 yards	300

N ↑

The old-fashioned shop front of Maquedano on Calle Sierpes

Cross the square to **Calle Sierpes**, one of Seville's oldest shopping streets (p81). *Check out Maquedano, which always has an impressive window display of hats for sale.*

Take a sharp right into Calle Hernando Colon for the beautiful **Ayuntamiento** *(p80).*

Turn left into Calle Guzman El Bueno and then cross into the Argote de Molina to walk behind the **Palacio Arzobispal** *(p84).*

Turning right near the top of Calle de Mateos Gago, you pass the 17th-century **Iglesia de Santa Cruz**.

Continue past the birthplace of painter Bartolomé Esteban Murillo and the **Convento San José del Carmen**.

Start at the **Jardines de Murillo** *(p87), where there is a monument to Columbus, before heading down Calle Santa Teresa.*

Stroll down Calle San Fernando, past the **Universidad** *(p114), to finish your walk back at the Jardines de Murillo.*

Across the Puente de San Telmo is the **Jardines de Cristina**, *a major bus hub.*

START

FINISH

↑ The towering Monumento a Colon in the Jardines de Murillo

Map labels:

DEL DUQUE DE LA VICTORIA
PL DE LA CAMPANA
Palacio de Lebrija
E RIOJA
LAGAR
CALLE SIERPES
CUNA
aquedano
PLAZA SALVADOR
VILLEGAS
SANTA CRUZ
AZA EVA
PL DE SAN FRANCISCO
yuntamiento
Plaza Nueva
CALLE AIRE
C. DE FRANCOS
GUZMAN EL BUENO
ARGOTE DE MOLINA
ABADES
ANGELES
Palacio Arzobispal
MATEOS GAGO
Santa Cruz
STA TERESA
JIMIOS
AVDA DE ROMA
HERNANDO COLON
Seville Cathedral
Birthplace of Bartolomé Esteban Murillo
Convento San José del Carmen
RCIA DE NUESA
PLAZA DEL CABILDO
AVDA DE LA CONSTITUCION
Archivo de Indias
PLAZA DEL TRIUNFO
PL. DONA ELVIRA
PLAZA ALFARO
SANTO TOMAS
Real Alcázar
TOMAS DE IBARRA
PLAZA CONTRATACION
NTANDER
Jardines del Alcázar
Jardines de Murillo
PUERTA DE JEREZ
Puerta de Jerez
Puerta de Jerez
M
Jardines de Cristina
Hotel Alfonso XIII
CALLE SAN FERNANDO
AVDA DE ROMA
Universidad (Fabrica de Tabacos)
PLAZA DON JUAN DE AUSTRIA
PALOS DE LA FRONTERA

LA MACARENA

Once orchards and farmland, La Macarena was settled by the Moorish Almohads in the 12th century. It became the most northern part of Seville and the city walls, remnants of which can still be seen today, were expanded to encompass this new settlement.

Between 1247 and 1248, the area was taken by the Christians as part of the *reconquista*. Shortly after, in a bid to boost the economy of this newly Christian district, a bustling market sprang up on Calle de la Feria, which still exists today in the form of the weekly El Jueves second-hand market.

By far the area's most famous and celebrated inhabitant is the 17th-century statue of the Virgen de la Esperanza Macarena, a magnificently resplendent depiction of the Madonna weeping. It has been housed in the purpose-built Basílica de la Macarena since 1949. Every year, during Semana Santa (Holy Week), the statue is brought out in the huge processions that fill the streets of La Macarena, where it is enthusiastically revered.

Today, while some of the area's old buildings lie in a state of disrepair, many have been carefully restored, including the 16th-century Hospital de las Cinco Llagas. A working hospital until 1978, it now serves as the seat of Andalucía's Parliament.

LA MACARENA

Experience
1. Alameda de Hércules
2. Monasterio de San Clemente
3. Torre de Don Fadrique
4. Parlamento de Andalucía
5. Cámara Oscura
6. Basílica de la Macarena
7. Murallas
8. Iglesia de San Marcos
9. Iglesia de San Pedro
10. Iglesia San Luís de los Franceses
11. Palacio de las Dueñas
12. Convento de Santa Paula
13. Iglesia de Santa Catalina
14. Metropol Parasol

Eat
1. ConTenedor
2. Eslava
3. Arte y Sabor

Drink
4. Bar Gigante
5. Linterna Ciega
6. Jazz Naima Sevilla

Shop
7. Botellas y Latas
8. Record Sevilla
9. Rompemoldes

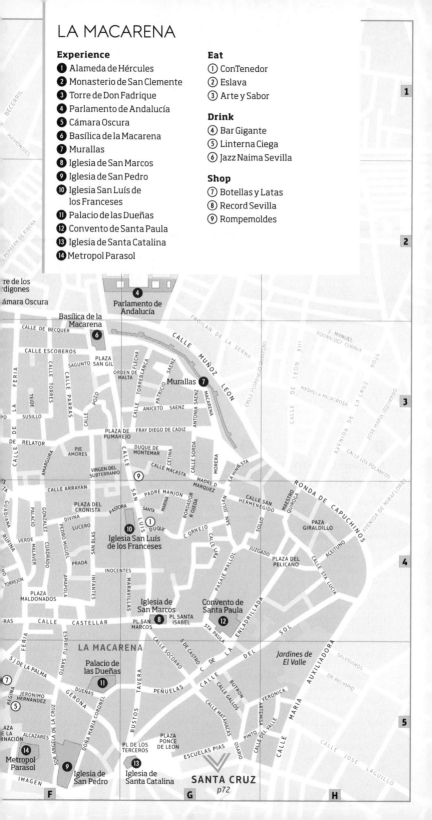

The two marble columns on the Alameda de Hércules, bathed in morning light

EXPERIENCE

1

Alameda de Hércules

📍E4 🚌A7, 13, 14

This tree-lined boulevard was originally laid out in 1574, transforming a former marshy area into a fashionable promenade for *sevillanos* in the 16th century. Today it's a trendy, clean promenade with a bohemian charm; there are walk-through fountains for hot days, and a children's playground. It is also a main centre of nightlife in Seville, with an eclectic mix of bars, cafés and restaurants.

At the southern end stand two marble columns brought here from a Roman temple dedicated to Hercules in what is now Calle Mármoles (Marbles Street), where three other columns remain. Time-worn statues of Hercules and Julius Caesar cap the Alameda's columns.

2

Monasterio de San Clemente

📍E3 🏠Calle Reposo 9 🚌C3, C4 ⛪Church: for Mass only 🌐sanclementesevilla.es

Behind the ancient walls of the Monasterio de San Clemente is a tranquil cloister and an arcade with a side entrance to the monastery's church. This atmospheric church can also be entered from Calle Reposo. Its features range from the 13th to 18th centuries, and include a fine Mudéjar *artesonado* ceiling (with a geometric pattern), *azulejos (p88)* dating from 1588, a Baroque main *retablo* by architect Felipe de Rivas and early 18th-century frescoes by painter Lucas Valdés.

At the times posted outside the gate, the nuns that live here sell a range of sweets, pastries and preserves.

DRINK

Bar Gigante
Quirky vintage decor, and tables on the plaza.

📍E4 🏠Alameda de Hércules 17 📞955 29 45 29

―――――――――

Linterna Ciega
Bijou microbrewery with pale ales, lagers, stouts and more.

📍F5 🏠Calle Regina 10 📞854 52 10 21

―――――――――

Jazz Naima Sevilla
Intimate bar featuring live jazz most evenings.

📍E4 🏠Calle Conde de Barajas 2 📞653 75 39 76

Renaissance building, the Hospital de las Cinco Llagas (Hospital of the Five Wounds). The hospital, founded in 1500 by nobleman Catalina de Ribera, was originally sited near Casa de Pilatos. In 1540 work began on the new site, and it became Europe's largest hospital. Designed by a succession of architects, its south front has a Baroque central portal by Asensio de Maeda.

The hospital was completed in 1613, and admitted patients until the 1960s. In 1992 it was restored for the Parliament.

At the heart of the complex, the Mannerist church, built by Hernán Ruiz the Younger in 1560, makes up the debating chamber.

---

⑤
Cámara Oscura

📍 F2 🏛 Calle Resolana 37 🚌 C1, C2, C3, C4, C5, 2, 13, 14 📞 679 09 10 73 🕐 Sep–mid-July: 11:30am–5pm Tue–Sun; mid-Jul–Aug: 10am–3:30pm Tue–Sun (closed when raining)

Housed in the Tower of Perdigones, this huge camera obscura uses mirrors and magnifying lenses to project a real-time image of the surrounding area.

③
Torre de Don Fadrique

📍 E3 🏛 Espacio de Santa Clara, Calle Becas 🚌 A2, A7, C3, 3, 6 🕐 10am–7pm Tue–Sun 🖥 espaciosanta clara.org

One of the best-preserved historical surprises in Seville, this 13th-century tower stands like a chess-piece castle in the courtyard of the Convento de Santa Clara and once formed part of the defences for the palace of the Infante Don Fadrique. There are fine views from the top of the tower.

---

④ 〈M5〉
Parlamento de Andalucía

📍 G2 🏛 Calle Parlamento de Andalucía 🚌 A2, 2, 10, 13 🕐 By appt only; see website 🖥 parlamentode andalucia.es

The Parliament of Andalucía has its seat in an impressive

⑥ 〈image〉
Basílica de la Macarena

📍 F3 🏛 Calle Bécquer 1 🚌 C1, C2, C3, C4, C5, 2, 10, 13, 14 📞 954 90 18 00 🕐 9am–2pm & 5–9pm daily (from 9:30am Sun) 🗓 Good Fri

Built in 1949, the Basílica de la Macarena houses the much-loved statue of the Virgen de la Esperanza Macarena, which stands above the main altar amid waterfalls of gold and silver. Paintings by Rafael Rodríguez Hernández have themes focusing on the Virgin. In the adjacent museum there are magnificent processional garments as well as gowns made from *trajes de luces* (matadors' outfits), donated no doubt by grateful bull-fighters. Huge floats used in Semana Santa, among them La Macarena's elaborate silver platform, can also be admired.

VIRGEN DE LA MACARENA

Devotions to the Virgen de la Macarena reach their peak during Semana Santa *(p46)*, when her statue is borne through the streets on a canopied float decorated with swathes of white flowers, candles and ornate silver-work. Accompanied by hooded penitents and cries of ¡guapa! (beautiful!) from her followers, the virgin travels from the Basílica de la Macarena to the Cathedral *(p76)* on Good Friday.

↑ The Murallas, or city walls, protecting Seville from invasion since medieval times

❼ Murallas

⊙ G3 ▥ A2, C2, C4, 13

A section of the defensive wall that once enclosed Seville survives along calles Andueza and Muñoz León. It runs from the rebuilt Puerta de la Macarena at the Basílica de la Macarena (p99) to the Puerta de Córdoba some 400 m (1,300 ft) further east.

Dating from the 12th century, it was constructed as a curtain wall with a patrol path in the middle. The original walls had over 100 towers; the Torre Blanca is one of seven that can be seen here. At the eastern end stands the 17th-century Iglesia de San Hermenegildo, named after a Visigothic king allegedly martyred on this site.

❽ Iglesia de San Marcos

⊙ G4 ⚑ Plaza de San Marcos
▥ C5 ☎ 954 50 26 16
⊙ 7-8:30pm (to 8pm in winter) Mon-Sat, 12:30-1:30pm & 7:30-8:30pm Sun

This 14th-century church retains several Mudéjar features, notably its Giralda-like tower (based on the minaret of an earlier mosque) and the decoration on the Gothic portal on Plaza de San Marcos. The restoration of the interior has highlighted unique horseshoe arches in the nave. A statue of St Mark with book and quill pen, attributed to Baroque sculptor Juan de Mesa, is in the far left corner.

In the plaza is the Convento de Santa Isabel, founded in 1490. It became a women's prison in the 19th century. The church within the convent dates from 1609. Its Baroque portal, facing onto Plaza de Santa Isabel, has a bas-relief of *The Visitation* by Andrés de Ocampo.

❾ Iglesia de San Pedro

⊙ F5 ⚑ Plaza de San Pedro
▥ C5, 27, 32 ☎ 954 21 68 58
⊙ 8:30am-1pm & 7-8:30pm Mon-Thu, 8:30-11:30am Fri, 8:30-9:30am & 10:30-11:30am Sat, 9:30am-2pm & 7:30-8:30pm Sun

The church where the painter Diego Velázquez was baptized in 1599 presents a typically Sevillian mix of architectural styles. Mudéjar elements survive in the lobed brickwork of its tower, which is surmounted by a Baroque belfry. The principal portal, facing Plaza de San Pedro, is another Baroque adornment added by stonemason Diego de Quesada in 1613. A statue of St Peter looks disdainfully down at the traffic below.

The poorly lit interior has a Mudéjar wooden ceiling and west door. The vault of one of its chapels is decorated with exquisite geometric patterns formed of interlacing bricks.

Behind the church, in Calle Doña María Coronel, cakes and biscuits are sold by nuns from a revolving drum in the wall of

---

SEVILLE'S BELL TOWERS

Bell towers rise above the rooftops of Seville like bookmarks flagging the passing centuries. The influence of La Giralda (p76) is seen in the Moorish arches and tracery adorning the 14th-century tower of San Marcos, and the Mudéjar brickwork which forms the base for San Pedro's belfry. The churches of Santa Paula (right) and La Magdalena reflect the ornate confidence of the Baroque period, while the towers of San Ildefonso illustrate the Neo-Classical tastes of the 19th century.

← The interior of the Iglesia San Luís de los Franceses, and *(inset)* its two domed towers and cupola

the Convento de Santa Inés. An arcaded patio fronts its restored church, which has frescoes by Francisco de Herrera and a nuns' choir separated from the public by a screen. The preserved body of Doña María Coronel, the convent's 14th-century founder, is honoured in the choir every 2 December.

10 ⊘ ⓜ

Iglesia San Luís de los Franceses

📍 G4 🏠 Calle San Luís 27
🚌 C5 📞 954 55 02 07
🕐 10am–2pm & 4–8pm Tue–Sun

One of the most remarkable examples of the Baroque style of architecture in Seville, the Iglesia San Luís de los Franceses was designed by Spanish architect Leonardo de Figueroa and built between 1699 and 1730. It was built for the Jesuits but, after the order was expelled from Spain in 1835, it had a variety of uses over the following years, including functioning as a convent, factory and hospital.

The church was built at an angle so that the main altar sits in the west. This means that the fabulous altarpiece by sculptor Duque Cornejo is usually bathed in light. The lesser altars of San Estanislao and San Francisco Borja are positioned so that they receive the most sunlight on their relevant saint's day.

As well as the main altar, the interior's other highlight is its dome, which is decorated with significant religious scenes from the old and new testaments. Some of these frescoes are the work of Spanish Baroque painter Lucas de Valdés.

EAT

ConTenedor
Linger over fresh, regional "slow food" delivered with flair.

📍 G4 🏠 Calle San Luís 50
🌐 restaurante contenedor.com

€€€

Eslava
You'll enjoy award-winning Andalucían dishes here.

📍 D4 🏠 Calle Eslava 3
🌐 espacioeslava.com

€€€

Arte y Sabor
This low-key eatery fuses Spanish, Moroccan and Mediterranean cuisine to create beautiful tapas.

📍 E4 🏠 Alameda de Hércules 85
🌐 arteysabor.es

€€€

← Dining room of the Palacio de las Dueñas, official residence of the Dukes of Alba

27 nuns from four continents. The public is welcome to enter through two different doors in the Calle Santa Paula. Knock on the brown one, marked No 11, to have a look at the convent museum. Steps lead to two galleries crammed with religious paintings and artifacts. The windows of the second door look onto the nuns' cloister, which echoes with laughter in the afternoon recreation hour. The nuns make a phenomenal range of marmalades and jams, which visitors may purchase in a room near the exit.

Ring the bell by a brick doorway nearby to visit the convent church, reached by crossing a meditative garden. Its portal vividly combines Gothic arches, Mudéjar brickwork, Renaissance medallions and ceramics by the Italian artist Nicola Pisano.

SHOP

Botellas y Latas

Gourmet shop overflowing with regional products such as artisan cheeses, Iberian ham, sausages, choice patés, preserves, olive oil, wine and beers.

📍F5 🏠 Calle Regina 14 🌐 elclubdelgourmet.es

Record Sevilla

Heaven for music aficionados, with a great selection of new and used vinyl, CDs, cassettes and merchandise.

📍E5 🏠 Calle Amor de Dios 17 🌐 record storeday.es

Rompemoldes

A complex of workshops where artists and craftsmen work, exhibit and sell to the public. Find ceramics, jewellery, clothing, sculptures, decorative pieces and paintings. Hours vary according to each individual space.

📍G4 🏠 Calle San Luís 70 🌐 rompemoldes.com

11
Palacio de las Dueñas

📍F5 🏠 Calle Dueñas 5 🚌C5 🕐 Apr–Sep: 10am–8pm daily; Oct–Mar: 10am–6pm daily 🌐 lasduenas.es

Built in Renaissance style with Mudéjar and Gothic influences, this late 15th-century palace is considered one of the most beautiful in Seville, with lovely courtyards and gardens. Famous Spanish poet Antonio Machado (1875–1939) was born here, and many of his verses highlight the beauty and grandeur of this extraordinary estate.

The palace is a treasure trove of antiques and grand rooms with elegant period furniture. There are also displays of family photos and personal letters. A room is dedicated to the history of the Feria de Abril (p47).

12
Convento de Santa Paula

📍G4 🏠 Calle Santa Paula 11 🚌C5 📞 954 53 63 30 🕐 10am–1pm Tue–Sun

Seville has many enclosed religious complexes, but only a few are accessible. This is one of them, a convent set up in 1475 and currently home to

The honeycombed Metropol Parasol leisure complex ↑

Inside, the nave has a wooden roof carved in 1623. Among its statues are St John the Evangelist and St John the Baptist, carved by sculptor Juan Martínez Montañés.

⑬ Iglesia de Santa Catalina

📍 G5 🏛 Plaza Ponce de Léon 🚌 C5 📞 954 21 74 41 🕐 For Mass at 10am & 8pm daily (also 9pm in summer)

Built on the former site of a mosque, this 14th-century church has a Mudéjar tower modelled on La Giralda (p76),

Did You Know?

The Metropol Parasol is claimed to be the largest wooden structure in the world.

which has been spared the customary Baroque hat. On the west side, by Calle Alhóndiga, the Gothic portal is originally from the Iglesia de Santa Lucía, knocked down in 1930. Within its entrance is a horseshoe arch. At the far left end of the nave, the Capilla Sacramental is by architect Leonardo de Figueroa. On the right, the Capilla de la Exaltación has a decorative ceiling and a figure of Christ by sculptor Pedro Roldán.

⑭ Metropol Parasol

📍 F5 🏛 Plaza de la Encarnación 🚌 C5, 10, 11, 12, 15, 16, 20, 24, 27, 32 🕐 Observation deck & walkways: 10am-11pm Sun-Thu, 10am-11:30pm Fri & Sat; Museum: 10am-7:30pm Tue-Sat, 10am-1:30pm Sun & public hols 🌐 setasdesevilla.com

Known locally as "Las Setas" (The Mushrooms), this

GREAT VIEW
Tower Tally

See how many of Seville's famous bell towers you can spot from the Metropol Parasol's observation deck - perhaps with a drink in hand from one of the skywalk bars.

ultramodern structure with a latticed canopy was built from 2005 to 2011. It presents a striking contrast of modern architecture and astounding archaeological finds: the Observation Deck provides a soaring view of the city, with skywalks circling around the core of gastrobars, while the first floor has an open-air plaza, which hosts cultural events. The market buzzes with life on the ground floor, and the Antiquarium Museum, housed in the basement, showcases the archaeological remains that were found when this project began in 1973, with extensive Roman ruins from the Tiberius era (c AD 14–AD 37), and a Moorish house from the 12th and 13th centuries.

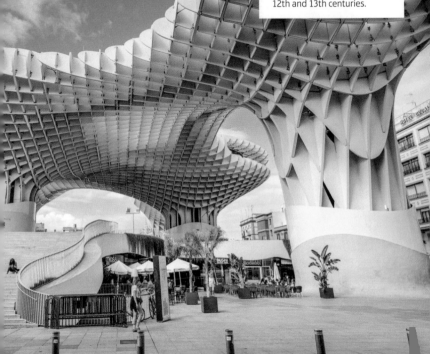

A SHORT WALK
LA MACARENA

Distance 1.5 km (1 mile) **Nearest bus route** C5
Time 20 minutes

A stroll in this area provides a glimpse of everyday life in a part of Seville that has so far avoided developing the rather tourist-oriented atmosphere that is found elsewhere. Calle de la Feria, the main street for shopping and browsing, is best visited in the morning when there is plenty of activity and its market stalls are filled with fresh fish and vegetables. Early evening, meanwhile, is a good time to discover the district's large number of fine churches, which are open for Mass. It is also the time when local people visit the bars for a drink and tapas.

Boxed in by the surrounding houses, the **Palacio de las Dueñas**, *a 15th-century Mudéjar palace, has an elegant patio (p102). It is an official residence of the Dukes of Alba, whose tiled coat of arms can be seen above the palace entrance.*

On Thursday mornings, El Jueves, Seville's oldest market, takes place on **Calle de la Feria**.

The **Iglesia San Juan de la Palma** *is a small Mudéjar church. Its brickwork belfry was added in 1788.*

Did You Know?

The name La Macarena is thought to derive from the Roman goddess, Macaria.

The nuns who live in the **Convento de Santa Inés** *make and sell cakes (p101).*

Velázquez was baptized at the **Iglesia de San Pedro** *(p100). The church is a mix of architectural styles.*

CALLE CASTELLAR

ESPIRITU SANTO

CALLE DE LA FERIA

DUEÑAS ▶ **START**

CALLE GERONA

JERONIMO HERNANDEZ

SOR ANGELA DE

DOÑA MARIA CORONEL

CALLE REGINA

LA CRUZ

The 14th-century **Iglesia de San Marcos**, built on the site of a mosque, has a Mudéjar tower and a beautiful Mudéjar-Gothic portal. The interior preserves unique horseshoe arches (p100).

Locator Map
For more detail see p96

The **Convento de Santa Paula** is one of the city's few cloistered complexes that is accessible to the public (p102).

PLAZA SAN MARCOS

FINISH

SANTA PAULA

ENLADRILLADA

BUSTOS

PEÑUELAS

TAVERA

CALLE DEL SOL

0 metres   75   N
0 yards   75   ↑

San Román is a 19th-century Mudéjar-Gothic church with a fine coffered ceiling.

PLAZA DE LOS TERCEROS

The Gothic **Iglesia de Santa Catalina** has a Mudéjar tower and apse and, inside, a statue of Santa Lucía, patron saint of the blind, by Roldán (p103).

El Rinconcillo is said to be the place where tapas were first invented. Dating back to 1670, it has a suitably old-fashioned atmosphere and a fine selection of food.

↑ Spending an evening in El Rinconcillo

PARQUE MARÍA LUISA

The area south of the city centre is dominated by the extensive, leafy Parque María Luisa, Seville's principal green area. A large part of it originally formed the grounds of the Baroque Palacio de San Telmo, dating from 1682. Today the park is devoted to recreation; with its fountains, flower gardens and mature trees it provides a welcome place to relax during the long, hot summer months. Just north of the park lies Prado de San Sebastián, the former site of the *quemadero*, the platform where many victims of the Inquisition were burnt to death. The last execution took place here in 1781.

Many of the historic buildings situated within the park were erected for the Ibero-American Exposition of 1929. This international jamboree sought to reinstate Spain and Andalucía on the world map. Exhibitions from Spain, Portugal and Latin America were displayed in attractive, purpose-built pavilions that are today used as museums, embassies, military headquarters and also cultural and educational institutions. The grand historic five-star Hotel Alfonso XIII and the crescent-shaped Plaza de España are the most striking legacies from this surge of Andalucían pride.

Nearby is the Royal Tobacco Factory, forever associated with the fictional Romani heroine, Carmen, who toiled in its halls. Today it is part of the Universidad, Seville's university.

D

0 metres 250
0 yards 250

N

PLAZA
CONTRATACION

EL ARENAL
p62

Real
Alcázar

Jardines
de Muril

Jardines del
Alcázar

JUDERIA

S GREGORIO

PUERTA DE
JEREZ

**Puerta de
Jerez**

CALLE SAN FERNANDO

SANTA CRUZ
p72

②

①

Jardines
de Cristina

❷ Hotel
Alfonso XIII

PALOS

AVENIDA DE ROMA

DE

Puente de
San Telmo

Universidad
(Fábrica de Tabacos)

❸

PL DON
JUAN DE
AUSTRIA

Prado d
San Sebastiá

❺ Palacio de
San Telmo

LA

FRONTERA

INFANTE DE RIVERA

CARLO

PASEO DE LAS DELICIAS

Jardines de
San Telmo

CALLE LA RABIDA

GLORIETA
SAN
DIEGO

AVENIDA

DE

9

CALLE

CALLE JUAN

DEL

CALLE DEL TURIA

MONTE

CARMELO

ELCANO

SEBASTIAN

G
u
a
d
a
l
q
u
i
v
i
r

AVENIDA DEL PERÚ

Teatro Lope
de Vega

❹

GRAL PRIMO

AVENIDA DE ISABEL LA CATOLICA

GRAN CAPITAN

Pabellón
de Chile

AVENIDA DE CHILE

Pabellón
de Perú

MARÍA LUISA

PLAZ
DE
ESPA

Pabellón
de Uruguay

AVENIDA

AVDA CONDE DE COLOMBIA

Costuero
de la Reina 𝒊

RODRIGUEZ

CASO

AVENIDA

10

V DE ARACELI

V DE ROBLEDO

GLORIETA
DE LA
CIGARRERA

GLORIETA
DE LOS
MARINEROS

Monumento a
los Marineros
Voluntarios

Puente del
Generalísimo

AVENIDA

DE

PIZARRO

DE

Parque
María Luisa

❶

HERNAN

CORTES

MUELLE

DE

LAS

DELICIAS

AVENIDA

SANTIAGO

MONTOTO

PASEO

DE

LAS

AVENIDA

DE

MAGALLANES

11

Museo de Artes y
Costumbres Populares

PLAZA D

AMÉR

**PARQUE
MARÍA LUISA**

Museo
Arqueológico

12

D

E

F

GLORIETA DE
MEXICO

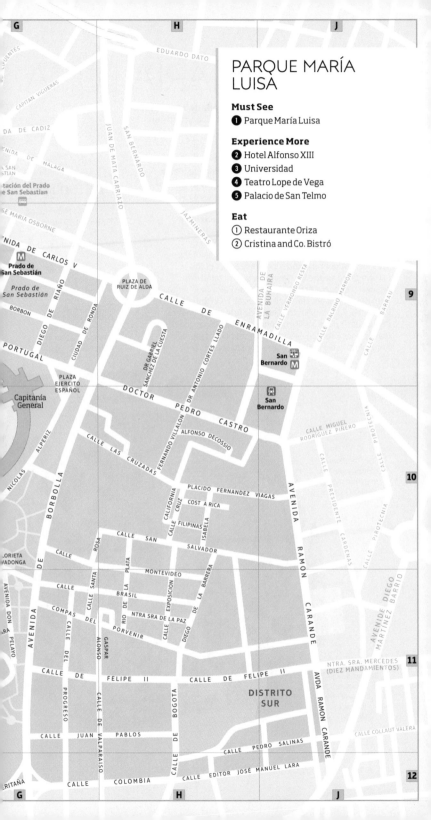

PARQUE MARÍA LUISA

Must See
1 Parque María Luisa

Experience More
2 Hotel Alfonso XIII
3 Universidad
4 Teatro Lope de Vega
5 Palacio de San Telmo

Eat
① Restaurante Oriza
② Cristina and Co. Bistró

❶ 🍴 🖵

PARQUE MARÍA LUISA

📍F10 🏠Paseo de las Delicias s/n Ⓜ🚃Prado de San Sebastián
☎955 47 12 32 🕐Jul & Aug: 8am-midnight daily; Sep-Jun:
8am-10pm daily

Sprinkling fountains, blooming flowers and cool,
tree-shaded avenues all help to make Parque María
Luisa a refreshing retreat from the heat and dust of
the city, particularly in summer.

Princess María Luisa donated part of the grounds of the
Palacio de San Telmo to the city for this park in 1893.
Landscaped by Jean Forestier, director of the Bois de
Boulogne in Paris, the park was the leafy setting for the
1929 Ibero-American Exposition. The legacies of this
extravaganza are the Plaza de España, decorated with
regional scenes on ceramic tiles, and the Plaza de América,
both the work of architect Aníbal González. On the latter,
in the Pabellón Mudéjar, the Museo de Artes y Costumbres
Populares displays traditional Andalucían folk arts. The Neo-
Renaissance Pabellón de las Bellas Artes houses the Museo
Arqueológico, exhibiting artifacts from Itálica (p144).

Did You Know?

Princess María Luisa
married 17-year-old
Leopold II at the
age of 14.

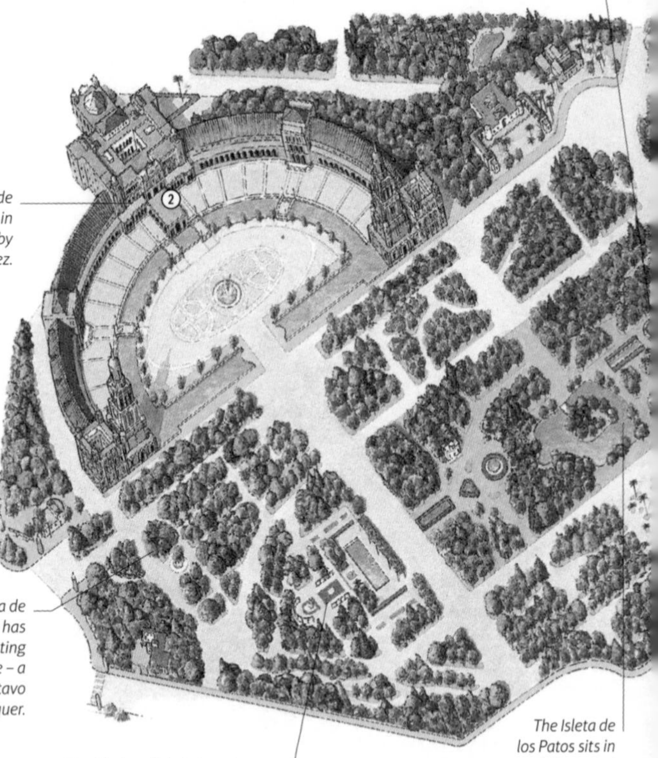

Ceramic lions guard the
Fuente de los Leones, which
was inspired by the fountain
in the Patio de los Leones at
the Alhambra (p216).

The Plaza de
España was built in
a theatrical style by
Aníbal González.

The Glorieta de
Bécquer arbour has
sculptures depicting
the phases of love – a
tribute to poet Gustavo
Adolfo Bécquer.

The Glorieta de la Infanta has a
bronze statue honouring the park's
benefactress, Princess María Luisa.

The Isleta de
los Patos sits in
a lake graced
by ducks and
swans.

↑ The curving Plaza de España and *(inset)* the emotive statue in the nearby Glorieta de Bécquer

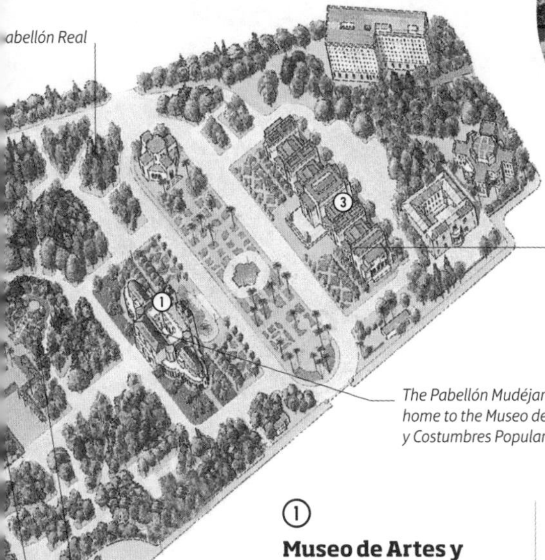

abellón Real

The Neo-Renaissance Pabellón de las Bellas Artes now houses the Museo Arqueológico.

The Pabellón Mudéjar is home to the Museo de Artes y Costumbres Populares.

The Monte Gurugú is a mini-mountain with a tumbling waterfall.

Plaza de América

↑ The tree-shaded avenues and pavilions that make up the Parque María Luisa

①
Museo de Artes y Costumbres Populares

🏠 Pabellón Mudéjar, Parque María Luisa 🚌 1, 3, 6, 30, 31, 34, 37 📞 955 54 29 51 🕐 Jun-mid-Sep: 9am-2:30pm Tue-Sun; mid-Sep-May: 9am-9pm Tue-Sat, 9am-3pm Sun

Housed in the Mudéjar Pavilion of the 1929 Ibero-American Exposition, this museum is devoted to the popular arts and traditions of Andalucía. Exhibits include workshop scenes detailing crafts such as leatherwork, goldsmithing and cooperage, with a re-creation of a Huelva wine cellar. Alongside collections of antique glassware and ceramics, both domestic and ornamental, there is also an informative account of the history of the *azulejo*. Upstairs is a display of 19th-century costumes, furniture, musical instruments and rural machinery. Romantic images of flamenco, bullfighting and the Semana Santa and Feria de Abril *(p47)* are a compendium of the Sevillian cliché.

② Plaza de España

🏠Parque María Luisa

This impressive semicircular plaza was designed by architect Aníbal González as the centrepiece for the 1929 Ibero-American Exposition (p54). González mixed elements of Art Deco, Renaissance and Baroque Revival and Neo-Mudéjar in his design for the building fronting the plaza. With its north and south towers, it's a major city landmark.

In the colonnade fronting the building, there are a series of alcoves decorated with stunning tiles, each representing a Spanish province and a moment in history. For example, the Barcelona alcove depicts Columbus being greeted by the Catholic Monarchs (Queen Isabel I of Castile and King Fernando II of Aragon) on his return from the New World. He bows to his king and queen while the indigenous people that he

brought back with him from the Caribbean lay gifts at their feet. The Madrid alcove, meanwhile, depicts the city's resistance to Napoleon's troops during the Peninsular War. Each alcove is flanked by a pair of bookshelves. Here, you'll find tomes about the province, as well as books left by other visitors. Spend some time browsing the titles.

A canal follows the curve of the building's façade and is crossed by colourful footbridges, which represent the four ancient kingdoms of Spain – Castile, León, Aragon and Navarre. For a fee, you

can jump aboard one of the boats that travel up and down this canal. It's a wonderful way to experience the grandeur of the main building and the atmosphere of the square itself. It'll come as no surprise that the Plaza de España has starred in many films, including *Lawrence of Arabia* (1962), *Star Wars II: Attack of the Clones* (2002) and *The Dictator* (2012).

The Plaza de España's arcade, and *(inset)* one of the tiled alcoves ↑

③
Museo Arqueológico

🏛 **Plaza de América, Parque María Luisa** 🚌**1, 3, 6, 30, 31, 34, 37** 📞**955 12 06 32** 🕐**Jun-mid-Sep: 9am-3pm Tue-Sun; mid-Sep-May: 9am-9pm Tue-Sat, 9am-3pm Sun**

Designed by González, the Pabellón del Renacimiento (Renaissance Pavilion) of the 1929 Ibero-American Exposition is now Andalucía's museum of archaeology. The basement houses Paleolithic to early-Roman exhibits, such as copies of the remarkable Tartessian Carambolo treasures.

←
Bust of the emperor Hadrian, born in Itálica, in the Museo Arqueológico

This hoard of 6th-century BC gold jewellery was discovered by a workman who was excavating a site for a new sports club near Seville in 1958. Oriental elements in its design have intrigued scholars of early civilizations.

Upstairs, the galleries are devoted to the Roman era, with statues and fragments rescued from Itálica *(p144)*. Highlights include a 3rd-century BC mosaic from Écija, a statue of the Venus of Itálica and sculptures of emperors Trajan and Hadrian. The rooms continue to Moorish Spain via Palaeo-Christian sarcophagi, Visigothic relics and artifacts from Medina Azahara.

Potted orange trees surround the elegant patio of the Hotel Alfonso XIII ↑

INSIDER TIP
Tour the High Cs

Seville is the setting for more than 100 operas. Learn about this musical heritage – and hear some of the famous tunes – on a city tour with a soprano (www.sevilla officialtours.com).

EXPERIENCE MORE

②
Hotel Alfonso XIII

📍 E8 🏛 Calle San Fernando 2 🚇Ⓜ Puerta de Jerez 🚌 C5 🌐 hotel-alfonso xiii-sevilla.com

This is Seville's best-known luxury hotel, named after King Alfonso XIII who reigned until 1931, when Spain became a republic. It was built for visitors to the 1929 Ibero-American Exposition. The building is in Regionalista style, decorated with *azulejos* (p88), wrought iron and ornate brickwork. Its centrepiece is a grand colonnaded patio with a fountain. Non-residents are welcome to visit the hotel's bars and restaurants.

③
Universidad

📍 F9 🏛 Calle San Fernando 4 🚇Ⓜ Puerta de Jerez or Prado de San Sebastián 🚌 5, 21, 34, C1, C2, C3, C4 🕐 8am–8:30pm Mon-Fri 🌐 us.es

Part of Seville University now occupies a building that was formerly the Real Fábrica de Tabacos (Royal Tobacco Factory). This was a popular attraction for 19th-century travellers in search of Romantic Spain. Three-quarters of Europe's cigars were manufactured here at that time, rolled by over 3,000 *cigarreras* (female cigar-makers). These women were the inspiration behind Mérimee's novella *Carmen*, and Georges Bizet's opera of the same name.

The factory complex is the largest building in Spain after El Escorial in Madrid and was built between 1728 and 1771. The moat and watchtowers show the importance given to protecting the king's lucrative tobacco monopoly. To the right of the main entrance is the former prison where workers caught smuggling tobacco were kept. To the left is the chapel.

The discovery of tobacco in the Americas is celebrated in the principal portal, which has busts of Columbus (p139) and Cortés. This part of the factory was once used as residential quarters – to either side of the vestibule lie patios with plants and ironwork. Ahead, the Clock Patio and Fountain Patio lead to the former working areas. The tobacco leaves were first dried on the roof, then shredded by donkey-powered mills below.

When Seville University took over the building in 1950, tobacco production moved to a less distinguished factory on the other side of the river. This new factory closed in 2007, bringing Seville's tobacco-making tradition to an end.

CARMEN

The hot-blooded *cigarreras* of Seville's tobacco factory inspired the French author Prosper Mérimée to create his famous Romani heroine, Carmen. The short story he wrote in 1845 tells the tragic tale of a wild, sensual woman who turns her affections from a soldier to a bullfighter and is then murdered by her spurned lover. Bizet based his famous opera of 1875 on this impassioned drama, which established Carmen as the incarnation of Spanish romance.

4

Teatro Lope de Vega

F9 Avenida María Luisa s/n Prado de San Sebastián 5, 21, 34, C1, C2, C3, C4 For performances only teatrolopedevega.org

Lope de Vega (1562–1635), often called "the Spanish Shakespeare", wrote more than 1,500 plays. This Neo-Baroque theatre, which honours him, was opened in 1929 as a casino and theatre for the Ibero-American Exposition. Its domed and colonnaded buildings are still used to stage performances and plays. Savour a coffee amid the faded opulence of the adjacent Café del Casino, housed in a 1920s ballroom.

5

Palacio de San Telmo

E9 Avenida de Roma Puerta de Jerez 3, 5, 21, 37, 41, C3, C4, C5 By appt only Thu & Sat juntadeandalucia.es

This imposing palace was built in 1682 to serve as a marine university, training navigators and high-ranking officers. It is named after St Telmo, patron saint of navigators. In 1849 the palace became the residence of the dukes of Montpensier – until 1893 its vast grounds included what is now Seville's glorious Parque María Luisa *(p110)*. The palace was a seminary from 1901 until 1989, when it became the presidential headquarters of the Junta de Andalucía (the autonomous Andalucían government).

Overlooking the Avenida de Roma is the palace's star feature, the exuberant Churrigueresque portal designed by architect Antonio Matías de Figueroa, and completed in 1734. Surrounding the Ionic columns are allegorical figures representing the nautical arts and sciences. St Telmo, the patron saint of sailors (also known as St Elmo), can be seen holding a ship and charts, flanked by the sword-bearing St Ferdinand and St Hermenegildo with a cross.

The north façade, which is on Avenida de Palos de la Frontera, is crowned by a row of sculptures of Sevillian celebrities. These sculptures were added in 1895 by Antonio Susillo. Among them are representations of several notable artists such as Murillo, Montañés and Velázquez.

EAT

Restaurante Oriza

Expect tantalizing and elegant Basque-Andalucían cuisine at this eatery. The setting is a delightful 20th-century mansion.

F8 Calle San Fernando 41 restauranteoriza.com

€€€

Cristina and Co. Bistró

Feast on a tempting choice of traditional dishes given a modern touch here. Whether you're in the mood for their flavourful vegetable dishes, savoury stews, juicy meats or fresh seafood, you won't be disappointed by Cristina and Co. Bistró.

F8 Calle San Fernando 19 606 41 64 58 D Wed, Sat & Sun

€€€

← The extraordinary sculpted portal in the façade of the Palacio de San Telmo

A SHORT WALK

AROUND THE UNIVERSIDAD

Distance 2.5 km (1.5 miles) **Nearest metro** Puerta de Jerez **Time** 35 minutes

South of the Puerta de Jerez, a cluster of stately buildings stands between the river and Parque María Luisa. The oldest ones owe their existence to the Guadalquivir itself – the 17th-century Palacio de San Telmo was built as a training school for mariners, while the arrival of tobacco from the New World prompted the construction of the monumental Royal Tobacco Factory, today the Universidad de Sevilla. The 1929 Ibero-American Exposition added pavilions in various national and historic styles and also the opulent Hotel Alfonso XIII, creating an area of proud and pleasing architecture that will entertain visitors as they walk towards the Parque María Luisa.

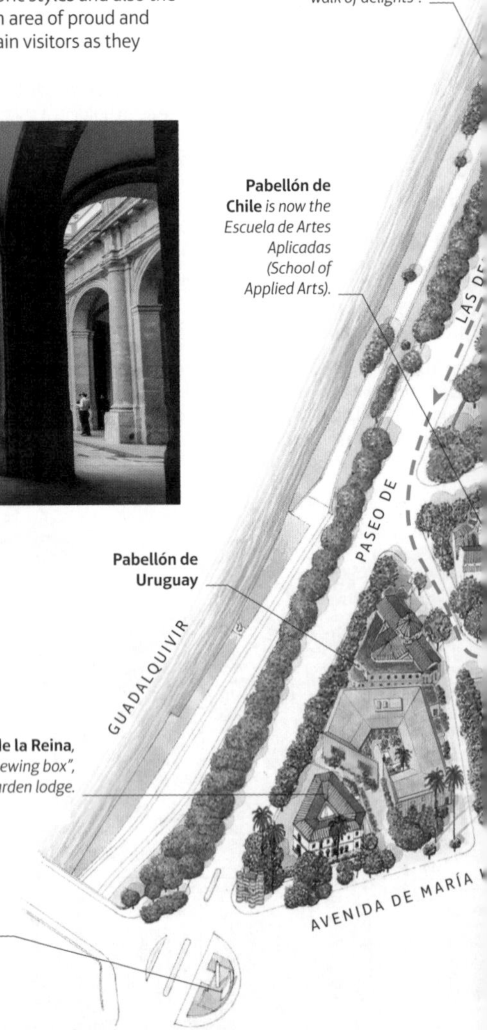

A riverside walk, the **Paseo de las Delicias** *flanks the Jardines de San Telmo. Its name means the "walk of delights".*

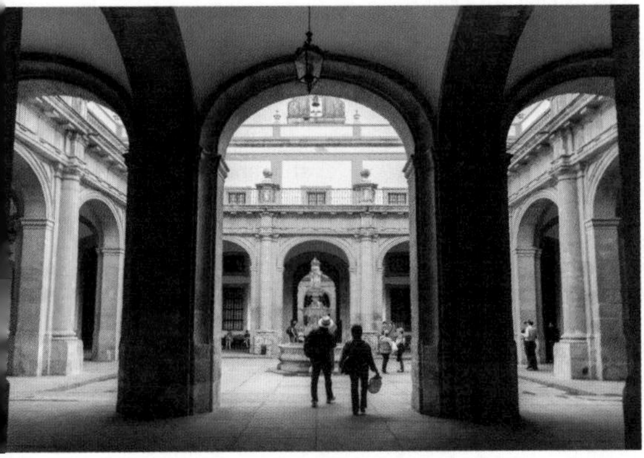

↑ A courtyard in the former Royal Tobacco Factory, now the Universidad

Pabellón de Chile *is now the Escuela de Artes Aplicadas (School of Applied Arts).*

Pabellón de Uruguay

The **Costurero de la Reina**, *or "Queen's sewing box", used to be a garden lodge.*

Monument to El Cano, *who completed the first world circumnavigation in 1522 after Magellan was killed en route.*

GUADALQUIVIR

PASEO DE

LAS DE

AVENIDA DE MARÍA

The **Palacio de San Telmo** houses
the *Junta de Andalucía* (p115).
Presiding over its Churrigueresque
doorway is a statue of St Telmo.
The impressive architecture is
the highlight.

**Around the
Universidad**

**PARQUE
MARÍA LUISA**

Locator Map
For more detail see p108

START

AVENIDA DE ROMA

Seville's premier hotel,
with a sumptuous
Neo-Mudéjar interior,
the **Hotel Alfonso XIII**
welcomes non-guests
to have a drink in its
elegant bar (p114).

FINISH

LA RABIDA

PALOS DE LA FRONTERA

AVENIDA DEL CID

Now part of the **Universidad**,
the vast 18th-century former
Royal Tobacco Factory has
many fine features, including
this Baroque fountain (p114).

Built as the 1929 *Pabellón de
Sevilla*, the **Teatro Lope de Vega**
is now a major venue for staging
concerts and shows (p115).

Modelled on the Archbishop's Palace in Lima, the
Pabellón de Perú has a vividly carved façade. It
is typical of the nationalistic designs used for the
Exposition buildings.

| 0 metres | | 75 |
| 0 yards | | 75 |

N
↑

Ceramic figure on a house in Triana

ACROSS THE RIVER

On the west bank of the Guadalquivir, old Seville meets new. Since Roman times, pottery has been made in Triana, an area named after the emperor Trajan. It has traditionally been a working-class district, famous as the home of bullfighters and flamenco artists. In the 15th century, a Carthusian monastery was built in what was then a quiet area north of Triana – hence the name that the district acquired: Isla de la Cartuja. Later Columbus resided here, planning his future exploits. Mainly due to this connection, La Cartuja was the site for Expo '92. The Expo site has been redeveloped to include the Isla Mágica theme park.

Must See

① Triana

Experience More

② Isla Mágica
③ PCT Cartuja
④ CaixaForum
⑤ Monasterio de Santa María de las Cuevas
⑥ Iglesia de Santa Ana
⑦ Iglesia de Nuestra Señora de la O
⑧ Torre Sevilla

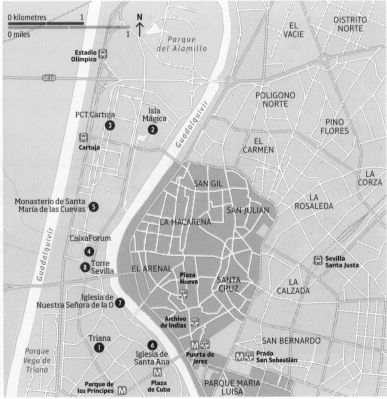

①

TRIANA

C Centro Cerámica Triana: 954 34 15 82; Museo de la Inquisición: 954 33 22 40
M Plaza de Cuba, Parque de los Príncipes **🚌** C1, C2, C3

Named after the Roman emperor Trajan, this quarter has, since early times, been famous for its potteries and plenty of workshops still produce and sell tiles and ceramics. Once Seville's Romani quarter, this *barrio* also has a reputation for producing great bullfighters, sailors and flamenco artists. It remains a traditional working-class district, with compact, flower-filled streets and a tangibly independent atmosphere.

Triana may seem a world away from the grandeur of central Seville, but it's just as enchanting as the areas on the other side of the Río Guadalquivir, and there is plenty to keep you occupied here. Visitors to Triana can buy tiles and wander through its narrow streets during the day, and enjoy the lively bars and romantic views across the river at night. Worth a visit is the museum dedicated to Triana's ceramic-making tradition – the Centro Cerámica Triana. On display here are tiles decorated by the architect Aníbal González, as well as 16th-century kilns, tools and materials. To discover a different side of Triana's history, head to the Museo de la Inquisición, in the Castillo de San Jorge, which examines the events of the Spanish Inquisition through paintings and dramatizations.

> 💬 INSIDER TIP
> **A Day on the Tiles**
>
> Take a two-and-a-half-hour workshop at Barro Azul, where you'll learn some basic ceramic techniques, before painting a tile that you can take home with you *(www.barroazul.es)*.

Boats on the Río Guadalquivir during Triana's Vela de Santa Ana festival ↑

Housed in the old Cerámica Santa Ana factory, the Centro Cerámica Triana examines the area's crafts.

Built by Aníbal González in 1926, the Capillita del Carmen stands at the west end of the Puente de Isabel II.

The Puente de Isabel II, an iron bridge also known as Puente de Triana, leads to El Arenal.

Museo de la Inquisición

At the west end of Puente de Isabel II, the Plaza del Altozano features glass-fronted, wrought-iron balconies called *miradores*.

CASTILLA

ANTILLANO CAMPOS

SAN JORGE

ADONGA

SAN JACINTO

PLAZA DEL ALTOZANO

RODRIGO DE TRIANA

FLOTA

CALLE BETIS

CALLE DE LA PUREZA

JUAN LUGO

TORRIJOS

PELAY CORREA

DUARTE

Calle Betis, a hub of nightlife, is lined with bars, cafés and clubs.

The Capilla de los Marineros is a sailors' chapel.

Calle Rodrigo de Triana is named after the sailor who first caught sight of the New World in 1492.

Founded in the 13th century by Alfonso X, the Iglesia de Santa Ana is the city's oldest parish church (p124).

Hung with flowers and often washing, Calle Pelay Correa evokes the close-knit flavour of old Triana.

↑ The atmospheric streets of Triana

SANTA JUSTA AND SANTA RUFINA

Two Christians working in the Triana potteries in the 3rd century became Seville's patron saints after they were thrown to the lions by the Romans for refusing to join a procession venerating Venus. Their martyrdom has inspired many works by Sevillian artists, including those by Antonio María Esquivel *(right)*.

EXPERIENCE MORE

② Isla Mágica

🏛 Pabellón de España, Isla de la Cartuja 🚌 C1, C2
🕐 Hours vary, check website 🗓 Nov–mid-Apr
🌐 islamagica.es

Opened in 1997, the popular Isla Mágica theme park occupies part of the Isla de la Cartuja, the island that was redeveloped for Expo '92. Elsewhere on the island are PCT Cartuja and the Monasterio de Santa María de las Cuevas (p124).

Isla Mágica recreates the exploits of the explorers who set out from Seville in the 16th century on voyages of discovery to the New World. The first of its six zones is Seville, Port of the Indies, followed by the Gateway to the Americas, the Pirate's Lair, the Fountain of Youth, El Dorado and Amazonia. The Jaguar is the most thrilling ride for visitors – a roller coaster hurtling at 85 km/h (53 mph) along its looping course, but head also for the Anaconda, a flume ride, the Orinoco Rapids, on which small boats are buffeted in swirling water, and El Desafío ("The Challenge"), a spectacular 68-m (223-ft) freefall tower designed as a minaret. There are terrific views from the top before the stomach-churning drop. The Fountain of Youth is designed for children, with carousels and fighting pirates.

For an additional fee, Agua Mágica offers four zones of water-based fun. Playa Quetzal has a large swimming pool with simulated waves and a beach; Isla de Tobagones is a maze of waterslides; Río Lento features a slow-moving river that visitors can float down; and Mini Paraiso has a pool and smaller slides aimed at younger children. Shows in the park include street performances and dance, as well as IMAX cinema screenings. Check the Isla Mágica website for up-to-date information on shows and times.

Did You Know?

Isla Mágica's most popular attraction, the Jaguar, was the first inverted roller coaster in Spain.

③ PCT Cartuja

🏛 Paseo del Oeste (renamed Calle Leonardo da Vinci) 🚌 C1, C2

The Parque Científico y Tecnológico Cartuja is a science and technology park that occupies the western side of the Expo '92 site. Visitors can walk along Calle Leonardo da Vinci and the service roads for close-up views of some of Expo '92's most spectacular pavilions.

→ Riding a traditional swing ride at the Isla Mágica theme park

CaixaForum's entrance, designed by Guillermo Vázquez Consuegra ↑

These striking buildings are, however, now part of the Andalucían World Trade Centre and belong to public and private companies, and as such are closed to visitors. Groups of buildings south and east of the Parque Alamillo are part of Seville University, which has links with PCT Cartuja. To its south lie the gardens surrounding the ancient Monasterio de Santa María de las Cuevas (p124), which now houses a contemporary art museum.

CaixaForum

🏛 Centro Comercial Torre Sevilla, Calle López Pintado s/n 🚌 5, C1 🕙 10am-8pm daily (to 6pm 5 Jan, Thu & Fri of Holy Week, 24 & 31 Dec) 🌐 caixaforum.es

This modern cultural centre sponsored by the CaixaBank financial group offers a smorgasbord of entertainments, including exhibitions, events, films, workshops, talks, storytelling, poetry readings, concerts and other activities. It is located below the shopping centre at the base of the 40-storey Torre Sevilla skyscraper (p125), which is owned by CaixaBank, who sponsor the complex.

The complex has two expansive exhibition areas, an amphitheatre with seating for up to 273 guests, two multi-use halls, a zone for children's activities, a gift shop with an excellent selection of art and design books and a restaurant with al fresco dining available. The exhibitions change four times a year, and focus on La Caixa's collection of contemporary art. Within these exhibitions are activities for children, based on the theme of the current displays.

EAT

Vega 10
Cosy restaurant offering a delectable range of creative tapas, an ample list of wines, attentive service with a smile and very good value.

🏛 Calle Rosario Vega 10 📞 954 23 77 48 🕙 Sun

€€€

Mariatrifulca
Magical spot on the river. Fresh seafood is the focus, but landlubbers will relish the prime cuts of meat on offer.

🏛 Plaza del Altozano 1 📞 954 33 03 47

€€€

Restaurante El Duende
Mediterranean fine dining taken to the next level - literally - with plates accompanied by commanding city views from the top of the Torre Sevilla.

🏛 34th floor, Torre Sevilla, Calle Gonzalo Jiménez Quesada 2 🕙 L 🌐 restauranteel duendesevilla.com

€€€

This is the eighth CaixaForum in the country, and the third largest, at over 8,000 sq m (86,000 sq ft), hosting some 1,200 events per year. Visit on a Sunday and complete your experience with the curated menu in the restaurant, offering select dishes from the region from which the current featured artist hails. There are dizzying upward views of the Torre Sevilla from the restaurant terrace.

Monasterio de Santa María de las Cuevas

 Calle Américo Vespucio 2, Isla de la Cartuja 🕙11am-9pm Tue-Sat, 11am-3:30pm Sun & public hols 🌐museosdeandalucia.es

This huge complex, built by the Carthusian monks in the 15th century, is closely tied to Seville's history. Columbus stayed and worked here, and even lay buried in the crypt of the church, Capilla Santa Ana, from 1507 to 1542. The Carthusians lived here until 1836 and commissioned some of the finest works of the Seville School (p50), including

> 💬 **INSIDER TIP**
> ## So Jazzy
>
> Visit the Centro Andaluz de Arte Contemporáneo on a Sunday morning. After contemplating the thought-provoking works, get your groove on to live jazz at the museum's outdoor café.

The Monasterio de Santa María de las Cuevas, and (inset) its alabaster tombs ↑

masterpieces by Zurbarán and Montañés, now in the Museo de Bellas Artes (p66).

In 1841 Charles Pickman, a British industrialist, built a ceramics factory on the site. After decades of successful business, production ceased in 1980 and the monastery was restored as a central exhibit for Expo '92.

Don't miss the Capilla de Afuera by the main gate, and the Casa Prioral, which has an exhibition of the restoration. There is a Mudéjar cloister, made of marble and brick. The chapter house has a number of tombstones of rich patrons of the monastery.

The monastery also houses the Centro Andaluz de Arte Contemporáneo, which features contemporary art exhibitions as part of the Museo de Arte Contemporáneo. The centre's permanent collection is mostly by 20th-century Andalucían artists, while its temporary exhibitions

include paintings, photographs, installations, sculpture, digital art and performance art by international artists.

Iglesia de Santa Ana

📍Entrance at Calle Vázquez de Leca 1 📞954 27 08 85 🕙10:30am-1:30pm Mon-Thu, 11am-1:30pm Fri

One of the first churches built in Seville after the reconquista (p50), Santa Ana was founded in 1276 but has been much remodelled over the centuries. Today it is a focal point for the residents and cofradías (the religious brotherhoods) of the Triana district.

In the baptistery is the *Pila de los Gitanos*, or Romani Font, which is believed to pass on the gift of flamenco song to the children of the faithful.

The vaulting of the nave is similar to that of Burgos Cathedral, suggesting that the same architect worked on both. The west end of the nave has a 16th-century *retablo*, richly carved by Alejo Fernández. In the baptistery is the *Pila de los Gitanos*, or Romani Font, which is believed to pass on the gift of flamenco song to the children of the faithful.

7

Iglesia de Nuestra Señora de la O

🏛 Calle de Castilla 📞 954 33 75 39 🕐 Daily

The Church of Our Lady of O, built in the late 17th century, has a belfry decorated with locally made *azulejos*. Inside, Baroque sculptures include a Virgin and Child with silver haloes, attributed to Duque Cornejo, in the far chapel to the left as you enter. On the other side of the high altar is a fine group by Pedro Roldán depicting St Anne, St Joachim and Mary, the Virgin; a Jesus of Nazareth bearing his cross in the main chapel is by the same sculptor.

The church is on Calle de Castilla, whose name comes from the notorious castle in Triana where the Inquisition had its headquarters from the 16th century. The castle now houses the **Museo de la Inquisición**.

Museo de la Inquisición

🏛 Plaza del Altozano s/n 📞 955 47 02 55 🕐 11am–6pm Tue–Sat, 10am–3pm Sat & Sun

8

Torre Sevilla

🏛 Calle Gonzalo Jiménez de Quesada 2 🚌 C1, C2, 6 & 43 🌐 torre-sevilla.com

Located on the southern edge of La Cartuja, the Torre Sevilla towers over the Guadalquivir river and commands superb views. Designed by Argentinian architect César Pelli, this 40-storey, 180-m (590-ft) tower was the subject of much controversy while in its planning stages and UNESCO voted against its construction, due to its obstruction of the skyline. The Eurostars five-star hotel occupies the top 12 storeys; the remaining floors are used as commercial office and retail space.

For a good view of the tower itself, visit the adjacent shopping centre's garden roof.

→ The Torre Sevilla (Seville Tower), the tallest building in Andalucía

125

EXPERIENCE
ANDALUCÍA

Huelva and Sevilla................................132

Córdoba and Jaén................................148

Cádiz and Málaga................................174

Granada and Almería........................210

GETTING TO KNOW
ANDALUCÍA

The autonomous region of Andalucía dominates southern Spain. It's a land of dramatic landscapes, with deserts, wetlands, snowcapped mountains and, of course, sunny beaches. The cities, too, are equally beguiling, with their intriguing mixture of architecture, from Moorish to modern.

PAGE 132

HUELVA AND SEVILLA

Steeped in ageless charm, Andalucía's western extremities are rarely explored by visitors. Here, you can imagine Roman gladiators roaring in the amphitheatre at Itálica or bask in the seductive town of Carmona, which exudes its Arabic past. Away from the towns and cities, there are wild, isolated beaches along Huelva's Atlantic coast. If you like wildlife, head for the dunes and marshes of the Parque Nacional de Doñana and, if walking is your thing, the craggy mountains of the northern sierras invite endless exploration.

Best for
Getting out in nature

Home to
Parque Nacional de Doñana

Experience
A 4WD tour of the Parque Nacional de Doñana

PAGE 148

CÓRDOBA AND JAÉN

Running across the north of these two provinces is the Sierra Morena, where deer and boar shelter in forest and scrub, while gold expanses of sunflowers and corn lie to the south. In between, you'll find some of Andalucía's best architecture. Home to the most UNESCO World Heritage sites in the world, including the vast great mosque La Mezquita, the city of Córdoba is a must-visit. If Córdoba province is a Moorish masterpiece, then Jaén is a Renaissance rival, with its enchanting twin cities of Úbeda and Baeza.

Best for
Amazing architecture

Home to
Córdoba, Jaén, Úbeda, Baeza

Experience
Stargazing in the Sierra Morena, a UNESCO Starlight Reserve

$\rightarrow$

PAGE 174

CÁDIZ AND MÁLAGA

Andalucía's southern provinces offer striking contrasts. Málaga's jagged cliffs, peppered with whitewashed villages and abandoned fortresses, drop off abruptly to fashionable seaside resorts. Inland from the Costa del Sol are forested mountains and awesome natural wonders, such as the Garganta del Chorro, and to the west are the verdant farmlands and vineyards of Cádiz, home to the age-old sherry industry. Here, the proximity of North Africa is palpable not just in the sight of Morocco across the Strait, but in the lingering Moorish aura.

Best for
Bodegas and beaches

Home to
Jerez de la Frontera, Cádiz, Ronda, Málaga

Experience
Grape stomping in Jerez de la Frontera

PAGE 210

GRANADA AND ALMERÍA

How many places offer the opportunity to go skiing on powdered pistes one day and swimming in crystal-clear waters the next? Bisected by the snowy Sierra Nevada mountain range and skirted by the golden beaches of the Costa Tropical, Granada province is unique. To the east, you can play cowboy in the dry deserts of Almería or relax on the secluded sands of the Parque Natural de Cabo de Gata. The cities, too, are equally enchanting. Don't miss Granada itself and its magical Moorish palace – the Alhambra.

Best for
Snow and sand

Home to
Granada, Almería

Experience
Skiing in the Sierra Nevada

HUELVA AND SEVILLA

Roman legions under Scipio Africanus founded Itálica, a formidable metropolis to the north of Seville, in the 3rd century BC. It became the first of many illustrious settlements. Later, the Moors held the region as part of the Emirate of al-Andalus. They peppered it with whitewashed, fortified towns, such as Carmona. After the Christian *reconquista*, Moorish traditions persisted through Mudéjar architecture, blending with Baroque and Renaissance in cities such as Osuna, which flourished in the 16th century.

Huelva province is inextricably bound up with another chapter in the history of world conquest – in 1492 Columbus set out on his epic voyage from Palos de la Frontera, which at the time was an important port.

Running along Huelva's northern border is a ridge of mountains, of which the forested Sierra de Aracena forms part. These mountains are home to the large reserves of iron, copper and other elements, that have been mined by Rio Tinto, an Anglo-Australian firm, since 1873. The pollution caused by this industry was first protested against in 1888, and hundreds of people are thought to have died in this "year of shots". But, today, Huelva and Sevilla are renowned for their natural beauty. In the Sierra Norte de Sevilla, goats forage, birds of prey fly overhead and streams gush through deep chasms. The Parque Nacional de Doñana preserves the dunes and marshlands near the mouth of the Guadalquivir to the south. Here, teeming bird life and wetland fauna thrive on the mudflats and shallow, saline waters.

PORTUGAL

Sierra

Morena

Moura

Fregenal de
la Sierra

Arroyomolinos
de León

Monest

Rosal de la
Frontera

Aroche

Embalse
de Aracena

Santa Olalla
del Cala

Cortegana

Jabugo

Aracena

Higuera
de la Sierra

Santa Bárbara
de Casa

4

**SIERRA DE
ARACENA**

El Ronquillo

Paymogo

Cabezas
Rubias

Zalamea
la Real

3 **MINAS DE
RIOTINTO**

El Castillo de
las Guardas

Calañas

HUELVA

Tharsis

Valverde
del Camino

Alosno

Aznalcóllar

Villanueva de
los Castillejos

Embalse
de Sancho

Sanlúcar de
Guadiana

San Bartolomé
de la Torre

EL CONDADO **15**

Sanlúcar
la Mayor

San Silvestre
de Guzmán

Gibraleón

Trigueros

Niebla

Palma del Condado

Villablanca

San Juan
del Puerto

Bollullos
del Condado

Pilas

Cartaya

HUELVA

6

8 **MOGUER**

Almonte

10

Lepe

**MONASTERIO DE
LA RÁBIDA**

9 **11**

**PALOS DE
LA FRONTERA**

AYAMONTE

2

**ISLA
CRISTINA**

**PUNTA
UMBRÍA**

5

7 **MAZAGÓN**

12 **EL ROCÍO**

Villafranca de
Guadalquiví

Golfo de Cádiz

21

MATALSCAÑAS

1

**PARQUE
NACIONAL DE
DOÑANA**

Sanlúcar de
Barrameda

Chipiona

Atlantic Ocean

El Puerto de
Santa María

Cádiz

San Fernando

Chiclana de
Fronte

0 kilometres   25
0 miles   25

N
↑

HUELVA AND SEVILLA

Must See

❶ Parque Nacional de Doñana

Experience More

❷ Isla Cristina
❸ Minas de Riotinto
❹ Sierra de Aracena
❺ Punta Umbría
❻ Huelva
❼ Mazagón
❽ Moguer
❾ Monasterio de la Rábida
❿ Ayamonte

⓫ Palos de la Frontera
⓬ El Rocío
⓭ Lebrija
⓮ Itálica
⓯ El Condado
⓰ Sierra Norte
⓱ Écija
⓲ Estepa
⓳ Osuna
⓴ Carmona
㉑ Matalascañas

→

Greater flamingos fishing
on a marsh in the Parque
Nacional de Doñana at dusk

1 (⅍)

PARQUE NACIONAL DE DOÑANA

🄰B4 🄰Huelva & Sevilla 🅸Carretera A-483, km 1, La Rocina; Carretera A-483 Almonte-Matalascañas, km 27.5, Palacio del Acebrón; Carretera A-483 del Rocío a Matalascañas, km 12, El Acebuche; www.reddeparquesnacionales.mma.es

Doñana National Park is ranked among Europe's greatest wetlands. Together with its adjoining protected areas, the park covers over 50,000 hectares (185,000 acres) of marshes and sand dunes, and is home to an abundance of wildlife.

The area used to be a hunting ground belonging to the Dukes of Medina Sidonia. As the land was never suitable for human settlers, wildlife was able to flourish and, in 1969, this large area became officially protected. In addition to a wealth of endemic species, such as fallow deer (*Dama dama*), red deer (*Cervus elaphus*) and the imperial eagle (*Aquila adalberti*), thousands of migratory birds, including the squacco heron (*Ardeola ralloides*) and the greater flamingo (*Phoenicopterus ruber*), stop here in winter when the marshes become flooded again, after months of drought.

Softly rounded dunes, up to 30 m (100 ft) high, fringe the park's coastal edge. Monte de Doñana, the wooded area behind these sand dunes, provides shelter for lynx, deer and boar, and the number of visitors to the park's interior is strictly controlled. The only way to access the area is on a tour (*www.donanareservas.com*).

THE LYNX'S LAST REFUGE

The lynx is one of Europe's rarest mammals and is only glimpsed with patience. In Doñana about 30 individual Iberian lynx (*Lynx pardinus*) have found refuge. They have yellow-brown fur with dark-brown spots and pointed ears with black tufts. Research is under way into this shy, nocturnal animal, which tends to stay hidden in scrub. It feeds mainly on rabbits and ducks, but might catch an unguarded fawn.

←
A squacco heron, with a bright blue bill during the breeding season

A spiny thrift (*Armeria pungens*) growing on
↓ Doñana's dunes

INSIDER TIP
Walk this Way

The park has three self-guided paths: La Rocina to Charco de la Boca is 3.5 km (2 miles) long, Charco del Acebrón is a 1.5-km (1-mile) route and there is a 1.5-km (1-mile) circuit around Laguna del Acebuche.

EXPERIENCE MORE

❷ Isla Cristina

🅰A3 🏠Huelva 🚌 ℹ️Calle San Francisco 12; www.islacristina.org

Once a distinct island, Isla Cristina is now surrounded by marshes. Situated near the mouth of the Guadiana river, it is an important fishing port, home to a fleet of tuna and sardine trawlers. With a fine sandy beach, Isla Cristina is also a popular summer resort. Situated along the main seafront is an excellent choice of restaurants, which serve delicious, freshly landed fish and seafood.

EAT

Casa Rufino
Our favourite Isla Cristina restaurant.

🅰A3 🏠Avenida de la Playa s/n, Isla Cristina 🌐restauranterufino.com

€€€

LPA The Culinary Bar
Tantalizing seafood in Ayamonte.

🅰A3 🏠Plaza la Lota 10, Ayamonte ☎633 66 76 03 🗓Mon

€€€

Restaurante Tapas Jesús Carrión
Regional cuisine is given a twist at this Aracena eatery.

🅱B2 🏠Calle Pozo de la Nieve 35, Aracena 🌐jesuscarrion restaurante.com

€€€

Did You Know?
NASA uses the extreme acid environment of Riotinto to simulate conditions on Mars.

---

❸ Minas de Riotinto

🅱B3 🏠Huelva 🚌 ℹ️Plaza de Minero s/n; www.ayto riotinto.es

A fascinating detour off the N435 between Huelva and the Sierra de Aracena leads to the opencast mines at Riotinto. These have been excavated since Phoenician times; the Greeks, Romans and Visigoths exploited their reserves of iron, copper, silver and mineral ores.

From the lip of the crater, the trucks at work in the mines appear toy-sized. The **Museo Minero** in the village explains the history of the mines and of the Rio Tinto company. At weekends and on public holidays there is a train tour in restored 1900 carriages.

Museo Minero

🕐🕙 🏠Plaza del Museo 🕐10:30am–3pm & 4–7pm daily 🗓1 & 6 Jan, 25 Dec 🌐parquemineroderiotinto.es

---

❹ Sierra de Aracena

🅰A3 🏠Huelva 🚂El Repilado 🚌Aracena ℹ️Calle Pozo de la Nieve, Aracena; www.aracena.es

This wild mountain range in northern Huelva province is one of the most remote and least visited corners of Andalucía. Its slopes, covered with cork, oak, chestnut and wild olive, are cut by rushing streams and many tortuous mountain roads. The main town here, Aracena, squats at the foot of a ruined Moorish fortress on a hillside pitted with caverns. One of these, the entrancing **Gruta de las Maravillas** ("Cave of Wonders"), can be entered to see its underground Emerald Lake and extraordinary stalactite and stalagmite formations.

Gruta de las Maravillas

🕐🕙 🏠Calle Pozo de la Nieve, Aracena ☎663 93 78 76 🕐10am–1:30pm & 3–6pm daily

---

❺ Punta Umbría

🅰A3 🏠Huelva 🚌 ℹ️Avenida Ciudad de Huelva; www.punta umbria.es

The largest beach resort in Huelva province, Punta Umbría sits at the end of a long promontory, with the

↑ Shaded boardwalk leading to the beach at Punta Umbría

Marismas del Odiel wetlands to one side and a sandy beach on the other. The Riotinto Company first developed the resort in the late 19th century for its British employees. Today, the beachside villas are popular with Spanish visitors.

A long bridge crosses the marshes, giving road access from Huelva, but it's more fun to follow the trail blazed by Riotinto expatriates seeking the sun and take the ferry across the bird-rich wetlands.

6
Huelva

🅰A3 🚉Huelva 🚌 🚌 🛈Calle Jesús Nazareno 21; www. turismohuelva.org

Founded as Onuba by the Phoenicians, Huelva had its grandest days as a Roman port. It prospered again in the early days of trade with the Americas, but Seville soon took over. Its decline culminated in 1755, when Huelva was almost wiped out by the great Lisbon earthquake. Today, industrial suburbs sprawl around the Odiel quayside, from which the Rio Tinto company once exported its products all over the commercial world.

That Columbus set sail from Palos de la Frontera, across the estuary, is Huelva's main claim to fame. This fact is celebrated in the excellent **Museo Provincial**, which also has several exhibitions charting the history of Riotinto.

Museo Provincial
🅰 Alameda Sundheim 13
📞959 65 04 24 🕘9am-8pm Tue-Sat, 9am-3pm Sun

COLUMBUS IN ANDALUCÍA

Believing that he could reach India by sailing westwards, Christopher Columbus (below) set off in that direction from Palos de la Frontera in 1492. When he landed in the Bahamas later that same year, he believed that he had fulfilled his ambition. He made three further voyages from Andalucía, reaching mainland South America and other islands in what are still termed the West Indies in deference to his mistake.

The Emerald Lake in the Gruta de las Maravillas, ↓ Sierra de Aracena

❼
Mazagón

🅰A4 🏠Huelva 🚌 ℹEdificio Mancomunidad, Avenida de los Conquistadores s/n; www.andalucia.org

One of the more remote beach resorts of the Costa de la Luz, Mazagón shelters among pine woods 23 km (14 miles) southeast of Huelva. Virtually deserted in winter, it comes to life in summer when mainly Spanish holiday-makers arrive to fish, sail and enjoy the huge, and often windswept, beach. Despite this seasonal influx, if you visit the resort in the summer months, you may still find some pleasure in Mazagón's solitude, while taking long walks along the endless Atlantic shoreline and among the sand dunes.

↑ Moguer, a maze of pretty streets and flower-filled shady courtyards

❽
Moguer

🅰A3 🏠Huelva 🚌 ℹCalle Andalucía 17; www.andalucia.org

A beautiful whitewashed town, Moguer is a delight to stroll around, exploring treasures such as the 16th-century hermitage of Nuestra Señora de Montemayor and the Neo-Classical town hall. Moguer is also the birthplace of the poet and 1956 Nobel laureate Juan Ramón Jiménez. The **Museo de Zenobia y Juan Ramón Jiménez** is located in his restored former home.

The walls of the 14th-century **Monasterio de Santa Clara** enclose some splendid, stone-carved Mudéjar cloisters. The nuns' dormitory, kitchen and refectory capture some of the atmosphere of their life here.

Museo de Zenobia y Juan Ramón Jiménez

♿🕐 🏠Calle Juan Ramón Jiménez 10 🕐Hours vary, check website 🌐fundacion-jrj.es

Monasterio de Santa Clara

♿🕐 🏠Plaza de las Monjas 🕐By guided tour only; Tue-Sun 🌐monasteriodesanta clara.com

---

❾ ♿ 🕐
Monasterio de la Rábida

🅰A3 🏠Diseminado de la Rábida s/n, Huelva 🚌From Huelva 🕐10am-6pm Tue-Sun 🌐monasteriodela rabida.com

In 1491, a dejected Genoese explorer found refuge in the

↑ Mazagón beach, irresistible for long walks along the Atlantic shore and among the sand dunes

Franciscan friary at La Rábida. King Fernando and Queen Isabel had refused to back his plan to sail west to the East Indies. The prior, Juan Pérez, who as the confessor of the queen had great influence, managed to get this decision reversed. The following year, this sailor, by the name of Columbus, became the first European to reach the Americas since the Vikings.

La Rábida friary, which was built on Moorish ruins in the 15th century, is now a shrine to Columbus. Frescoes painted by Daniel Vásquez Díaz in 1930 glorify his life and the Sala de las Banderas contains a small casket of soil from every Latin American country.

---

⑩
Ayamonte

🅰A3 🏛Huelva 🚌 ⓘPlaza de España 1; 959 32 07 37

Before the road bridge over the Guadiana river opened in 1992, anyone who was crossing between Andalucía and the Algarve had to pass through Ayamonte. The car ferry across the jellyfish-infested river still operates. Nowadays,

you can also cross the border into Portugal by zip-line with **Límite Zero**.

Límite Zero
⊛ 🏛Avenida de Portugal, Sanlúcar de Guadiana ⏰Book online in advance 🇼limite zero.com

---

⑪
Palos de la Frontera

🅰A3 🏛Huelva 🚌 ⓘParaje de la Rábida s/n; 959 49 46 64

Despite appearing to be an unprepossessing agricultural town, Palos de la Frontera is a major attraction on the Columbus trail. On 3 August 1492, the conquistador set sail from here in his ship, the *Santa María*, with the caravels the

> ## Did You Know?
>
> The drinking water for the *Santa María* was drawn from the well in Palos de la Frontera.

Pinta and the *Niña*, whose captains were Martín and Vicente Pinzón, brothers from Palos. A statue of Martín Pinzón stands in the town's main square, and his former home has been turned into a small museum of exploration, the **Casa Museo de Martín Alonso Pinzón**.

Columbus heard Mass at the Gothic-Mudéjar Iglesia San Jorge before boarding the *Santa María* at a pier that is now forlornly silted up.

Casa Museo de Martín Alonso Pinzón
⊛ 🏛Calle Colón 24 ☎959 10 00 41 ⏰10am-2pm Mon-Fri

A pretty square, with a bougainvillea-covered pergola, in Ayamonte

→

Parading the Virgin to the Santuario de Nuestra Señora del Rocío (inset)

⑫ El Rocío

🅰B4 🏠Huelva 🚌 ℹ️Calle Alonso Pérez, Almonte; 959 45 15 03

The village of El Rocío is famous for its annual *romería* (p47), when almost a million people converge here. Many are pilgrims who travel from distant parts of Spain by bus, car, horse, gaudily decorated ox-carts or even on foot. They come to visit the Santuario de Nuestra Señora del Rocío, where a statue of the Virgin is said to have performed miraculous healings since 1280. Pilgrims are joined by revellers, enticed by the promise of plentiful wine, music and a great party.

📷 PICTURE PERFECT
Pilgrims' Progress

Find a spot along the Quema river to capture the colourful ox-carts and horse-drawn traps crossing the hump-backed bridge into El Rocío during the annual *romería* (pilgrimage).

---

⑬ Lebrija

🅰B4 🏠Sevilla 🚂🚌 ℹ️Casa de Cultura, Calle Tetuán 15; 955 97 40 68

The pretty, walled town of Lebrija enjoys panoramic views over the neighbouring sherry-growing vineyards of the Jerez region. Narrow cobbled streets lead to the Iglesia de Santa María de la Oliva, a 12th-century mosque with many original features, which was later consecrated as a church by Alfonso X.

---

⑭ Itálica

🅰B3 🏠Avenida de Extremadura 2, Santiponce, Sevilla 📞600 14 17 67 🚌From Seville ⏰9am-6pm Tue-Sat (Apr-mid-Jun: to 9pm; mid-Jun-mid-Sep: to 3pm), 9am-3pm Sun & public hols

Scipio Africanus established Itálica in 206 BC as one of the first cities founded by the Romans in Hispania. Later, it developed, both as a military headquarters and as a cultural centre. Emperors Trajan and Hadrian were both born in Itálica, the latter adding marble temples and other fine buildings.

Archaeologists have speculated that the changing course of the Guadalquivir may have led to the demise of Itálica. Certainly, the city declined steadily after the fall of the Roman Empire.

At the heart of the complex are the crumbling remains of a vast amphitheatre, which once seated 25,000. Next to it is a display of finds from the site, although many of the treasures are displayed in the Museo Arqueológico in Seville (p113). Visitors can wander among the traces of streets and villas. Little remains of the city's temples or baths, as most stone and marble was plundered by builders over the subsequent centuries.

15

El Condado

🅰B3 🅰Huelva 🚆🚌Palma del Condado 🛈Plaza de España 14, Palma del Condado; www.lapalma delcondado.org

The rolling hills to the east of Huelva produce several of Andalucía's finest wines. El Condado, defined roughly by Niebla, Palma del Condado, Bollullos Par del Condado and Rociana del Condado, is the heart of this wine region.

Around Niebla, vineyards spread out over the landscape, which is dotted with villages close to the main *bodegas*. At the **Centro del**

Vino Condado de Huelva you can learn about wine-growing techniques and taste wines before making a purchase.

Bollullos and Palma del Condado are good examples of the popular young white wines produced in the region.

Centro del Vino Condado de Huelva

🅰Calle San José 2, Bollullos Par del Condado 📞959 41 38 75 🕐9am–3pm Mon, 9am–3pm & 4–7pm Tue–Fri, 10am–2pm & 4–7pm Sat

---

16

Sierra Norte

🅰C2 🅰Sevilla 🚆Estación de Cazalla y Constantina 🚌Constantina; Cazalla 🛈Plaza del Dr Manuel Nosea 1, Cazalla de la Sierra; 954 88 35 62

An austere mountain range flanks the northern border of Sevilla province. Known as the Sierra Norte de Sevilla, it is a part of the greater Sierra Morena, which forms a natural

> At the Centro del Vino Condado de Huelva you can learn about wine-growing techniques and taste wines before making a purchase.

frontier between Andalucía and the plains of La Mancha and Extremadura. The region is sparsely populated and, as it is relatively cool in summer, it can offer an escape from the relentless heat of Seville.

Cazalla de la Sierra, the main town of the area, seems surprisingly cosmopolitan and is popular with young *Sevillanos* at weekends. It has made a unique contribution to the world of drink, Liquor de Guindas. A concoction of cherry liqueur and aniseed, its taste is acquired slowly, if at all.

Constantina, to the east, is more peaceful and has superb views across the countryside. A romantic aura surrounds the ruined castle that stands high above the town.

→
Hidden lake within a pristine landscape in the Sierra Norte

🔟 Écija

🗺️ C3 🚍 Sevilla 🚌 ℹ️ Calle
Elvira 1A, Palacio de
Benamejí; 955 90 29 33
🌐 turismoecija.com

Écija is nicknamed "the frying
pan of Andalucía" owing to its
famously torrid climate. In the
searing heat, the palm trees
which stand on the Plaza de
España provide some blissful
shade. This is an ideal place to
sit and observe daily life,
especially in the evening.

Écija has 11 Baroque church
steeples, many adorned
with gleaming *azulejos (p88)*,
and together they make an
impressive sight. The most
florid of these is the Iglesia de
Santa María, overlooking the
Plaza de España. The Iglesia
de San Juan, adorned with an
exquisite bell tower, is a very
close rival.

The **Palacio de Peñaflor** is
also in Baroque style. Its pink
marble doorway is topped by
twisted columns, while a
pretty wrought-iron balcony
runs along the front façade.

Palacio de Peñaflor

🗺️ Calle Caballeros 32 📞 954
83 02 73 🕐 10am-2:30pm
Mon-Fri, 10am-2:30pm &
8-10pm Sat, 10am-3pm Sun

↑ Plaza de España in Écija, popular for a stroll
and a coffee in the cool of the evening

20,000

tonnes of *mantecados*,
polvorones and other
treats are produced in
Estepa each year.

🔟 Estepa

🗺️ D3 🚍 Sevilla 🚌 ℹ️ Calle
Aguilar y Cano; 955 91 27 17
🌐 estepa.es

Legend has it that when the
invading Roman army closed
in on Estepa in 207 BC, the
townsfolk committed mass
suicide rather than surrender.
These days, life in this small
town in the far southeast of
Sevilla province is far less
dramatic. Its fame today
lies in the production of its
renowned biscuits, *mantecados*
and *polvorones*. Wander
among the narrow streets of
iron-grilled mansions, and sit
on the main square to admire
the beautiful black-and-white
façade of the Baroque church,
the Iglesia del Carmen.

🔟 Osuna

🗺️ C3 🚍 Sevilla 🚊🚌 ℹ️ Calle
Sevilla 37; 954 81 57 32

In 2014 the sleepy town of
Osuna was thrust into the
limelight when *Game of
Thrones* and its mighty
entourage descended to film
key scenes. While not all the
locals welcomed the influx,
most appreciated the boost
to business and the resulting
tourism boom. Eager fans flock
here to see locations including
the bullring, which featured
as the fighting pit of Meereen.
The local museum now has an
entertaining section featuring
costumes and memorabilia
from the sets.

This is Osuna's third period
of glory, albeit of a very
modern kind this time. It was
once a key Roman garrison
town, before being eclipsed
during the Moorish era. The
dukes of Osuna, who wielded
immense power, restored the
town to prominence in the 16th
century, founding the grand
collegiate church, Colegiata de
Santa María. Inside is a Baroque
retablo, and paintings by José
de Ribera. The dukes also
founded Osuna's Universidad,
a rather severe building with a
graceful patio. Fine mansions,
among them the Palacio del
Marqués de la Gomera, also
testify to Baroque splendour.

← The bell tower of the Iglesia
de San Juan in Écija, a
confection in Baroque style

20

Carmona

🅰C3 🚉Sevilla 🚌 ℹAlcázar de la Puerta de Sevilla; 954 19 09 55 🌐turismo. carmona.org

Travelling east from Seville on the NIV A4 across expansive agricultural plains, Carmona is the first major town you come to. Sprawling suburbs spill out beyond the Moorish city walls, entered through the old Puerta de Sevilla. Inside, there is a dense concentration of mansions, Mudéjar churches, squares and cobbled streets.

The grandeur of Plaza de San Fernando is epitomized by the strict Renaissance façade of the old Ayuntamiento. The present town hall, located just off the square, dates from the 18th century; in its courtyard are some fine Roman mosaics. Close by lies the Iglesia de Santa María la Mayor. Built in the 15th century over a mosque, whose patio still survives, this is the finest of the churches. Dominating the town, however, are the imposing ruins of the Alcázar del Rey Pedro, once a palace of Pedro I, also known as Pedro the Cruel. Parts of it now form a parador, or guesthouse.

Just outside Carmona is the **Necrópolis Romana**, the extensive remains of a Roman burial ground. A site museum displays worldly goods buried with the bodies – statues, glass and jewellery – as well as urns.

Necrópolis Romana

🏛 Avenida Jorge Bonsor 9 ☎600 14 36 32 🕐9am-6pm Tue-Sat, 9am-3pm Sun

---

Matalascañas

🅰B4 🚉Huelva 🚌 ℹParque Dunar; 959 43 00 86

Matalascañas is the closest beach to Seville, lying west of the Guadalquivir river. Thousands holiday here, lying in the sun, riding, sailing or water-skiing by day and dancing to the latest hits at night. Matalascañas is totally self-contained. To one side there are dunes and forests stretching as far as Mazagón, to the other the wild peace of the Doñana (p136).

↓ The floodlit Alcázar in Carmona, seen from the bell tower of San Pedro

EAT

Casa Curro
Meticulously prepared tapas in Osuna.

🅰C3 🏛Plaza Salitre 5, Osuna 🚫Mon

€€€

Aires de Doñana
Lovely, rustic El Rocío eatery, with a locally sourced menu.

🅰B4 🏛Avenida de la Canaliega 1, El Rocío 🌐airesdedonana.com

€€€

La Yedra
Romantic Carmona restaurant, serving exquisite desserts.

🅰C3 🏛Calle General Freire 6, Carmona 🌐restaurante layedra.es

€€€

CÓRDOBA AND JAÉN

The areas that are now called Córdoba and Jaén have been inhabited since prehistoric times, but their histories took a turn with the arrival of the Romans. The importance of these settlements was cemented when Córdoba was made the capital of the Roman province of Baetica (which roughly corresponds to the area defined as Andalucía today).

Although the Romans left their mark on these regions, it was under the Moors that they flourished. Córdoba became the centre of the Iberian caliphate, and swiftly became perhaps the largest and most culturally significant city in all of Europe. Its excellence in scholarship, particularly science, mathematics and literature, was felt throughout the continent.

With the *reconquista* in the 13th century, Córdoba and Jaén were subsumed into Christian Spain, and with Christian wealth and might focused further north, they declined. Both areas were invaded and occupied by the French during the Peninsular War from 1808 to 1814. More warfare was not far away as just over a century later the Spanish Civil War ravaged Andalucía. Jaén in particular was brutally punished for siding with the ultimately unsuccessful Republican cause.

Today, tourism is a major part of both areas' economies, and Jaén is renowned as one of Spain's, if not the world's, best producers of olive oil.

Castuera

Alamillo

Puertollano

A420 · Belalcázar

N502 · Santa Eufemia

Hinojosa del Duque

Torrecampo

Embalse de Montoro I

N420

Añora · Pedroche

Conquista

Alcaracejos · Pozoblanco

Peñarroya-Pueblonuevo

N432

N502

Villanueva de Córdoba

A420

M o r e n a

Cardeña

Fuente Obejuna

Bélmez

S i e r r a

SANTUARIO VIRGEN DE LA CABEZA

Espiel

Embalse de Puente Nuevo

A421

N420

Bembézar

Villaviciosa de Córdoba

Embalse del Guadalmellato

ANDÚJAR

Embalse del Bembézar

CÓRDOBA

Adamuz

8 MONTORO

Hornachuelos

MEDINA AZAHARA **6**

N432

1 CÓRDOBA

Villa del Río

Arjona

Embalse del Retortillo

Posadas

7

Guadajoz

Bujalance

Porcuna

A433

CASTILLO DE ALMODÓVAR DEL RÍO

A4

A306

Lora del Río

A431

La Carlota

N331

A309

Castro del Río

A305

10 PALMA DEL RÍO

NIV

Fernán Núñez

N432

Espejo

BAENA

La Campana

La Rambla

5 MONTILLA

15

Alcaudete

Écija

A4

Doña Mencía

HUELVA AND SEVILLA p132

AGUILAR DE LA FRONTERA **9**

A318

12 CABRA

A333

A364

A309

A45

14 LUCENA

11 PRIEGO DE CÓRDOBA

A340

Puente Genil

Embalse de Cordobilla

Rute

A331

A388

Estepa

Iznájar

A391

A92

Benamejí

Genil

Embalse de Iznájar

Hu Ta

A361

Morón de la Frontera

A92

Riofrío

A406

Campillos

A384

CADIZ AND MALAGA p174

A92M

Embalse de Guadalhorce

Alhama Grana

CÓRDOBA AND JAÉN

A343

AP46

Colmenar

A357

Pizarra

A45

Véle Mala

Cártana

Málaga

A7

Tou del

N340a

0 kilometres   25

0 miles   25

N

CÓRDOBA AND JAÉN

Must Sees
1 Córdoba
2 Jaén
3 Úbeda
4 Baeza

Experience More
5 Montilla
6 Medina Azahara
7 Castillo de Almodóvar del Río
8 Montoro
9 Aguilar de la Frontera
10 Palma del Río
11 Priego de Córdoba
12 Cabra
13 Alcalá la Real
14 Lucena
15 Baena
16 Cástulo
17 Baños de la Encina
18 La Carolina
19 Cazorla
20 Desfiladero de Despeñaperros
21 Andújar
22 Santuario Virgen de la Cabeza
23 Parque Natural de Cazorla, Segura y Las Villas
24 Segura de la Sierra

Córdoba's Puente Romano, stretching across the Río Guadalquivir ↑

❶
CÓRDOBA

🗺️D3 🚌Córdoba 🚉🚌 ℹ️Plaza del Triunfo s/n; www.turismodecordoba.org

This city has had a long and illustrious history. Under the Romans Córdoba was famed as the birthplace of philosopher Seneca and in the 10th century Abd al Rahman III made the city the capital of his powerful caliphate. Today, Córdoba is still as awe-inspiring.

①
Museo Arqueológico

🏛️Plaza de Jerónimo Páez 7 📞957 35 55 17 🕐Jul-Aug: 9am-3pm Tue-Sun & public hols; Sep-Jun: 9am-9pm Tue-Sat, 9am-3pm Sun & public hols

Located in a Renaissance mansion, this excellent museum displays the remains of a Roman theatre found beneath the building, including mosaics and pottery, as well as impressive finds from the Moorish era. Highlights include a 10th-century bronze stag found at Medina Azahara (p164). Also on display is a marble sculpted head of the Emperor Augustus, dating to the 1st century AD, which was found in the area.

②
Alcázar de los Reyes Cristianos

🏛️Calle Caballerizas Reales s/n 📞957 42 01 51 🕐Mid-Jun-mid-Sep: 8:30am-3pm Tue-Sat, 8:30am-2:30pm Sun; mid-Sep-mid-Jun: 8:30am-8:45pm Tue-Sat, 8:30am-2:30pm Sun

This palace-fortress was built in 1328 for Alfonso XI. Fernando II and Isabel stayed here during their campaign to conquer Granada from the Moors. Later it was used by the Inquisition, and then as a prison. The gardens are particularly lovely, with their ponds and fountains, and stay open into the evenings in July and August. Behind the palace's walls are Roman mosaics.

③
Sinagoga

🏛️Calle Judíos 20 📞957 20 29 28 🕐Mid-Jun-mid-Sep: 9am-3:30pm Tue-Sun & public hols; mid-Sep-mid-Jun: 9am-8:30pm Tue-Sat, 9am-3:30pm Sun & public hols

Constructed around 1315, this Mudéjar-style synagogue is one of three in Spain preserved from that era. The other two are in Toledo. The women's gallery and decorative plasterwork, with Hebrew script, are of particular interest. The synagogue lies in the Judería, the Jewish quarter, which has hardly changed since Moorish times. In a plaza nearby is a bronze statue of Maimonides, a 12th-century Jewish sage who has become a popular local figure.

Did You Know?

The name Córdoba may have derived from *Kartuba*, Phoenician for "prosperous city".

④ ⧉ Torre de la Calahorra

🏛 Puente Romano 🕐 Oct-Apr: 10am-6pm daily; May-Sep: 10am-2pm & 4:30-8:30pm daily 🌐 torre calahorra.es

This 14th-century tower is located at the end of the Puente Romano – an arched bridge with Roman foundations that was rebuilt by the Moors. The tower now houses a museum about the life, culture and philosophy of 10th-century Córdoba, when Abd al Rahman III created the independent caliphate.

⑤ ⧉ Museo de Bellas Artes

🏛 Plaza del Potro 1 📞 957 10 36 59 🕐 Mid-Jun–mid-Sep: 9am-3:30pm Tue-Sun; mid-Sep–mid-Jun: 9am-9pm Tue-Sat, 9am-3pm Sun

Located in a former charity hospital, this museum exhibits sculptures by local artist Mateo Inurria and Seville School paintings by Zurbarán.

⑥ ⧉ Palacio de Viana

🏛 Plaza Don Gome 2 🕐 Jul & Aug: 9am-3pm Tue-Sun; Sep-Jun: 10am-7pm Tue-Sat, 10am-3pm Sun 🌐 palaciodeviana.com

Tapestries, furniture, porcelain and paintings are displayed in this 17th-century mansion, which was once the home of the affluent Viana family. Purchased by a savings bank in 1981, it has been kept much as the family left it. Outside, you'll find 14 beautiful patios and a delightful garden.

⑦ ⧉ Baños del Alcázar Califal

🏛 Campo Santo de los Mártires 🕐 Hours vary, check website 🌐 banosdel alcazarcalifal.cordoba.es

These Arab baths were once part of the Umayyad palace, which was later replaced by the Alcázar de los Reyes Cristianos. Built under the orders of al-Hakam II, these

10th-century well-preserved Arab baths reflect the classical order of Roman baths: cold rooms, warm rooms and hot rooms. A museum recreates the social and religious history and uses of the baths.

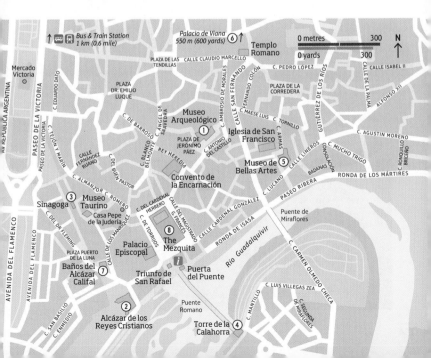

⑧ 🏛️

THE MEZQUITA

🏠 Calle Torrijos 10 🕐 Mar-Oct: 10am-7pm Mon-Sat, 8:30-11:30am & 3-7pm Sun; Nov-Feb: 10am-6pm Mon-Sat, 8:30-11:30am & 3-6pm Sun 🌐 mezquita-catedraldecordoba.es

Córdoba's Great Mosque, dating back 12 centuries, embodied the power of Islam on the Iberian Peninsula. As you tread beneath its rows of hallowed arches, you'll be transported back to the affluent age of Moorish rule.

Abd al Rahman I, the founder of the caliphate of Córdoba, built the original mosque on the site of a Visigothic church between AD 785 and 787. The building evolved over the centuries, blending many architectural forms. In the 10th century al-Hakam II made some of the most lavish additions, including the elaborate *mihrab* (prayer niche) and the *maqsura* (caliph's enclosure). Later, during the 16th century, a cathedral was built in the heart of the recon-secrated mosque, under the orders of Carlos I, to complete the city's "Christianization".

Torre del Alminar, a bell tower 93 m (305 ft) high, is built on the site of the original minaret. Steep steps lead to the top for a fine view of Córdoba.

Orange trees grow in the Patio de los Naranjos – the courtyard where the faithful washed before prayer.

The Puerta del Perdón is a Mudéjar-style entrance gate, built during Christian rule in 1377.

← The Mezquita, seen from across the Río Guadalquivir

The Puerta de San Esteban is set into a wall that has survived from the Visigothic church.

← Walking among the red-and-white striped Caliphal arches

MOORISH ARCHES

The Visigoths were the first to use horseshoe arches in the construction of churches. The Moors modified these arches and used them as the basis of great architectural endeavours, as seen in the Mezquita. Subsequent arches show more sophisticated ornamentation and the slow demise of the basic horseshoe shape.

Caliphal arch, the Mezquita

Almohad arch, Real Alcázar (p78)

Mudéjar arch, Real Alcázar (p78)

Nasrid arch, the Alhambra (p216)

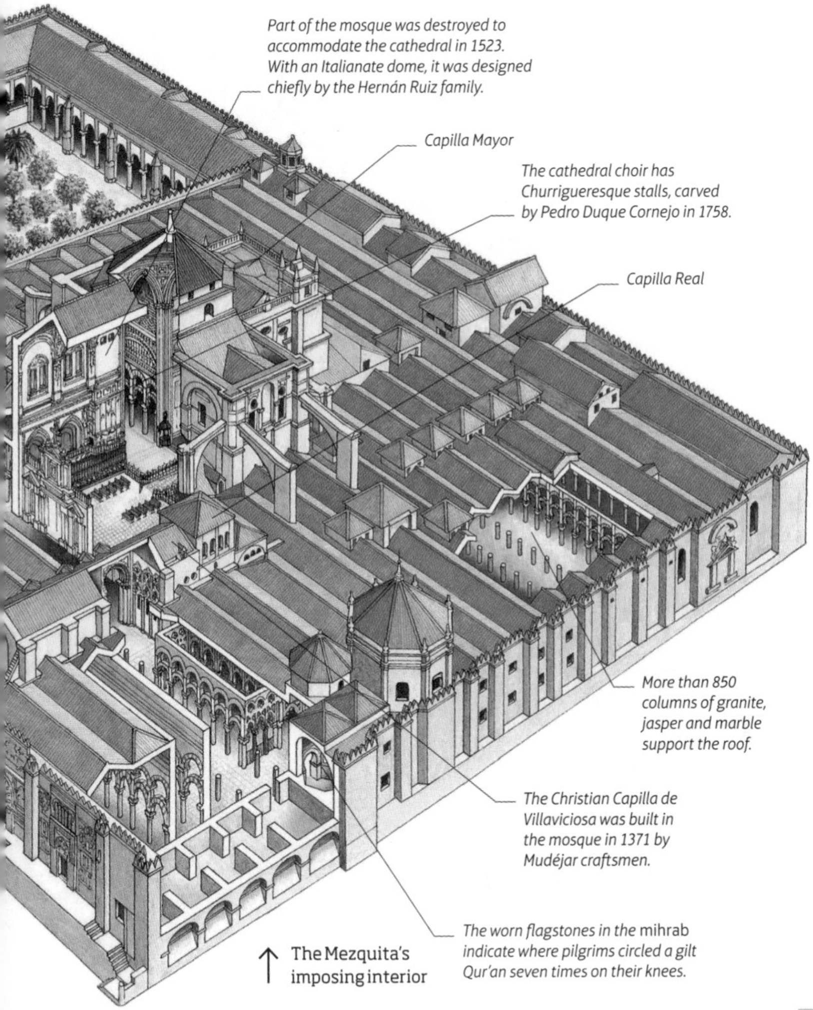

Part of the mosque was destroyed to accommodate the cathedral in 1523. With an Italianate dome, it was designed chiefly by the Hernán Ruiz family.

Capilla Mayor

The cathedral choir has Churrigueresque stalls, carved by Pedro Duque Cornejo in 1758.

Capilla Real

More than 850 columns of granite, jasper and marble support the roof.

The Christian Capilla de Villaviciosa was built in the mosque in 1371 by Mudéjar craftsmen.

The worn flagstones in the mihrab indicate where pilgrims circled a gilt Qur'an seven times on their knees.

↑ The Mezquita's imposing interior

A SHORT WALK
CÓRDOBA

Distance 2 km (1 mile) **Nearest train station** Córdoba **Time** 30 minutes

The heart of Córdoba is the old Jewish quarter, situated to the west of the Mezquita's towering walls. A walk around this area gives the sensation that little has changed since the 10th century, when this was one of the greatest cities in the Western world. Wrought ironwork decorates cobbled streets too narrow for cars, where silversmiths create fine jewellery in their workshops. Most of the chief sights are here, while modern city life takes place some blocks north, around the Plaza de las Tendillas.

Built in the Gothic-Mudéjar style, the **Capilla de San Bartolomé** *is decorated with elaborate tiles.*

Hebrew script covers the **Sinagoga** *(p152). Spain's other major synagogues are in Toledo, Madrid and Barcelona.*

Casa de Sefarad *is a cultural centre with exhibits on Judeo-Spanish history, in the heart of the Jewish quarter.*

Water terraces and fountains add to the tranquil atmosphere of the gardens belonging to the **Alcázar de los Reyes Cristianos** *(p152).*

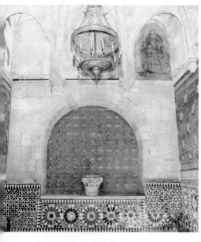

↑ Bright *azulejos* decorating the Capilla de San Bartolomé

The **Callejón de las Flores** *brims with colourful geraniums, which contrast with the whitewashed walls.*

↑ The Puente Romano stretching over the Guadalquivir river to the Torre de la Calahorra

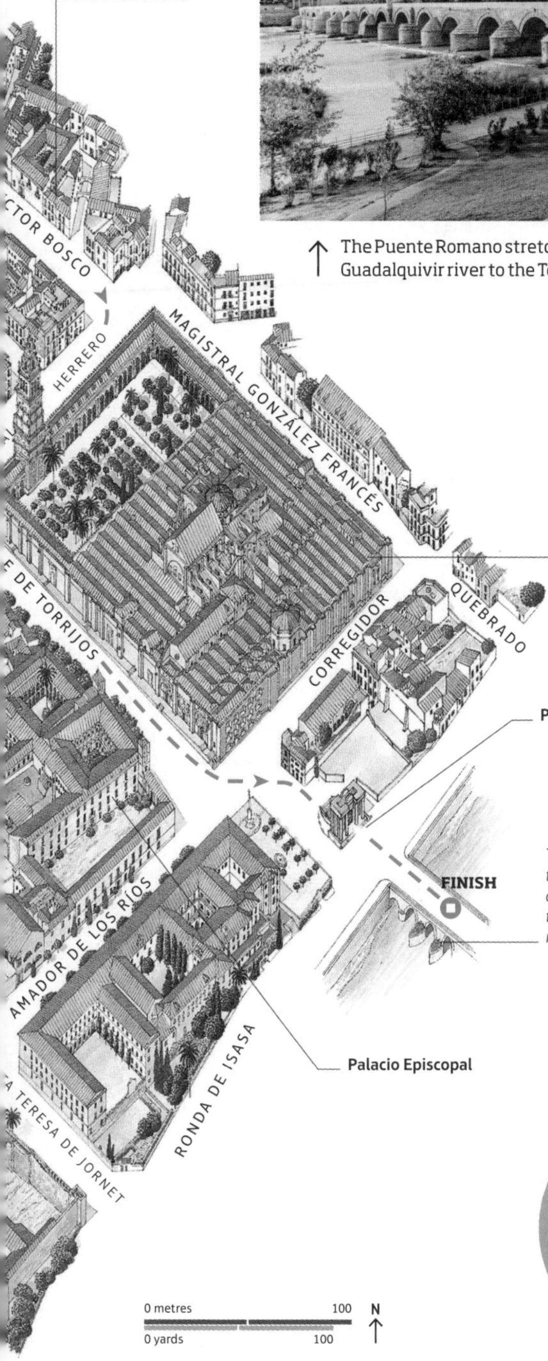

The mighty walls of **The Mezquita** *hide a forest of delicate arches, pillars and a dazzling mihrab (p154).*

Puerta del Puente

FINISH

The **Puente Romano** *spans the Río Guadalquivir. A museum on its southeast side explores the different cultures of medieval Córdoba.*

Palacio Episcopal

0 metres 100
0 yards 100

N ↑

Did You Know?

Córdoba hosts the Fiesta de los Patios (Festival of the Patios) every May.

❷
JAÉN

ⒶE3 **Ⓐ**Jaén **ⒶⒶ** **𝒊** Calle Maestra 8; 953 31 32 81

The Moors knew Jaén as Geen, meaning "way station of caravans", and for centuries this area was a battleground between Moors and Christians. Today, the city centre is filled with smart shops, and in the evenings people take to the narrow streets to enjoy the *tapeo*.

①
Catedral

ⒶPlaza Santa María **Ⓒ**953 23 42 33 **Ⓒ**10am–2pm & 4–8pm Mon–Fri, 10am–2pm & 4–7pm Sat, 10am–noon & 4–7pm Sun

Andrés de Vandelvira, who was responsible for many of Úbeda's fine buildings (*p160*), designed Jaén's cathedral in the 16th century. Later additions include the two 17th-century towers that flank the west front. Inside are carved choir stalls and a museum of sacred art. Every Friday, from 10:30am to noon and 5 to 6pm, worshippers can view the Lienzo del Santo Rostro. St Veronica is said to have used this piece of cloth to wipe Christ's face, which left a permanent impression.

②
Centro Cultural Baños Árabes

ⒶPalacio Villardompardo, Plaza Santa Luisa de Marillac **Ⓒ**9am–10pm Tue–Sat, 9am–3pm Sun **Ⓒ**Public hols **ⓦ**bañosarabesjaen.es

Noteworthy features of these 11th-century baths include tiny star-shaped windows, a hemispherical dome and two clay vats in which bathers once immersed themselves.

③
Capilla de San Andrés

ⒶCalle San Andrés s/n

Tucked away in a narrow alley, this 16th-century chapel was founded by Gutiérrez González,

who was treasurer to Pope Leo X. A magnificent gilded iron screen by Maestro Bartolomé de Jaén is the highlight of the chapel.

④
Real Monasterio de Santa Clara

ⒶCalle Santa Clara 7

Founded in the 13th century, just after the Reconquest of the city, the Real Monasterio de Santa Clara has a curious 16th-century bamboo image

---

OLIVE OIL

Since the Phoenicians, or possibly the Greeks, brought the olive tree to Spain it has flourished in Andalucía, particularly in Jaén, which today has an annual production of more than 200,000 tonnes of oil. Harvesting, mostly by hand, takes place from December onwards.

←
Jaén, dominated by the Catedral and surrounded by olive groves

of Christ made in Ecuador. You can buy sweet cakes made by the nuns from the convent.

---

⑤
Basílica Menor de San Ildefonso

📍 Plaza San Ildefonso s/n

This church's façades are in three different styles. One is Gothic, with a mosaic of the Virgin descending on Jaén during a Moorish siege in 1430. A second is partly Plateresque and the third is Neo-Classical. Inside, the high altar is by Pedro and José Roldán. There is also a chapel which enshrines the Virgen de la Capilla, Jaén's patron saint.

⑥
Castillo de Santa Catalina

📍 Carretera al Castillo
📞 953 12 07 33 🕐 Jul-Sep: 10am-2pm & 5-9pm Mon-Sat, 10am-3pm Sun; Oct-Jun: 10am-6pm Mon-Sat, 10am-3pm Sun

Hannibal is believed to have erected a tower on this rocky pinnacle, high above the city. Later the Moors established a mighty fortress, only to lose it to the crusading King Fernando III in 1246. A larger castle was then built with huge ramparts. This has been restored and a medieval-style parador (inn) built next door.

Take the sinuous road up to the Torre del Homenaje for stunning views of the city, and the surrounding landscape, including the olive-tree-clad Sierra Morena and the mountains of the Sierra Nevada.

⑦
Museo Provincial

📍 Paseo de la Estación 29
🕐 Mid-Jun-mid-Sep: 9am-3pm Tue-Sun; mid-Sep-mid-Jun: 9am-8pm Tue-Sat, 9am-3pm Sun 🌐 museosde andalucia.es

This building incorporates the remains of the Iglesia de San Miguel and the façade of a 16th-century granary. A Palaeo-Christian sarcophagus and Greek and Roman ceramics are among the articles on display.

Nearby is the Plaza de las Batallas and a memorial to the defeats of both Napoleon and the Moors.

SHOP

Pepitina Ruiz Silk
Natural silk garments, scarves, fans and accessories are made and sold here.

📍 Paseo de la Estación 14
🌐 pepitinaruizseda.com

Oleoteca Jaén
Olive oil, the liquid gold of Andalucía, is sold here in more than 50 different varieties. Expect top-shelf extra virgin oil, as well as gourmet foods and artisan souvenirs.

📍 Calle Maestra 9 📞 953 82 34 24

Galería de vinos Caldos
Dedicated exclusively to the world of wine, Caldos stocks both local and international varieties.

📍 Calle Cerón 12
🌐 vinosjaen.com

→ The imposing façade of the Hospital de Santiago, fronted by gardens

❸

ÚBEDA

🅰 E2 🏠 Jaén 🚌🚍 ℹ️ Plaza de Andalucía 5; 953 77 92 04

A UNESCO World Heritage Site, Úbeda is a showcase of Renaissance magnificence, thanks to the patronage of some of Spain's most influential men of the 16th century, including such dignitaries as Juan Vázquez de Molina. The Old Town is contained within city walls that were first raised by the Moors in AD 852.

① 🖥️

Hospital de Santiago

🏛️ Calle Obispo Cobos s/n 📞 953 75 08 42 🕐 10am-2pm & 5-9pm daily (Jul: Mon-Sat; Aug: Mon-Fri)

Created on the orders of the Bishop of Jaén around 1562, the colossal Hospital de Santiago was designed by Andrés de Vandelvira, who refined the Spanish Renaissance style into its more austere characteristics. The façade is flanked by square towers. Today the building hosts cultural exhibitions.

②

Museo Arqueológico

🏛️ Casa Mudéjar, Calle Cervantes 6 📞 953 10 86 23 🕐 Jun-mid-Sep: 9am-3:30pm Tue-Sun; mid-Sep-May: 9am-8:30pm Tue-Sat, 9am-3:30pm Sun

This archaeological museum exhibits artifacts from Neolithic to Moorish times, including tombstones from the 1st century AD. It is located in the grand Casa Mudéjar, a 15th-century palace.

③

Iglesia de San Pablo

🏛️ Plaza Primero de Mayo 39 🕐 6:30-7:30pm Tue-Sat, 10:30am-1pm Sun

This church is remarkable for its 13th-century apse and beautiful 16th-century chapel. The church is surmounted by a Plateresque tower that was completed in 1537.

> 💬 INSIDER TIP
> ### Twin Towns
> Úbeda's sister town, Baeza (p162), is a short drive away and is equally stunning, with a wealth of Renaissance architecture. Be sure to visit both while you're in the area.

④

Capilla del Salvador

🏛 **Plaza Vázquez de Molina**
🕐 **Hours vary, check website**
🌐 **fundacionmedinaceli.org**

The Capilla del Salvador was designed in the 16th century for Francisco de los Cobos, then secretary of state. Although the church was pillaged during the Civil War, it retains a number of treasures, including a golden chalice that was given to Cobos by Carlos I. Behind the chapel stand Cobos' palace, with a Renaissance façade, and the Hospital de los Honrados Viejos (Hospital of the Honoured Elders). Both of these buildings can only be visited on a pre-arranged guided tour.

⑤

Santa María de los Reales Alcázares

🏛 **Plaza Vázquez de Molina s/n** 🕐 **Hours vary, check website** 🌐 **santamaria deubeda.es**

Built on the site of an original mosque, this church, which

dates mainly from the 13th century, has a Gothic cloister and a noteworthy Romanesque doorway. Nearby is the Cárcel del Obispo (Bishop's Jail), so-called because nuns who had been punished by the bishop were confined here.

⑥

Parador de Úbeda

🏛 **Plaza Vázquez de Molina s/n** 🌐 **parador.es**

Built in the 16th century but much altered in the 17th, this was the residence of Fernando Ortega Salido, dean of Málaga and chaplain of the Capilla del Salvador. The austere palace is now a hotel that is also known as the Condestable Dávalos, in honour of a warrior. The patio is open to non-guests.

⑦

Palacio de las Cadenas

🏛 **Plaza Vázquez de Molina s/n** 📞 **953 75 04 40** 🕐 **8am-2:30pm Mon-Fri**

Two stone lions guard Úbeda's town hall, which occupies the

STAY

Zenit El Postigo Inn

This modern hotel offers spacious, comfortable rooms, as well as a pool and garden.

🏛 **Calle de El Postigo 5**
🌐 **elpostigo.zenit hoteles.com**

€€€

Hotel Palacio de Úbeda

A luxurious five-star hotel with coffered ceilings and four-poster beds. There is a spa and restaurant on site.

🏛 **Calle de Juan Pasqua 4**
🌐 **palaciodeubeda.com**

€€€

Palacio de las Cadenas, a mansion built for Vázquez de Molina by de Vandelvira. It gets its name from the iron chains *(cadenas)* once attached to the columns supporting the main doorway.

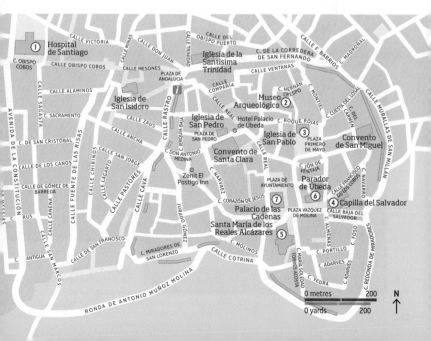

❹

BAEZA

🅰 E2 📍 Jaén 🚌 🚍 ℹ️ Plaza del Pópulo s/n; 953 77 99 82

Nestled amid olive groves that characterize much of Jaén province, beautiful Baeza is a small town that's unusually rich in Renaissance architecture. As you wander its winding streets, you'll stumble upon unique examples of this opulent period of building design. With palaces, churches and stately buildings on almost every corner, Baeza is a treat to explore.

Called Beatia by the Romans and later the capital of a Moorish fiefdom, Baeza is portrayed as a "royal nest of hawks" on its coat of arms. It was conquered by Fernando III in 1226 – the first town in Andalucía to be definitively won back from the Moors – and was then settled by Castilian knights. An era of medieval splendour followed, reaching a climax in the 16th century, when Andrés de Vandelvira's splendid buildings were erected. Perhaps the most impressive of these is the town's cathedral, which was rebuilt by de Vandelvira in 1567. Inside, look out for the Capilla Sagrario, within which is a beautiful choir screen by Bartolomé de Jaén. Baeza was designated a UNESCO World Heritage Site in 2003, along with its twin town, the slightly larger Úbeda (p160).

Did You Know?

The province of Jaén is responsible for 20 per cent of the world's olive oil production.

←

A narrow town street, with the Antigua Universidad rising at the end

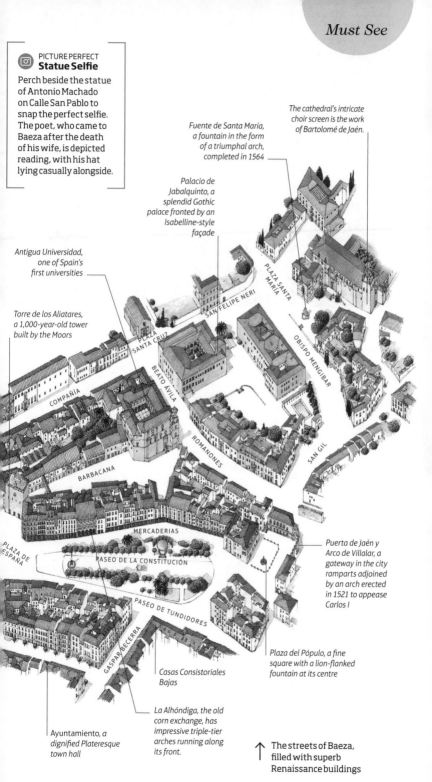

PICTURE PERFECT
Statue Selfie

Perch beside the statue of Antonio Machado on Calle San Pablo to snap the perfect selfie. The poet, who came to Baeza after the death of his wife, is depicted reading, with his hat lying casually alongside.

Fuente de Santa María, a fountain in the form of a triumphal arch, completed in 1564

The cathedral's intricate choir screen is the work of Bartolomé de Jaén.

Palacio de Jabalquinto, a splendid Gothic palace fronted by an Isabelline-style façade

Antigua Universidad, one of Spain's first universities

PLAZA SANTA MARÍA

SAN FELIPE NERI

OBISPO MENGIBAR

Torre de los Aliatares, a 1,000-year-old tower built by the Moors

PLAZA SANTA CRUZ

BEATO AVILA

COMPAÑÍA

ROMANONES

SAN GIL

BARBACANA

MERCADERIAS

PLAZA DE ESPAÑA

PASEO DE LA CONSTITUCIÓN

Puerta de Jaén y Arco de Villalar, a gateway in the city ramparts adjoined by an arch erected in 1521 to appease Carlos I

PASEO DE TUNDIDORES

GASPAR BECERRA

Casas Consistoriales Bajas

Plaza del Pópulo, a fine square with a lion-flanked fountain at its centre

La Alhóndiga, the old corn exchange, has impressive triple-tier arches running along its front.

Ayuntamiento, a dignified Plateresque town hall

↑ The streets of Baeza, filled with superb Renaissance buildings

EXPERIENCE MORE

5
Montilla

🅰D3 🅰Córdoba 🚲🚌
ℹCalle Capitan Alonso de Vargas 3; 957 65 24 62

Montilla is the centre of an important wine-making region that produces an excellent smooth white fino. Unlike sherry, fino does not need fortifying with alcohol. Some *bodegas*, including Bodega Alvear, are happy to welcome visitors.

The town's castle dates from the 18th century. The town library is in the Casa del Inca, so named because the writer Garcilaso de la Vega, "El Inca" – the son of a

Did You Know?

Indoor plumbing was a feature of Medina Azahara as far back as the 10th century.

conquistador and an Inca noblewoman – lived there in the 16th century.

6
Medina Azahara

🅰D3 🅰Carretera Palma del Rio, km 5.5, Córdoba 🕐Apr-Jun: 9am-9pm Tue-Sat, 9am-3pm Sun; Jul-mid-Sep: 9am-3pm Tue-Sun; mid-Sep-Mar: 9am-6pm Tue-Sat, 9am-3pm Sun 🌐medina azahara.org

Northwest of Córdoba lie the remains of a Moorish palace built in the 10th century for Caliph Abd al Rahman III, who named it after his favourite wife, Azahara. More than 10,000 workers and 15,000 mules ferried building materials from as far as North Africa. Alabaster, ebony, jasper and marble adorned its many halls, but the palace was sacked by Berber invaders in 1010. Now, the ruins give only glimpses of its former splendour. The palace is being restored, but progress is slow.

📷 PICTURE PERFECT
Game On

Have your camera at the ready on the road to Castillo de Almodóvar del Río. As its massive bulk looms into view you'll recognize it as Highgarden, seat of House Tyrell in *Game of Thrones*.

7
Castillo de Almodóvar del Río

🅰C3 🅰Córdoba 🕐Apr-Sep: 11am-2:30pm & 4-8pm Mon-Fri, 11am-8pm Sat & Sun; Oct-Mar: 11am-2:30pm & 4-7pm Mon-Fri, 11am-7pm Sat, Sun & public hols 🌐castillodealmodovar.com

One of Andalucía's most dramatic silhouettes breaks the skyline as you approach Almodóvar del Río. The Moorish castle, with parts dating back to the 8th century, overlooks the whitewashed town and surrounding fields

Harvesting Pedro Ximénez wine grapes in the Montilla district

of cotton. The themed tours are highly recommended, particularly the theatrical one.

8

Montoro

🅰 D2 🏛 Córdoba 🚌
ℹ Calle Corredera 25; www.montoro.es

Spread over five hills that span a bend in the River Guadalquivir, Montoro dates from the times of the Greeks and Phoenicians. Today the economy of this restful town depends on its olive groves, and on fine leather bags and embossed saddlery.

Steep streets give the town charm. In Plaza de España are the Ayuntamiento, former seat of the ducal rulers, and the Gothic-Mudéjar Iglesia de San Bartolomé.

9

Aguilar de la Frontera

🅰 D3 🏛 Córdoba 🚉🚌
ℹ Cuesta de Jesús 2; 957 66 17 71

Ceramics, wine and olive oil are important products in Aguilar, which was settled in Roman times. The town centres on the eight-sided Plaza de San José. Built in 1810, it is home to the town hall, a Baroque clock tower and several manor houses.

10

Palma del Río

🅰 C3 🏛 Córdoba 🚉🚌
ℹ Plaza Mayor de Andalucía s/n; www.palmadelrio.es

The Romans established a settlement here, on the route from Córdoba to Itálica (p144), almost 2,000 years ago. The remains of the 12th-century city walls are a reminder of the town's frontier days under the Almohads.

The Baroque Iglesia de la Asunción dates from the 18th century. The Monasterio de San Francisco is now a delightful hotel, where guests dine in the 15th-century refectory of the Franciscan monks. Palma is the home town of the late El Cordobés, one of Spain's most famous matadors. His biography, *Or I'll Dress You in Mourning*, paints a vivid picture of life in the town and of the hardship that followed the end of the Civil War.

DRINK

Mirador Tierra de Frontera

Enjoy house-brewed craft beers and great views on the terrace bar of this friendly guesthouse in Alcalá la Real. There's a small but well-chosen food menu, too.

🅰 E3 🏛 Calle Santo Domingo de Silos 30, Alcalá la Real
📞 650 68 35 60

Bodega Alvear

The oldest winery in Andalucía is renowned for its Pedro Ximénez grapes, which produce sweet fino, oloroso and amontillado wines. You can take a tour, with a tasting, at this Montilla institution on Sundays and Mondays.

🅰 D3 🏛 Avenida María Auxiliadora, Montilla
🌐 alvear.es

← A gathering outside the Iglesia de la Asunción, Palma del Río

EAT

La Pianola Casa Pepe

Hearty stews, fish and choice cuts of meat are king at this homey restaurant in Priego de Córdoba. Paella is served for Sunday lunch.

🅐D3 🏠Calle Obispo Caballero 6, Priego de Córdoba 📞957 70 04 09 🗓Mon

€€€

Bar Carrasquilla

This Montilla eatery specializes in juicy, fall-off-the-bone roasted meats and succulent seafood. The desserts are equally delicious.

🅐D3 🏠Calle Feria 1, Montilla 📞957 65 00 50 🗓Tue

€€€

⓫

Priego de Córdoba

🅐D3 🏠Córdoba 🚌 ℹ️Plaza de la Constitución 3; www.turismodepriego.com

This pleasant small town lies on a fertile plain at the foot of La Tiñosa, the highest mountain in Córdoba province. Despite Priego de Córdoba's unassuming air, it more than deserves the title of the capital of Córdoba Baroque. The self-assertion is easy to accept in view of the dazzling work of local carvers, gilders and ironworkers.

The town's labyrinthine old quarter was the site of the original Arab settlement. But the 18th century, when silk manufacture prospered, was Priego's golden age. During this time elegant houses were built and money was lavished on fine Baroque churches.

A restored Moorish fortress, on Roman foundations, introduces visitors to the fine medieval quarter, Barrio de la Villa. Whitewashed buildings line its narrow streets and flower-decked squares. Paseo Colombia leads to the Adarve, a long promenade with views over the countryside.

The nearby Iglesia de la Asunción is an outstanding structure. Originally Gothic in style, it was converted to a Baroque church in the 18th century. Its *pièce de résistance* is the sacristy chapel, with its sumptuous, almost overwhelming ornamentation in the form of sculpted figures and plaster scrolls.

The Iglesia de la Aurora is another fine Baroque building. At midnight every Saturday the cloaked brotherhood of Nuestra Señora de la Aurora parades the streets singing songs to the Virgin and collecting alms.

> **Despite Priego de Córdoba's unassuming air, it more than deserves the title of the capital of Córdoba Baroque.**

Flower-filled passage in the old quarter, Priego de Córdoba ↑

At the end of the Calle del Río is the Fuente del Rey, or King's Fountain. This is a Baroque extravaganza, with three pools, and includes Neptune among its exuberant statuary.

May is one of the liveliest months to visit Priego: every Sunday a procession is held to celebrate the town's deliverance from a plague many centuries ago.

12 Cabra

🅐 D3 🅐 Córdoba 🚌 🅘 Calle Mayor 1; www.turismo. cabra.eu

Set amid fertile fields and vast olive groves, Cabra was an episcopal seat in the 3rd century. On a rise stands the former castle, which is now a school. There are also some noble mansions and the Iglesia Santo Domingo, with a Baroque façade.

Just outside the town, the Fuente del Río, source of the Río Cabra, is a pleasantly leafy spot in which to picnic.

13 Alcalá la Real

🅐 E3 🅐 Jaén 🚌 🅘 Palacio Abacial, Avenida de las Mercedes; 953 10 28 68

Alcalá was a strategic point held by the military Order of Calatrava during Spain's *reconquista (p50)*. On the hilltop of La Mota are the ruins of the Moorish Fortaleza de la Mota, built by the rulers of Granada in the 14th century, with later additions. Nearby are ruins of the town's former main church. There are splendid views over the countryside and the historic town, with its air of past glories. The Renaissance Palacio Abacial and Fuente de Carlos V are the chief attractions to be found around the plaza in the centre of the town.

↑ Baroque ornamentation in the Capilla del Sagrario of the Iglesia de San Mateo, Lucena

14 Lucena

🅐 D3 🅐 Córdoba 🚌 🅘 Calle San Pedro 42; www.turlucena.com

Under the caliphs of Córdoba, Lucena was an important trading and intellectual centre, with a dynamic independent Jewish community. Nowadays, the town is known for its furniture, its brass and copper ware, and some interesting ceramic creations.

The Iglesia de Santiago, with its Baroque turret, was built on the site of a synagogue in 1503. The Torre del Moral is the only remaining part of a Moorish castle. Nearby, the 15th-century Iglesia de San Mateo has a flamboyant Baroque sacristy.

On the first Sunday in May Lucena stages an elaborate ceremony, which honours the Virgen de Araceli.

15 Baena

🅐 D3 🅐 Córdoba 🚌 🅘 Virrey del Pino 5; 957 67 17 57

This town's olive oil has been famed since Roman times. At the top of Baena is the Iglesia Santa María la Mayor. On the Plaza de la Constitución, next to the modern town hall, is the Casa del Monte, an arcaded 18th-century mansion. Easter week is spectacular here, when thousands of drummers take to the streets.

Did You Know?

More than 2,000 drums make up the cacophony in Baena on the Wednesday of Holy Week.

⑯
Cástulo

🅰 E2 🅰 Carreta Linares-Torreblascopedro (JV-3003), km 3.3, Jaén 🚌 From Linares & Jaén ⏰ Mid-Jun-Aug: 9am-3pm Tue-Sun; Sep-mid-Jun: 9am-9pm Tue-Sat, 9am-3pm Sun 🌐 www.museosde andalucia.es

Around 7 km (4 miles) from Linares are the ruins of the ancient city of Cástulo. Evidence of human life dating to the Neolithic period has been discovered here, along with traces of late Neolithic-Chalcolithic huts and tools from the Bronze Age. The site's museum, the Museo Arqueológico de Linares, displays exhibits found in the area. Highlights include the Ibero-Roman León and the Patena de Cristo, considered one of the earliest representations of Christ.

⑰
Baños de la Encina

🅰 E2 🅰 Jaén 🚌 From Linares & Jaén 🛈 Avenida José Luis Messía 2; www. bdelaencinaturismo.com

This charming village is dominated by its Moorish fortress, the Castillo de Burgalimar. Caliph al Hakam II ordered its construction in AD 967. Rising above Baños de la Encina, it is a daunting sight, with its 15 towers and soaring ramparts.

> **GREAT VIEW**
> **Burgalimar Battlements**
>
> If you look down from the Castillo de Burgalimar's ramparts, you'll see the tiled roofs and windmills of Baños de la Encina, surrounded by a thick carpet of olive trees.

Sitting on its rocky perch, the castle of La Iruela outside Cazorla ↑

⑱
La Carolina

🅰 E2 🅰 Jaén 🚌 🛈 Plaza del Ayuntamiento; 953 66 00 34

Founded in 1767, La Carolina was populated by settlers from Germany and Flanders in a plan to develop the area and to make it safer for travellers. The person in charge, Carlos III's minister Pablo de Olavide, had a palace built on the main square. Just outside town is a monument to a battle that took place in 1212. Alfonso VIII, king of Castile, was led by a shepherd over the hills to Las Navas, where he crushed the Moors. His victory began the reconquest of Andalucía.

⑲
Cazorla

🅰 F3 🅰 Jaén 🚌 🛈 Paseo de Santa María; www.cazorla. es/turismo

Cazorla was wealthy in ancient times when the Romans mined the surrounding mountains for silver. Today it is better known as the jumping-off point for visiting the Parque Natural de Cazorla, Segura y Las Villas (p170).

Modern buildings have proliferated, but it is pleasant to stroll along the crooked streets between Plaza de la Corredera and the charming Plaza Santa María. Above this popular meeting place stands the **Castillo de la Yedra**, which houses a folklore museum.

On the road leading to the park are the remains of La Iruela, a much-photographed fortress atop a rocky spur.

On 14 May the locals pay homage to a former resident of Cazorla, San Isicio, one of seven apostles who preached Christianity in Spain before the arrival of the Moors.

Castillo de la Yedra
🅰 Camino Ángel s/n 📞 953 10 14 02 ⏰ Jun-mid-Sep: 9am-3pm Tue-Sat, 10am-3pm Sun & public hols; mid-Sep-May: 9am-9pm Tue-Sat, 10am-3pm Sun & public hols

SHOP

Sierra Sur Artesanos

This charming store in Alcalá la Real specializes in hand-carved wooden items, as well as other gifts.

E3 Calle Fernando el Católico 12, Alcalá la Real 953 45 77 55

Arciri s.c.a

Beautiful hand-painted ceramics are crafted at this Andújar workshop. Pick up the perfect gift or souvenir here.

E2 Calle Juan Ramón Jiménez 3, Andújar 953 51 13 71

Casa Mohedo

The rich scent of freshly tanned leather greets you in this Montoro workshop full of hand-tooled footwear and leather accessories.

D2 Calle Corredera 39, Montoro mohedo.es

20

Desfiladero de Despeñaperros

E2 Jaén Visitors' Centre, Carretera JA-7102 Santa Elena-Miranda del Rey, km 2, Santa Elena, Jaén; 658 56 05 07

A spectacular mountain pass, the Desfiladero de Despeñaperros is the only natural break in the Sierra Morena. In the 19th century, armies, stage-coaches and mule-trains all used the pass, so hold-ups were common. Today the Autovía de Andalucía and a railway line thread their way through the chasm, with views of rock formations – *Los Organos* (the organ pipes) and the *Salto del Fraile* (monk's leap). This is a popular area for hiking and camping.

21

Andújar

E2 Jaén Torre del Reloj, Plaza de Santa Maria; www.andujar.es

This strategically situated town was once the site of Iliturgi, an Iberian town that was destroyed by Scipio's army in the Punic Wars. A 15-arched bridge built by the Roman conquerors still spans the Guadalquivir river.

In the central plaza is the Gothic Iglesia San Miguel, with paintings by Alonso Cano. The Iglesia Santa María la Mayor features a Renaissance façade and a splendid Mudéjar tower. Inside is *Christ in the Garden of Olives* (c 1605) by El Greco.

The town is renowned for its potters, who still turn out ceramics in traditional style.

A spectacular mountain pass, the Desfiladero de Despeñaperros is the only natural break in the Sierra Morena.

22

Santuario Virgen de la Cabeza

D2 Padres Trinitarios, Jaén Daily santuario virgencabeza.org

North of Andújar, amid the oak trees and bull ranches of the Sierra Morena, this grim 13th-century stone temple houses a much-venerated Virgin, an image that, according to tradition, was sent to Spain by St Peter himself. On the last Sunday in April, thousands make a pilgrimage to the sanctuary to pay homage to the Virgin, who is carried, in a flower-decked float, through the crowds.

㉓

Parque Natural de Cazorla, Segura y Las Villas

🅰F2 🅰Jaén 🚌Cazorla
🛈Paseo de Santa María, Cazorla; 953 72 01 02

First-time visitors are amazed by the spectacular scenery of this 214,336-ha (529,409-acre) nature reserve, with its thick woodland, tumbling streams and abundant wildlife. Bristling mountains rise over 2,000 m

Did You Know?

Parque Natural de Cazorla, Segura y Las Villas is the largest national park in Spain.

(6,500 ft) above the source of the Río Guadalquivir. The river flows north through a valley before reaching the Tranco de Beas dam, where it turns to run down towards the Atlantic.

Cars are allowed only on the main road. Many visitors explore on foot, but the **Centro de Recepción e Interpretación de la Naturaleza** in the reserve can supply contacts for bike hire. There are also opportunities for hunting and angling.

Centro de Recepción e Interpretación de la Naturaleza

🅰Carretera del Tranco, km 49, Torre del Vinagre 🛈953 71 30 17 🕐Summer: 10am–2pm & 5–8pm daily; winter: 10am–2pm & 4–7pm daily

㉔

Segura de la Sierra

🅰F2 🅰Jaén 🚌 🛈Paseo P Genaro Navarro 1; 953 48 07 84 🌐seguradelasierra.es

This tiny village, at 1,200 m (4,000 ft) above sea level, is dominated by the **Castillo de Segura de la Sierra**, its restored Moorish castle. From the ramparts there are splendid views of the mountains. Below is an unusual bullring, partly chipped out of rock.

Olive oil in the Segura de la Sierra area is one of four which bear Spain's prestigious *Denominación de Origen Controlada* label.

Castillo de Segura de la Sierra

◉ 🅰Calle Castillo 🛈627 87 79 19 🕐Mar–mid-Oct: daily; mid-Oct–Mar: Fri–Sun (hours vary, call to check)

STAY

Spa Hotel Coto del Valle de Cazorla

Unwind at this tranquil retreat in the heart of Cazorla Natural Park, soaking up the views and taking advantage of the spa.

🅰F2 🅰Carretera del Tranco, km 34.3, Cazorla 🌐cotodelvalle.com

€€€

Molino la Nava

Idyllic B&B set in an 18th-century olive mill, in lovely gardens with an inviting pool. Ask about star-gazing events.

🅰D2 🅰Camino La Nava 6, Montoro 🌐molinonava.com

€€€

↑ River gorge walkway in the Parque Natural de Cazorla, Segura y Las Villas

WILDLIFE IN CAZORLA, SEGURA AND LAS VILLAS

The craggy limestone heights and riverside meadows of the Parque Natural de Cazorla, Segura y Las Villas protect a profusion of wildlife. Most is native to the region, but some species have been introduced or reintroduced for hunting. More than 100 species of birds live in Cazorla, some very rare, and it is the only habitat in Spain, apart from the Pyrenees, where the lammergeier can be seen. The extensive forests are home to a range of plant life, such as the indigenous *Viola cazorlensis*, a little purple flower, which grows among rocks.

Feathered Creatures

Of the multitude of birds that roam the skies, there are a couple of super-star species. One of the largest of these is the golden eagle *(Aquila chrysaetus)*. Known as the "king of the air", this raptor preys on small mammals living in the reserve and is often seen soaring in the skies. Griffon vultures *(Gyps fulvus)* also circle high above the reserve, descending rapidly when they catch sight of their prey. If you're lucky, you may catch sight of the park's rarest inhabitant, the lammergeier *(Gypaetus barbatus)*. This vulture drops bones from a height on to rocks to smash them and eat the marrow.

Mammals

The varied terrain of the reserve makes it a haven for a variety of mammals. Red deer *(Cervus elaphus)* were reintroduced to the area in 1952 and are most commonly seen in the autumn months, grazing on the grassland. The amazingly sure-footed Iberian ibex *(Capra pyrenaica)*, meanwhile, roams the reserve's rocky terrain. Today, the few that remain only emerge at dusk in order to feed. Otters *(Lutra lutra)* are also most likely to be spotted at dusk, as well as dawn, around the reserve's lakes and streams. Wild boar *(Sus scrofa)* hide in woodland by day and forage at night for anything from acorns to roots.

1 A trio of griffon vultures sit on a branch in the park.

2 Male red deer have antlers, while the females have none.

3 The Iberian ibex can live at heights of 3,000 m (10,000 ft).

4 Otters live in the park's rivers.

5 Wild boar will even eat birds' eggs and small mammals.

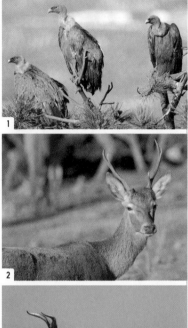

A DRIVING TOUR
SIERRA MORENA

Length 190 km (118 miles) **Stopping-off points**
Some of the villages along this route, such as
Fuente Obejuna, have restaurants and bars.
Terrain Some steep and winding roads

The austere Sierra Morena runs across northern
Andalucía. This route through Córdoba province
takes in a region of oak- and pine-clad hills, where
hunters stalk deer and boar. It also includes the
open plain of Valle de los Pedroches, where storks
make their nests on church towers. The area, little
visited by tourists, is sparsely populated. Its
individual character is more sober than the usual
image of Andalucía and it makes a delightful
excursion on a day out from Córdoba.

*An immense tower, part of a
ruined castle built in 1466,
can be found in* **Belalcázar**.
*In around 1480, Sebastián de
Belalcázar, conqueror of
Nicaragua, was born here.*

*The "Catedral de la Sierra",
the vast Gothic-Renaissance
Iglesia San Juan Bautista,
dominates the town of*
Hinojosa del Duque.

**Peñarroya-
Pueblonuevo** *was
once an important
copper- and iron-
mining centre.*

The Plaza Lope de Vega in
Fuente Obejuna *is often the
venue for Lope de Vega's
famous play about an
uprising in this village.*

Zújar

A422

A3280

Belalcázar

A422

A3279

A3

Hinojo
del Du

CO8406

A449

A3277

A430

Los Blázquez   Valsequillo

CO7405

La Granjuela

CO8404   A3276   A449

CO8405   A430

Peñarroya-Pueblonuevo

N432   Fuente
Obejuna   Guadiato   Embalse de
Sierra Boyera   Bélmez

La Cardenchosa   N432

A447   CO7403   Guadia

Aldea de los Rubios   Cañada
del Gamo

Argallón   Ojuelos   CO7403
Altos   Villanueva
del Rey

*There are fine
views to be enjoyed
from the remains
of the 13th-century
castle at* **Bélmez**.

←

Bélmez, crowned by
its castle, sitting on
top of a rocky hill

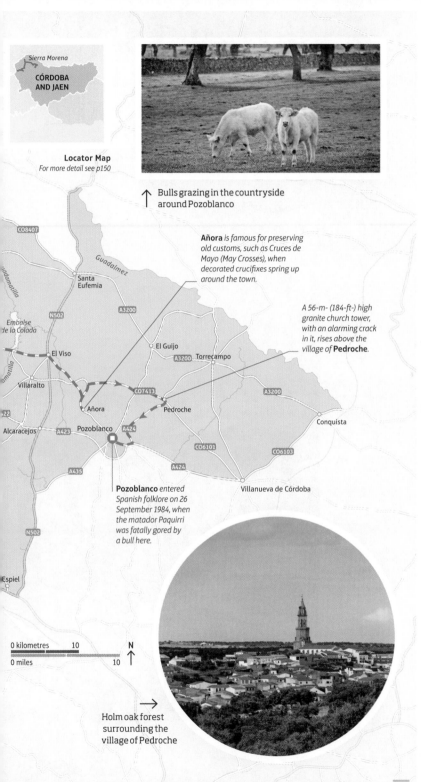

Sierra Morena

CÓRDOBA AND JAEN

Locator Map
For more detail see p150

↑ Bulls grazing in the countryside around Pozoblanco

Añora *is famous for preserving old customs, such as Cruces de Mayo (May Crosses), when decorated crucifixes spring up around the town.*

A 56-m- (184-ft-) high granite church tower, with an alarming crack in it, rises above the village of **Pedroche**.

Pozoblanco *entered Spanish folklore on 26 September 1984, when the matador Paquirri was fatally gored by a bull here.*

0 kilometres   10
0 miles   10

N ↑

→ Holm oak forest surrounding the village of Pedroche

CÁDIZ AND MÁLAGA

The cities of Cádiz and Málaga are two of the oldest in Europe, having been founded by the Phoenicians in around 1100 BC and 770 BC respectively, and continuously inhabited ever since. Their prime coastal locations made them attractive to foreign forces and the cities were occupied by the Greeks, Carthaginians, Romans, Visigoths and Byzantines before the Muslim invasion of Iberia in AD 711.

This was one of the last corners of the peninsula to fall to the *reconquista*. Cádiz remained under Muslim control until 1262, and Málaga was part of the Nasrid Kingdom of Granada until 1487.

Cádiz's port brought wealth and status to the province over the following centuries. In 1493 and 1502, Columbus sailed from there on his second and fourth voyages to the Americas and the Puerto de Indias trade monopoly transferred from Seville to Cádiz in 1717. The city's importance was cemented in 1812, when it briefly became Spain's capital and the first constitution was declared here.

In the 19th century, Málaga became a popular wintering place for English travellers seeking warmer climes. Then, in the 1960s, the narrow strip of coast to its east and west was claimed by the nascent tourism industry as the "Costa del Sol". A rash of high-rise developments around the beaches of grey sand at Torremolinos's eastern end soon made the resort's name synonymous with package holidays for the mass market. Meanwhile, further southwest at Marbella, an exclusive playground for international film stars and Arab royalty took shape. Today, these popular beach resorts are surrounded by charming hilltop villages, sprawling vineyards and hidden coves.

CÁDIZ AND MÁLAGA

Must Sees

1 Jerez de la Frontera
2 Cádiz
3 Ronda
4 Málaga

Experience More

5 Medina Sidonia
6 Chipiona
7 Sanlúcar de Barrameda
8 El Puerto de Santa María
9 Vejer de la Frontera
10 Baelo Claudia
11 Tarifa
12 Barbate
13 Parque Natural de Los Alcornocales
14 Gibraltar
15 La Línea de la Concepción
16 Sotogrande
17 Arcos de la Frontera
18 Ronda la Vieja
19 Parque Natural Sierra de las Nieves
20 Garganta del Chorro
21 Parque Natural del Torcal
22 Álora
23 Archidona
24 Antequera
25 Fuente de Piedra
26 Nerja
27 Axarquia
28 Montes de Málaga
29 Benalmádena
30 Marbella
31 Fuengirola
32 Torremolinos
33 Estepona
34 Ceuta
35 Melilla
36 Tangier

↑ A geometrically tiled square in Jerez de la Frontera at dusk

1

JEREZ DE LA FRONTERA

9 B4 **A** Cádiz **✈**🚌🚆 *i* Plaza del Arenal, Edificio Los Arcos; www.turismojerez.com

The capital of sherry production, Jerez is surrounded by chalky countryside blanketed with long rows of vines. To best appreciate the city, take a tour of one of its many *bodegas*, where you'll walk through cellars piled high with barrels and learn how to distinguish between a fino, an amontillado and an oloroso sherry.

1 🏇 Ⓜ

Real Escuela Andaluza de Arte Ecuestre

A Avenida Duque de Abrantes s/n **◷** 10am-2pm Mon-Sat **W** realescuela.org

Set in a magnificent 19th-century palace, the Royal Andalucían School of Equestrian Art is one of the most prestigious riding academies in the world. The school plays a significant role in preserving the Andalucían horse, a breed known for its dressage prowess. On selected days, in a display of exquisite dressage, the school's horses

dance to music amid colourful pageantry. Complete your visit with a tour of the on-site Equestrian Art Museum and Carriage Museum.

2 🏇 Ⓜ

Museos de la Atalaya

A Calle Cervantes 3 **◷** By guided tour only 9:30am, 10:30am, 11:30am, 12:30pm & 1:15pm Mon-Fri **W** museosdelaatalaya.com

Khronos, the God of Time, commands over this unusual clock museum. Considered to be one of the most original

museums in Spain, the Palace of Time displays over 300 Spanish, English and French time pieces, dating from as far back as the 17th century. During the 50-minute tour, you'll hear the symphony of sound created when all of the clocks chime together on the hour and half hour – an amazing sensory experience.

3 🏇

Catedral del Salvador

A Plaza de Encarnación **◷** Apr-Aug: 11am-2pm & 4-8pm daily; Sep: 10am-6:30pm Mon, 10am-8pm Tue-Sat, 1:30-8pm Sun; Oct-Mar: 10am-6:30pm Mon-Sat, 1:30-6:30pm Sun **W** catedraldejerez.es

This old Collegiate Church, dating from the Christian conquest of Jerez in 1264, combines Gothic, Baroque and Neo-Classical architectural styles. It was granted cathedral status by Pope John Paul II in 1984. The cathedral museum contains many original works of art, including *The Virgin Girl* by Zuburán.

Other highlights of the cathedral include the fragrant Patio de Naranjos (patio of orange trees) and the "secret staircase", a spiral stairway that doesn't actually lead anywhere today.

An essential part of any visit is to climb up the bell tower, built on the site of the minaret of the old mezquita. Those who venture to the top are rewarded with magnificent views of Jerez.

---

④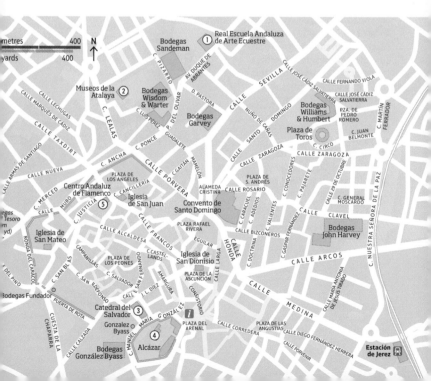

Alcázar

🏠 Alameda Vieja s/n
📞 956 14 99 55 🕐 Jul-Sep: 9:30am-5:30pm Mon-Fri, 9:30am-2:30pm Sat & Sun; Oct-Jun: 9:30am-2:30pm daily 🗓 1 & 6 Jan, 25 Dec

Considered to be one of only a few examples of Almohad architecture left in Spain, the Alcázar of Jerez de la Frontera is one of the city's most emblematic monuments. A stroll through the beautiful gardens, scented with olive and cypress trees, jasmine and orange blossom, transports you back to the 12th-century Almohad world.

The Mezquita, with its minaret, ablutions patio and prayer room, and the Arabic Baths are just two of the original areas of the fortress that can be visited. You can also take in the Baroque Villavicencio Palace, which was built during renovations of the Alcázar in 1664. Its tower contains a camera obscura, offering a bird's-eye view of Jerez de la Frontera and the surrounding area.

---

⑤

Centro Andaluz de Flamenco

🏠 Palacio de Pemartín, Plaza de San Juan 1
🕐 9am-2pm Mon-Fri
🗓 Public hols 🌐 centro andaluzdeflamenco.es

The 15th-century Palacio de Pemartín serves as the Centre of Andalucían Flamenco, which, through exhibitions and audio-visual shows, offers an insight into this musical tradition (p85). There are often performances in the palace's central patio.

Must See

DRINK

Bodegas Real Tesoro
Take a tour of this award-winning *bodega*, founded in 1897 by the Marques del Real Tesoro.

🏠 Carretera Nacional IV, km 640 🌐 grupo estevez.es

Bodegas González Byass
A train ride through this 19th-century *bodega* is the highlight here.

🏠 Calle Manuel María González 12 🌐 tiopepe.com

Bodegas Fundador
This 18th-century winery is home to the famous Harvey's brand.

🏠 Calle Puerta de Rota s/n 🌐 grupo emperadorspain.com

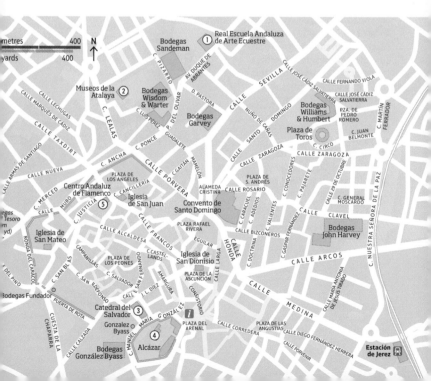

The seafront of Cádiz, with the cathedral towering behind ↑

②

CÁDIZ

🄰B4 🄲Cádiz 🚆🚌 🄸Avenida José León de Carranza s/n; www.cadizturismo.com

Jutting out of the Bay of Cádiz, and almost entirely surrounded by water, Cádiz lays claim to being Europe's oldest city. Legend names Hercules as its founder, although history credits the Phoenicians with establishing the town of Gadir, as Cádiz was known, in 1100 BC. In 1812 Cádiz briefly became Spain's capital when the nation's first constitution was declared here.

Today the joy of visiting this city is to wander along the waterfront with its neat gardens and open squares, before exploring the narrow alleys of the Old Town. The pride of the city is its Carnival – a riotous explosion of festivities, fancy dress, singing and drinking.

①
Catedral
🄰Plaza de la Catedral s/n
🄲Hours vary, check website
🌐catedraldecadiz.com

Known as the Catedral Nueva (New Cathedral) and built on the site of an older one, this Baroque and Neo-Classical church is one of Spain's largest. Its treasures are stored in the Casa de la Contaduria, behind the cathedral.

Baroque vaults

The presbytery altar, partly sponsored by Isabel II

Neo-Classical façade

Neo-Classical tower

→ Cádiz Cathedral, with a splendid cupola built by architect Juan Daura

Andalucía. On the third floor is a collection of puppets made for village fiestas.

---

③

Torre Tavira

⌂ Calle Marqués del Real Tesoro 10 🕐 Hours vary, check website 🌐 torre tavira.com

The city's official 18th-century watchtower is now a camera obscura, offering great views.

---

④

Oratorio de San Felipe Neri

⌂ Calle Santa Inés s/n 📞 956 80 70 18 🕐 Sep-Jun: 10:30am-2pm & 4:30-8pm Tue-Fri, 10:30am-2pm Sat, 10am-1pm Sun; Jul & Aug: 10:30am-2pm & 5:30-8:30pm Tue-Fri, 10:30am-2pm Sat, 10am-noon Sun

In 1812, as Napoleon tightened his grip on Spain, a provisional parliament assembled at this 18th-century church to try to lay the foundations of Spain's first constitutional monarchy.

Did You Know?

Lord Byron dubbed Cádiz the "Siren of the Ocean".

②

Museo de Cádiz

⌂ Plaza de Mina 📞 856 10 50 23 🕐 9am-9pm Tue-Sat, 9am-3pm Sun 🚫 1 Jan, 1 May, 25 Dec
This museum charts the history of Cádiz and houses the largest art galleries in

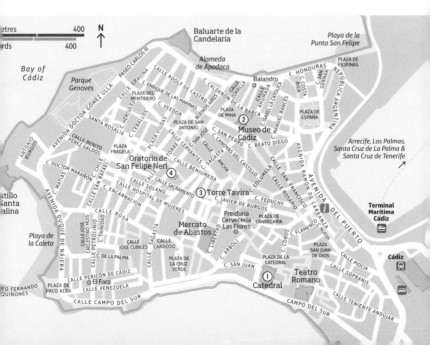

A LONG WALK
HISTORIC CÁDIZ

Distance 4 km (3 miles) **Walking time** 90 minutes
Difficulty Easy **Nearest station** Cádiz

This walk begins at the Ayuntamiento (town hall) and takes in 3,000 years of Cádiz history, most of which is defined by the surrounding sea. The route starts in the Plaza San Juan de Dios, on the eastern flank of the Bay of Cádiz, and then heads into the heart of the city's warren of small alleys and squares via the stunning topiary gardens by the university. You are rarely out of sight of the sea, passing Cádiz's fish market, its most famous fish restaurant and the Atlantic seafront. What better to place to end than at the city's cathedral, with its golden-coloured dome overlooking the ocean?

The **Alameda Apodaca** gardens boast vast dragon trees.

The **Baluarte de la Candelaria** is now a contemporary arts centre.

Baluarte de la Candelaria

Alameda de Apodaca

Turn left into Avenida Carlos III, passing the lovely **Parque Genovés**, with its avenue of symmetrical topiary trees, open-air theatre and café.

At the end of the gardens is Cádiz's modern **parador hotel**. From here, visitors can head into the heart of the Old Town.

Bay of Cádiz

Parque Genovés

Parador Hotel

The **Oratorio de San Felipe Neri** (p181)

Oratorio de San Felipe Neri

The unusual 18th-century **Torre Tavira** is named after its first keeper, Antonio Tavira (p181).

Castillo de Santa Catalina

Torre Tavira

On the city's most famous beach, **Playa de la Caleta**, is a 19th-century bathing station (now government offices) and a nautical college.

Playa de la Caleta

Mercato de Abastos

El Faro

It is worth turning left on Calle Venezuela and heading into the fishermen's quarter, which is home to the most famous fish restaurant in the region, **El Faro** (p181). Both the restaurant and the tapas bar here live up to the local saying, "Don't leave Cádiz before eating at El Faro."

Head towards the seafront and turn left into **Campo del Sur**, where pastel-coloured buildings stretch to the cathedral.

| 0 metres | 300 |
| 0 yards | 300 |

N ↑

Sitting at café tables
on a sunny street
near Cádiz Catedral

*Across the plaza, take
Fernando El Católico, which
leads to the seafront*
Murallas de San Carlos,
*the city walls overlooking
the Bay of Cádiz.*

Follow **Calle
Honduras**
*to the left,
hugging
Cádiz's sea
walls.*

Murallas de
San Carlos

CALLE HONDURAS
C. COSTA RICA
C. SAN GERMÁN
REPÚBLICA ARGENTINA
C. AHUMADA
C. MANUEL RANCES
PLAZA DE ESPAÑA
AZA DE SAN ANCISCO
C. BEATO DIEGO
AVENIDA RAMÓN DE CARRANZA
CALLE SAN FRANCISCO
C. COLUMELA
CALLE
ROSARIO
AVENIDA DEL PUERTO
C. FEDUCHY
C. JAVIER DE BURGOS
PLAZA DE CANDELARIA
C. COBOS
C. FLAMENCO
C. NUEVA
PLAZA SAN JUAN DE DIOS
PLAZA DE LA CATEDRAL
SAN JUAN
FINISH
Catedral
START
Ayuntamiento
CAMPO DEL SUR
CALLE PIOCIA
CALLE SOPRANIS
CALLE TENIENTE ANDÚJAR
Terminal
Marítima
Cádiz
Cádiz
Station

Pause in the **Plaza de España**. *The
square is dominated by the Monumento
a las Cortes, which commemorates the
short-lived parliament of 1812.*

*Calle Nueva runs into Calle San Francisco
up to the* **Plaza de San Francisco**, *one of
many tiny neighbourhood squares.*

*Head north from the square,
taking* **Calle Nueva**, *part of
Cádiz's busy shopping district.*

*Finish your walk at the
magnificent* **Catedral**,
*climbing one of its bell
towers to enjoy the
view (p180).*

*Start at the
Neo-Classical*
Ayuntamiento.
*Built in 1799, it is
chiefly the work
of architect
Torcuato
Benjumeda.*

↑ The Ayuntamiento in the
Plaza San Juan de Dios

183

Did You Know?

Orson Welles, perhaps best known as the director of *Citizen Kane*, is buried in Ronda.

③

RONDA

🅐 C4 🏠 Málaga 🚉🚌 ℹ️ Paseo de Blas Infante s/n; www.turismoderonda.es

One of the most spectacularly located cities in Spain, Ronda sits on a huge rocky outcrop, straddling a precipitous limestone cleft. This dramatic setting seems appropriate for a place which has historically sheltered outlaws and rebels. This rich history and its spectacular location have drawn visitors for years and the city was a favourite haunt of author Ernest Hemingway and actor and director Orson Welles.

Because of its impregnable position on the region's rocky landscape, Ronda was one of the last Moorish bastions, finally falling to the Christians in 1485. On the south side perches La Ciudad, a classic Moorish *pueblo blanco* (white town) of cobbled alleys, window grilles and dazzling whitewash. Most historic sights are in this part of the city, including the Palacio Mondragón, which features an arcaded patio adorned with original Moorish mosaics and plasterwork (although much of the rest of the palace was rebuilt following the *reconquista*). Located in El Mercadillo, the newer district, is one of the oldest and most important bullrings in Spain – the Plaza de Toros, which was inaugurated in 1785. In September, aficionados travel from all over the country for the singular atmosphere of the Corrida Goyesca, while millions watch it on television.

BULLFIGHTING IN RONDA

Ronda's Plaza de Toros is the spiritual home of bullfighting. The sport is an integral part of southern Spanish life, but it is highly controversial due to the prolonged nature of the kill purely for entertainment. If you decide to attend a *corrida*, try to see a big-name matador, who is likely to make a "clean" kill *(p245)*.

> **Because of its impregnable position on the region's rocky landscape, Ronda was one of the last Moorish bastions, finally falling to the Christians in 1485.**

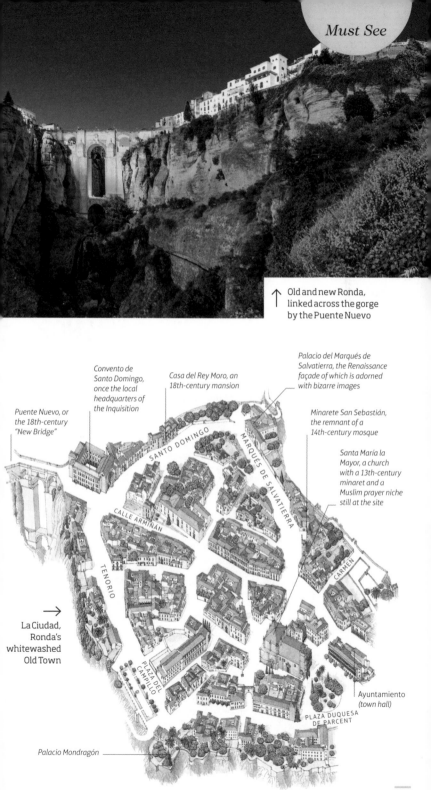

↑ Old and new Ronda, linked across the gorge by the Puente Nuevo

Convento de Santo Domingo, once the local headquarters of the Inquisition

Casa del Rey Moro, an 18th-century mansion

Palacio del Marqués de Salvatierra, the Renaissance façade of which is adorned with bizarre images

Puente Nuevo, or the 18th-century "New Bridge"

Minarete San Sebastián, the remnant of a 14th-century mosque

Santa María la Mayor, a church with a 13th-century minaret and a Muslim prayer niche still at the site

SANTO DOMINGO

MARQUÉS DE SALVATIERRA

CALLE ARMIÑÁN

TENORIO

CARMEN

→ La Ciudad, Ronda's whitewashed Old Town

PLAZA DEL CAMPILLO

Ayuntamiento (town hall)

PLAZA DUQUESA DE PARCENT

Palacio Mondragón

The Málaga skyline, dominated by the city's bullring ↑

4

MÁLAGA

🅰D4 🏠Málaga ✈ 🚂 🚌 ℹ️Plaza de la Marina 11; www.malagaturismo.com

A thriving port, Málaga is Andalucía's second largest city. Initial impressions tend to be of ugly suburbs and high-rise blocks, but this belies a city that is rich with history and filled with magnificent monuments.

① 🎨 🅜

Museo Carmen Thyssen Málaga

🏠 Calle Compañía 10
🕙 10am-8pm Tue-Sun
📅 1 Jan, 25 Dec 🌐 carmen thyssenmalaga.org

Opened in 2011, the Museo Carmen Thyssen Málaga is housed in the 16th-century Palacio de Villalón. It is so named because the gallery houses 285 late 19th- and early 20th-century pieces

Did You Know?

Baroness Carmen von Thyssen-Bornemisza sold John Constable's *The Lock* (1824) for £22 million in 2012.

from Baroness Carmen von Thyssen-Bornemisza's personal collection, which are on loan to the museum until 2025.

The museum has four main collections: Old Masters, Romantic Landscapes and Costumbrismo, Précieux and Naturalist, and Fin-de-Siècle, featuring Spanish artists such as Zurbarán, Julio Romero de Torres, Sorolla and Iturrino among others. In addition, there are often temporary exhibitions, focusing on particular artists or certain themes, such as Spanish Pop Culture, Realism and Cubism.

Construction work during the renovation of the palace revealed Roman ruins dating from the 2nd century AD. Archaeological work to preserve these ruins is on-going and it is hoped that these ruins will be open to the public in the near future.

SHOP

Mercado de Atarazanas

Take a trip to Málaga's market to shop like a local. As well as the fresh fish and vegetables, check out the stained glass at the back of the market, which depicts the city's history.

🏠 Calle Atarazanas 10
📞 951 92 60 10
🕙 9am-2pm Mon-Sat

② 🎨

Museo Automovilístico y de la Moda

🏠 Avenida de Sor Teresa Prat 15 🕙 10am-7pm daily
📅 1 Jan, 25 Dec 🌐 museo automovilmalaga.com

Let yourself get carried away with the old-world glamour and nostalgia on show at Málaga's Automobile and Fashion Museum. Bugatti, Rolls Royce, Bentley, Jaguar, Mercedes, Ferrari, Chanel, Dior – they're all represented at this quirky museum.

Located near Málaga's port, the Museo Automovilístico y de la Moda is housed in the former Royal Tobacco Factory. This 1930s building seems an appropriate setting for a collection which captures the glamour of the early 20th century, showcased on the racetrack and the catwalk. The museum houses nearly 100 meticulously restored classic cars, arranged in 13 themed rooms, charting the evolution of the automotive industry. Alongside these exclusive automobiles, you'll find over 200 haute-couture pieces. It's the perfect place to spend an afternoon escaping from the modern day.

↑ A blue-hued gallery in the Palacio de la Aduana, now the Museo de Málaga

③ ✥

Museo de Málaga

🏛 Plaza de la Aduana 1
🕐 Mid-Jun-mid-Sep: 9am-9pm Tue-Sat, 9am-3pm Sun; mid-Sep-mid-Jun: 9am-8pm Tue-Sat, 9am-3pm Sun 🚫 1 & 6 Jan, 1 May, 4, 25 & 31 Dec 🌐 museos deandalucia.es

When Málaga's Fine Arts Museum and Archaeological Museum merged in 2016 to become the Museo de Málaga, and moved to the 18th-century Palacio de la Aduana, they formed the biggest museum in Andalucía and the fifth largest in the country.

The archaeological collection houses more than 15,000 pieces, dating from the 8th century BC through to the Middle Ages. Amassed from digs carried out throughout Andalucía, the collection includes artifacts from the Egyptian, Greek, Roman, Arab, Phoenician, Christian and Byzantine civilizations that have inhabited this part of southern Spain. Some of the most interesting exhibits were once part of the Museo Loringiano, the antiquities amassed by the eminent Marquises of Casa-Loring in the 19th century.

On the second floor, there are over 200 works of art from some of Spain's most famous artists, including Murillo, Velazquez, Goya, Sorolla and, of course, Picasso, who was born in the city.

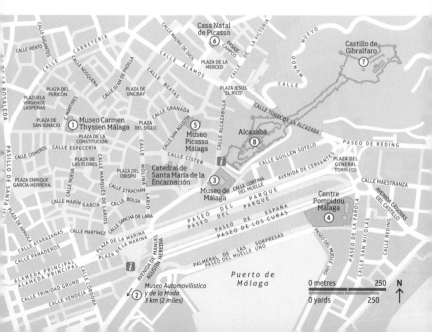

④ Centre Pompidou Málaga

📍 Pasaje Doctor Carrillo Casaux s/n, Muelle Uno
🕐 9:30am-8pm Wed-Mon
🚫 1 Jan, 25 Dec 🌐 centre pompidou-malaga.eu

Thought-provoking spaces, objects and sounds aim to inspire creativity at the Centre Pompidou Málaga, the first site of the Georges Pompidou National Centre of Art and Culture to be opened outside of France. Located on the promenade of Málaga's fashionable docklands development, Muelle Uno, this contemporary art museum exhibits around 70 selected works from the Centre Pompidou's unrivalled collection of 20th- and 21st-century art. The artworks are rotated every two to three years and there are also two or three temporary exhibitions every year.

The museum, which opened in 2015, is popularly known as "The Cube" due to its enormous steel and stained-glass skylight, which resembles a Rubik's® Cube. As well as guided tours, which are themed and interactive, you can borrow an audio guide to listen to extensive English commentary.

⑤ Museo Picasso Málaga

📍 Calle San Agustín 8
🕐 Mar-Jun, Sep & Oct: 10am-7pm daily; Jul & Aug: 10am-8pm daily; Nov-Feb: 10am-6pm daily 🚫 1 & 6 Jan, 25 Dec 🌐 museopicasso malaga.org

Málaga's Picasso Museum is dedicated to the life's work of the city's most famous son, and one of Spain's most prolific and renowned artists: Pablo Picasso. Through his paintings, sculptures and ceramics, the museum charts the artist's progression from his early sketches, through the Blue and Rose periods, to the creation of Cubism. Some of Picasso's world-famous works are displayed alongside lesser-known pieces that go some way to explain his creative process and allow visitors to gain an insight into the inner workings of one of the greatest artists that the world has ever seen.

The collection also examines Picasso's depiction of women, particularly his muses, his use of facial asymmetry and the impact of the World Wars and Spanish Civil War on his work.

⑥ Casa Natal de Picasso

📍 Plaza de la Merced 15
🕐 9:30am-8pm daily
🚫 1 Jan, 25 Dec 🌐 fundacion picasso.malaga.eu

Picasso's birthplace became a museum dedicated to the family background of the artist in 1991. It is a must see for anyone wanting to better understand one of the world's best-known artists.

The highlight of the museum is the lounge, which is so elaborately decorated because this is where the Picasso family would receive their guests. Other rooms display a variety of objects from Picasso's early life. One room is dedicated to the personal memories of his parents, displaying family memorabilia and some of Picasso's early work, while another explores the everyday life of Málaga's population in the 19th century. Photographs, postcards and documents from this time present the environment in which the artist was born and where he grew up.

The colourful Cube of the Centre Pompidou Málaga on the waterfront promenade ↓

Did You Know?

Picasso's full name is 23 words long and includes the names of many saints.

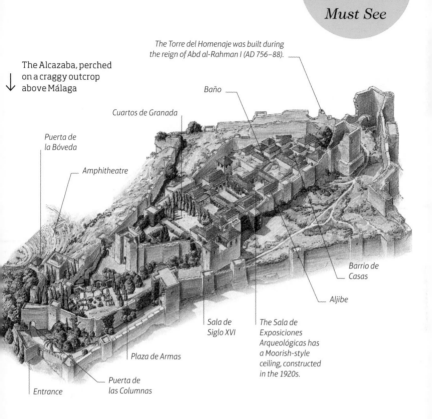

The Torre del Homenaje was built during the reign of Abd al-Rahman I (AD 756–88).

The Alcazaba, perched on a craggy outcrop above Málaga

Baño

Cuartos de Granada

Puerta de la Bóveda

Amphitheatre

Barrio de Casas

Aljibe

Sala de Siglo XVI

The Sala de Exposiciones Arqueológicas has a Moorish-style ceiling, constructed in the 1920s.

Plaza de Armas

Puerta de las Columnas

Entrance

⑦
Castillo de Gibralfaro

🏛 Camino Gibralfaro 11
📞 952 22 72 30 ⏰ Jun-Sep: 9am-8pm daily; Oct-May 9am-6pm daily

Built by the Cordoban emir Abd al-Rahman I during the 8th century, this fortress was designed to protect the Alcazaba. Following the *reconquista*, the castle acted as a temporary residence for the Catholic Monarchs.

An exhibition in the castle's arsenal displays military memorabilia and a small model showing the evolution of the Castillo de Gibralfaro from the 16th to 20th century, when the castle fell into disuse.

A walk along the Castillo de Gibralfaro's ramparts reveals fine views over Málaga and the Mediterranean. On a clear day, you can even catch a glimpse of Morocco.

⑧
Alcazaba

🏛 Calle Alcazabilla 2 📞 951 92 61 89 ⏰ Apr-Oct: 9am-8pm daily; Nov-Mar: 9am-6pm daily ⏰ 1 Jan, 24, 25 & 31 Dec

Crowning Gibralfaro hill is the majestic Alcazaba, a fortified Moorish palace that was built between the 8th and 11th centuries on the site of a Roman town. The two are curiously juxtaposed, with the Roman amphitheatre, discovered in 1951 and now almost fully excavated, just outside the entrance.

The outer citadel is accessed through the Puerta de la Bóveda, which doubles back on itself – a deliberate design feature intended to slow down the invasion of attacking forces. Through the gates are the gardens, a fragrant paradise of flowers and bubbling fountains that is typical of Moorish architectural values.

The inner enclosure contains the palace, which was built around three consecutive patios during the 11th, 13th and 14th centuries, as well as other dwellings. The real attraction in the citadel, however, is the Sala de Exposiciones Arqueológicas, which houses Phoenician, Roman and Moorish artifacts, including fine ceramics.

🔺 GREAT VIEW
Beyond the Buttresses

Climb to the top of the Alcazaba for a magical panorama of the Mediterranean, stretching out beyond Málaga's port, and the spectacular countryside that surrounds the city.

EXPERIENCE MORE

5

Medina Sidonia

🅰B5 🏛Cádiz 🚌 ℹPlazadeAbastos, Calle San Juan;www.turismomedinasidonia.es

As you drive along the N440 between Algeciras and Jerez, Medina Sidonia appears startlingly white atop a conical hill. The town was taken from the Moors in 1264 by Alfonso X, and during the 15th century the Guzmán family were established as the dukes of Medina Sidonia to defend the territory between here and the Bay of Cádiz. After the *reconquista* the family grew rich from investments in the Americas, and Medina Sidonia became one of the most important ducal seats in Spain. Many parts of the town's medieval walls still stand and cobbled alleys nestle beneath them.

The Iglesia de Santa María la Coronada is the town's most impressive building. Begun on the foundations of a castle in the 15th century, after the *reconquista*, it is a fine example of Andalucían Gothic. Inside is a collection of religious works of art dating from the Renaissance, including paintings and a charming *retablo* with beautifully carved panels.

6

Chipiona

🅰B4 🏛Cádiz 🚌 ℹCalle delCastillo 5; www.turismodechipiona.es

A lively little resort town, Chipiona is approached through sherry vineyards. It has a great beach and a holiday atmosphere in the summer. Days on the beach are followed by a *paseo* along the quay or in the Moorish old town, where cafés and ice-cream parlours stay open well past midnight. There are also street entertainers and horse-drawn carriages. The Iglesia de Nuestra Señora de Regla, the main church, has a natural spring feeding a fountain, and an adjoining cloister decorated with 17th-century *azulejos*.

7

Sanlúcar de Barrameda

🅰B4 🏛Cádiz 🚌 ℹCalleCalzada Duquesa Isabel s/n;www.sanlucarturismo.com

A fishing port at the mouth of the Guadalquivir river, Sanlúcar is overlooked by the Moorish Castillo de Santiago. The Parque Nacional de Doñana *(p136)*, over the river, can be reached by boat from the riverside quay. From here Columbus set off on his third trip to the Americas, in 1498, and in 1519 Ferdinand Magellan left the port with the intention of circumnavigating the globe.

However, Sanlúcar is now best known for its *manzanilla*, a light, dry sherry from, among other producers, **Bodegas Barbadillo**. Visitors to this *bodega* can sip a *copita* (little

322

Steps lead to the top of the Chipiona lighthouse, the tallest in Spain.

Sunset over the shore at Chipiona, with its 19th-century lighthouse

↑ The Museo de Manzanilla at the Bodegas Barbadillo in Sanlúcar de Barrameda

glass) of *manzanilla* and enjoy the local shellfish, *langostinos*. There are guided tours in Spanish and English every day but Monday, as well as a museum on site, the Museo de Manzanilla, which traces the history of the drink. It's a must for any sherry lover.

Other sights in the town include the Iglesia de Nuestra Señora de la O, which has superb Mudéjar portals, with heavily worked stone reliefs.

Bodegas Barbadillo

🕸️🕸️ 🏠 Calle Luis de Eguilaz 11 ⏰ Apr-Oct: 10am-3pm daily; Nov-Mar: 10am-3pm Mon-Sat 🌐 barbadillo.com

⑧
El Puerto de Santa María

🅰️B4 🚍 Cádiz 🚗🚌📧 ℹ️ Palacio de Aranibar, Plaza de Alfonso X El Sabio 9; www.turismo elpuerto.com

Sheltered from the Atlantic wind and waves of the Bay of Cádiz, El Puerto de Santa María is a tranquil town which has burgeoned as one of the main ports for the export of sherry. The *bodegas* of sherry companies, such as **Terry** and **Osborne**, can be visited for tours and tasting.

Among the town's sights are the 13th-century **Castillo San Marcos** and the **Plaza de Toros** – one of the largest and most famous bullrings in Spain. Whatever your opinion is of bullfighting, it's an impressive building. The main square, the Plaza Mayor, is presided over by the 13th-century, Gothic Iglesia Mayor Prioral, which is worth a look for its unusual choir. Scattered around the town are fine old *palacios* bearing the coats of arms of wealthy families who prospered in the port during colonial times.

Bodegas Terry

🕸️🕸️ 🏠 Calle de los Toneleros 1 📞 956 15 15 00 ⏰ Mon-Fri (phone to arrange)

EAT

Casa Bigote
Salty air and sandy planks set the mood at this seafood eatery in Sanlúcar de Barrameda.

🅰️B4 🏠 Calle Pórtico Bajo de Guia 10, Sanlúcar de Barrameda 🌐 restaurantecasa bigote.com

€€€

Pantalán G
Enjoy views of the marina and lots of fish at this El Puerto de Santa María eatery. There's live music at the weekend.

🅰️B4 🏠 Avenida de la Libertad, El Puerto de Santa María 🌐 pantalang.com

€€€

El Jardín del Califa
Mouthwatering Moroccan dishes are served in the jasmine-scented courtyard of this restaurant in Vejer de la Frontera.

🅰️B5 🏠 Plaza de España 16, Vejer de la Frontera 🌐 califavejer.com

€€€

Bodegas Osborne
🕸️🕸️ 🏠 Calle de los Moros 7 📞 956 86 91 00 ⏰ Daily (reservation required)

Castillo San Marcos
🕸️ 🏠 Plaza Alfonso X El Sabio 📞 956 85 17 51 ⏰ For tours, Jul-mid-Sep: 11:30am Wed-Mon & 6pm Mon-Sat; mid-Sep-Jun: 11:30am Tue, Thu & Sat

Plaza de Toros
🕸️ 🏠 Plaza Elias Ahuja 7 📞 956 86 11 88 ⏰ 10am-2pm & 4-7pm Mon-Fri

191

⑨
Vejer de la Frontera

🅰B5 🅰Cádiz 🅸Avenida Los Remedios 2, Parque Municipal Los Remedios; www.turismovejer.es

Attractively located on a hilltop above Barbate, Vejer de la Frontera was one of the first places occupied by the Muslim invaders in AD 711, shortly after they had defeated the Visigoths in battle close by.

The oldest part of town is enclosed by an irregular wall that is protected by three towers and entered by four gates. Within the walled area are the Arab castle and the parish church, the Iglesia Parroquial del Divino Salvador, which was built on the site of a mosque between the 14th and 16th centuries, in a mix of Gothic and Mudéjar styles.

Later buildings outside the walls include the Palacio del Marqués de Tamaron, which is a 17th- to 18th-century stately home.

SHOP

Barbate Mercado de Abastos

The tuna at Barbate is said to be the finest in the world. Grab yourself a slab or a slice from the catch-of-the-day displays at this local market, where an abundance of fresh, locally sourced seafood, produce and meats are sold underneath hand-painted ceiling murals of seascapes.

🅰B5 🅰Avenida de Andalucía 1, Barbate 📞956 06 36 25 🕘9am-2pm Mon-Sat

---

⑩
Baelo Claudia

🅰C5 🅰Bolonia, Cádiz 🕘Apr-mid-Jun: 9am-9pm Tue-Sat, 9am-3pm Sun; mid-Jun-Jul: 9am-3pm & 6-9pm Tue-Sat, 9am-3pm Sun; Aug-mid-Sep: 9am-3pm Tue-Sun; mid-Sep-Mar: 9am-6pm Tue-Sat, 9am-3pm Sun 🌐juntade andalucia.es

The Roman settlement of Baelo Claudia was established on the seashore in the 2nd century BC and gradually grew in importance through trade with North Africa and its fish salting and pickling works. Emperor Claudius (AD 41–54) elevated Baelo Claudia to the status of a municipality, but its prestige was short-lived, since it was effectively destroyed by an earthquake in the 2nd century AD and finally abandoned in the 6th century. The ruins, which include a theatre, a necropolis and several erect columns, sit in a picturesque spot next to a beautiful beach beside the small settlement of Bolonia.

WINDFARMS

You'll see windfarms aplenty around Tarifa; the wind blows with such reliable force here that it is used to drive electricity-generating wind turbines. Spain has the world's second-highest installed capacity of windpower after Germany. Look out for Tarifa's giant tuna weathervane on the sea front; the names of all the winds that blow in this region are inscribed at its base.

---

⑪
Tarifa

🅰C5 🅰Cádiz 🚌 🅸Paseo de la Alameda s/n; www.cadizturismo.com

Europe's wind- and kitesurfing capital takes its name from Tarif ben Maluk, an 8th-century Moorish commander.

The 10th-century **Castillo de Guzmán el Bueno** is the site of a legend. In 1292, Guzmán, who was defending Tarifa from the Moors, was told his hostage son would die if he did not surrender. Rather than give in, he threw down his dagger for the captors to use.

Castillo de Guzmán el Bueno

⊘ 🅰Calle Guzmán el Bueno 📞607 98 48 71 🕘Winter: 10am-4pm Tue-Sun; summer: 10am-4pm daily

---

←

The atmospheric ruins of the ancient Roman town of Baelo Claudia

Watching the sunset from a bar at Zahara de los Atunes, near Barbate ↑

⑫
Barbate

🅰 B5 🏛 Cádiz ℹ Paseo Marítimo 5; www.turismo barbate.es

The largest coastal settlement between Cádiz and Tarifa, Barbate stands at the mouth of the eponymous river, in an area of marshes and saltflats. There is not much of interest in the town itself, but two small tourist resorts attached to it are worth visiting.

A short way south down the coast is Zahara de los Atunes, which has grown up along one of the coast's best beaches. Barbate's culinary speciality is *mojama*, tuna *(atún)* that has been cured in the same way as *jamón serrano*. Inland from Zahara, around the main N340 coast road, are large swathes of wind turbines generating electricity for the national grid. The road north out of Barbate (past the fishing port) climbs over a headland fringed by cliffs and planted with dense pine woods to drop down to the small holiday resort of Los Caños de Meca, which began as a hippy hideaway in the 1970s and still has a carefree feel to it.

On a short sand spit nearby stands a lighthouse marking the Cabo de Trafalgar (Cape Trafalgar), which gave its name to the naval battle fought on 21 October 1805, when Britain's Admiral Nelson decided to take on – and defeat – the combined, vastly superior fleet of Spanish and French ships.

---

⑬
Parque Natural de Los Alcornocales

🅰 C5 🏛 Cádiz and Málaga ℹ Carretera C-2112, km 1, Alcalá de los Gazules; 856 58 75 08

This nature reserve is named after the *alcornocales*, cork oak

trees, that are prevalent in many parts of it. They are easily identified because they will have been stripped of their lower bark, leaving the vivid red heartwood showing. The far south of the natural park is crossed by deep valleys called *canutos*, in which rare vestiges of Europe's ancient fern-rich forests cling on.

Natural beauty aside, the area has a few towns worth visiting, including Jimena de la Frontera, Castellar de la Frontera and Medina Sidonia *(p190)*, plus several caves.

Hiking on the slopes of Parque Natural de Los Alcornocales ↑

GREAT VIEW
Strait Ahead

If you climb the high El Aljibe massif in the Los Alcornocales park, or take the N340 coast road that skirts it from Los Barrios to Facinas, you'll get superb views across the Strait of Gibraltar to Africa.

The Rock of Gibraltar, known to the Romans as one of the two Pillars of Hercules ↑

14

Gibraltar

C5 **Overseas Territory** **Duke of Kent House, Cathedral Square; www.visitgibraltar.gi**

The high, rocky headland of Gibraltar was signed over to Britain at the Treaty of Utrecht in 1713. Today, about 4 million people stream to and fro across the border between Gibraltar and La Línea de la Concepción in Spain every year to visit this speck of England, only 6.7 km² (2.6 sq miles) in area, bolted on to Andalucía. Pubs, British high street names and "bobbies" on the beat all give a quaint air.

Built on the foundations of Moorish baths, the **Gibraltar Museum** charts the territory's history, which has been shaped by its strategic position and geography. The territory is dominated by the so-called Rock of Gibraltar. Halfway up this promontory are an 8th-century Moorish castle, known as **The Keep**, which was used as a prison until 2010, and the **Siege Tunnels**, an 80-km (50-mile) network housing store-rooms and barracks, used when Spanish and French forces blockaded Gibraltar in the late 18th century.

During World War II, Gibraltar was of enormous strategic importance, controlling and defending the gateway to the Mediterranean Sea (today, half the world's shipping trade uses this narrow strait). Most of the civilian population was evacuated, mainly to London but also to Jamaica, for the duration of the conflict. **St Michael's Cave**, which then served as a military hospital, is now used as a venue for classical concerts.

A cable car runs from the centre of Gibraltar town to the Top of the Rock, at 450 m (1,475 ft). The **Apes' Den**, north of Europa Point – Gibraltar's southernmost tip – is home to the Rock's famous tailless apes. (Strictly speaking they are monkeys, a five-troop colony of Barbary macaques, which originate from Morocco.) Legend says that the British will keep Gibraltar only as long as the apes remain here.

Gibraltar Museum
18 Bombhouse Lane
10am–6pm Mon–Fri, 10am–2pm Sat Public hols
gibmuseum.gi

GIBRALTAR CONTROVERSY

Anglo-Dutch forces seized Gibraltar in 1704, as part of the War of the Spanish Succession, and Britain was then granted the Rock "in perpetuity". An attempt to wrestle it back by Spanish and French forces during the American War of Independence failed. As the gateway to the Mediterranean, Gibraltar was essential to Britain in the age of Empire. In a 1967 referendum, residents voted overwhelmingly to stay under British rule. Tensions over Gibraltar eased for a while, but the spectre of Britain's exit from the European Union has caused renewed hostility.

⓯
La Línea de la Concepción

🗺 C5 🏛 Cádiz 🚌 🛈 Avenida de 20 Abril; 956 78 41 35

La Línea is a town on the Spanish side of the border with Gibraltar. Its name, "The Line", refers to the old walls that once formed the frontier, but were demolished during the Napoleonic wars to prevent the French using them for defence. Now it is a lively trading town, with several hotels popular with those wishing to avoid the higher prices in Gibraltar.

⓰
Sotogrande

🗺 C5 🏛 Cádiz 🚌 San Roque 🛈 Palacio de los Gobernadores, Calle Rubín de Celis s/n; 956 69 40 05

Lying just above Gibraltar on the Costa del Sol, this

HIDDEN GEM
Bunker Down

World War II buffs can explore several bunkers while strolling around Reina Sofia Park in La Línea de la Concepción. To enter the bunkers, book a guided tour through the tourist information centre.

exclusive residential seaside town is popular with wealthy Gibraltarians, who commute to the Rock, and with affluent financiers, politicians and minor royalty from elsewhere in Europe. The best place to get an idea of the affluence of this area is at Sotogrande's marina, which is filled with expensive, gleaming yachts and lined with excellent seafood restaurants.

Nearby, as one might expect, there are several immaculately manicured golf courses, including the Real Club de Sotogrande.

The Keep, Siege Tunnels, St Michael's Cave, Apes' Den

⊗ 🏛 Upper Rock Area
🕐 9:30am–6:15pm daily

The Siege Tunnels formed an ingenious defence system.

The Keep, the remains of a Moorish castle

St Michael's Cave, used as a hospital in World War II

The Apes' Den, home to the Rock's semi-wild macaques

Europa Point, with views across the strait to North Africa

The 100-Ton Gun, brought from England in the 1880s

Gibraltar Museum charts the history of the colony.

↑ The runway of Gibraltar's airport and the key sights found on the Rock

↑ Classic whitewashed buildings at Arcos de la Frontera, once a well-defended hill town

17

Arcos de la Frontera

A B4 **A** Cádiz **🚌** **ⓘ** Calle Cuesta de Belén 5; 956 70 22 64

Arcos has been inhabited since prehistoric times. Its strategic position encouraged settlement, first as the Roman town of Arcobriga, and later as the stronghold of Medina Arkosh under the Caliphate of Córdoba.

An archetypal white town, Arcos de la Frontera has a labyrinthine Moorish quarter that twists up to its ruined castle. At its centre is the Plaza de España, with the superb Iglesia de Santa María de la Asunción, a late Gothic-Mudéjar building with extravagant Baroque choir stalls and a Renaissance

> An archetypal white town, Arcos de la Frontera has a labyrinthine Moorish quarter that twists up to its ruined castle. At its centre is the Plaza de España.

altarpiece. A small museum displays the church treasures. More striking is the massive 14th-century Gothic Parroquia de San Pedro. Its thick-set tower provides a view over the sheer drop down to the Guadalete river. Nearby is the **Palacio del Mayorazgo** with an ornate Renaissance façade.

Palacio del Mayorazgo
A Calle San Pedro 2 **C** 956 70 30 13 (Casa de Cultura) **🕐** 10:30am-1:30pm & 4:30-7:30pm Mon-Fri, 11am-2pm Sat & Sun

18

Ronda la Vieja

A C4 **A** Málaga **🚂🚌** Ronda **ⓘ** Paseo de Blas Infante, Ronda; www.turismode ronda.es

Ronda la Vieja is the modern name for the remains of the Roman city of Acinipo. An important town in the 1st century AD, it later declined, unlike the growing town of

Ronda (p184), which was called Arunda by the Romans. The ruins are on a hillside where only a fraction of the town has been excavated. The most significant sight is the theatre, but lines of stones also mark the foundations of houses, the forum and other buildings.

Along the C339, 22 km (12 miles) from Ronda la Vieja, are the **Cuevas de la Pileta**, the site of prehistoric cave paintings dating from about 25,000 BC.

Cuevas de la Pileta
🚫 **A** Benaoján **⊙** By appt only **🌐** cuevadelapileta.org

19

Parque Natural Sierra de las Nieves

A D4 **A** Málaga **ⓘ** Calle Jacaranda 1, Cortes de la Frontera; 952 15 45 99

One of Andalucía's least accessible areas, this UNESCO biosphere reserve southeast of Ronda extends between

Parauta (to the east), Tolox (west), El Burgo (north) and Istán (south). It features both extreme highs and lows, reaching up to the peak of Torrecilla (1,919 m/ 6,295 ft) and down to one of the world's deepest potholes, GESM, which is 1,100 m (3,608 ft) deep. The sierra is popular for caving and rock climbing, and has moderate to difficult signposted walking trails.

A short way south, near Ojén, is the Refugio de Juanar, which offers woodland walks.

---

⑳
Garganta del Chorro

🅐D4 🅜Málaga 🚇El Chorro 🚌Parque Ardales 🛈Plaza Fuente de Arriba 15, Álora; 952 49 61 00

The Guadalhorce valley is home to one of Spain's geographical wonders. The Garganta del Chorro is a gaping chasm 180 m (590 ft) high, slashing through a limestone mountain. In some places, where the Guadalhorce river hurtles through the gorge, waters foaming white, it is only 10 m (30 ft) wide. Visitors can access the **Caminito del Rey** walkway, attached to the walls of the gorge over 100 m (330 ft) above the river. A limited number of hikers is allowed at any one time, so reservations are essential.

Caminito del Rey
◈ 🕐Apr-Oct: 10am-5pm Tue-Sun; Nov-Mar: 10am-2pm Tue-Sun 🅦camino delrey.info

Did You Know?

The Caminito del Rey is 8 km (5 miles) long and known as "the scariest path in the world".

STAY

Parador de Arcos de la Frontera
Perched high on a bluff at the edge of Arcos de la Frontera, this parador offers amazing views and an excellent restaurant.

🅐B4 🅜Plaza del Cabildo, Arcos de la Frontera 🅦parador.es

€€€

Hotel La Luna Blanca
East meets West in this unique Japanese-style hotel in a quiet part of Torrremolinos only five minutes' walk from the beach. Relax in the rooftop Jacuzzi.

🅐D4 🅜Pasaje Cerrillo 2, Torremolinos 🅦hotel lalunablanca.es

€€€

La Villa Marbella
This fully refurbished 200-year-old house in Marbella's historic centre has old-time romantic charm. After breakfast by the pool it's only an eight-minute walk to the beach.

🅐D5 🅜Calle Príncipe 10, Marbella 🅦lavillamarbella.com

€€€

↓ The Caminito del Rey across the breathtaking Garganta del Chorro

Stark white dwellings in Arcos de la Frontera

㉑
Parque Natural del Torcal

🅰D4 🅜Málaga
🚉🚌Antequera ℹCarretera A-7075, 10 km (6 miles) S of Antequera; www. torcaldeantequera.com

A huge exposed hump of limestone upland battered into bizarre formations by wind and rain, El Torcal is popular with hikers. Most follow a network of footpaths leading from a visitors' centre; short walks (up to two hours) are marked by yellow arrows; longer walks in red. There are caves, canyons, mushroom-shaped rocks and other geological curiosities to see. The park also has fox and weasel populations, as well as eagles, hawks and vultures.

㉒
Álora

🅰D4 🅜Málaga 🚉🚌
ℹPlaza Fuente de Arriba 15; www.alora.es

Situated in the Guadalhorce river valley, Álora is an important agricultural centre. It is a classic *pueblo blanco*, or white town, perched on a hillside overlooking wheat fields, citrus orchards and olive groves.

The town's cobbled streets radiate from the 18th-century Iglesia de la Encarnación. At the bustling weekly market, stalls of farm produce and clothing fill nearby streets. On the higher of Álora's twin hills stands the **Castillo Árabe**, with a cemetery of niche tombs set in neat blocks.

Castillo Árabe
🅰Calle Ancha 📞952 49 61 00 🕐8am–3pm daily

㉓
Archidona

🅰D4 🅜Málaga 🚉🚌
ℹPlaza Ochavada 2; 952 71 64 79

This small town is worth a stop to see its extraordinary Plaza Ochavada – an octagonal square built in the 18th century in a French style, which also incorporates traditional Andalucían features. From the Ermita Virgen de Gracia on a hillside above the town, there are commanding views over rolling countryside.

㉔
Antequera

🅰D4 🅜Málaga 🚉🚌Calle Encarnación 4; www. turismo.antequera.es

This busy market town has long been strategically important; first as Roman Anticaria, and later as a Moorish border fortress defending Granada. The Iglesia de Nuestra Señora del

→

The Ephebe of Antequera, one of the finest Roman statues in Spain

↑ People taking in the weathered limestone formations at the Parque Natural del Torcal

DRINK

Bar Restaurante Tejada Dani-Denis

Cool off with a cold beer at a table on the terrace, while enjoying views of Fuente de Piedra's reservoir. There's plenty of choice of brews, as well as a food menu. Try the grilled prawn and octopus skewer.

🅐D4 🏠Plaza de la Constitución 10, Fuente de Piedra 📞952 73 53 32

Belvue Rooftop Bar

Enjoy views over the Mediterranean and fancy cocktails at this glamorous, adults-only bar in Marbella. Come here for a tipple at sunset or head over later for live music and DJ sounds. The bar serves snacks and there are four restaurants in the hotel if you get peckish.

🅐D5 🏠Amare Hotel, Paseo Alfonso Cañas Nogueras, Marbella 🌐amarehotels.com

Carmen, with its massive Baroque altarpiece, is not to be missed.

High on a hill overlooking the town is the Castillo Árabe, a 13th-century Moorish castle, built on the site of a Roman fort. Visitors cannot go inside, but you can walk round the castle walls to appreciate the scale of this fortress – the approach is through the 16th-century Arco de los Gigantes. There are fine views from the 16th-century Torre del Papabellotas, one of the towers in the castle walls. In the town below, the 18th-century **Palacio de Nájera** is the setting for the Municipal Museum, whose star exhibit is the Ephebe, a 2,000-year-old statue of a Roman boy.

On the outskirts of town are three large prehistoric **dolmens** that may have been the burial chambers of tribal leaders. Two of them – Viera and Menga – stand together, the latter the oldest and most impressive of all, dated at between 4,000 and 4,500 years old. The Menga Dolmen is also interesting because it is positioned so that, on the summer solstice, the sun shines straight into its entrance. A short distance away is the Dolmen de Romeral, which has a vaulted central chamber.

Palacio de Nájera

⊘ 🏠Plaza del Coso Viejo 📞952 70 83 00 🕐Mid-Jun–mid-Sep: 9am-2pm Tue-Sun; mid-Sep-mid-Jun: 10am-2pm & 4:30-6:30pm Tue-Sat, 9:30am-2pm Sun

Dolmens

⊘ 📞952 71 22 06 🕐Apr-May: 9am-8pm Tue-Sat, 9am-2pm Sun; Jun-mid-Sep: 9am-2pm Tue-Sat, 9am-2pm Sun; mid-Sep-Mar: 9am-5:30pm Tue-Sat, 9am-2pm Sun

---

㉕
Fuente de Piedra

🅐D4 🏠Málaga 🚊🚌 ℹ️Calle Cerro del Palo; 952 71 25 54

The largest of several lakes in an expanse of wetlands north of Antequera, the Laguna de la Fuente de Piedra teems with bird life, including huge flocks of flamingos. Every March, up to 25,000 of these birds arrive to breed before migrating back to West Africa. However, if there is drought in the region, there will be fewer birds breeding.

Apart from flamingos, there are cranes, herons, bee-eaters, snow-white egrets, as well as many species of ducks and geese. Their numbers have been on the increase since conservation and anti-hunting laws were introduced and the area declared a sanctuary. A road off the N334 leads to the lake side, from where visitors can watch the birds. Restraint is required: it is forbidden to join the waders in the lake. Information is available from a visitors' centre near the village of Fuente de Piedra.

↑ The seafront promenade at Nerja, shaded by palms and arcades

EAT

Espetos (grilled sardines) are the local speciality in Málaga province. Try this salty dish at one of these authentic eateries.

Merendero Moreno
🅰E4 🏠 Playa Burriana, Nerja 📞 952 52 54 80

€€€

El Canarias
🅰D4 🏠 Plaza del Remo, Torremolinos
🌐 elcanariasplaya.com

€€€

Miguel Cerdán
🅰D4 🏠 Paseo Marítimo, Torremolinos 📞 952 38 69 13

€€€

Pepe Oro
🅰E4 🏠 Diseminado Pago Carlaja 1867, Torrox 🌐 pepeoro.com

€€€

26

Nerja

🅰E4 🏠 Málaga 🚌 🛈 Calle Carmen 1 (ground floor of Ayuntamiento); www. turismo.nerja.es

This fashionable resort at the eastern extremity of the Costa del Sol lies at the foot of the beautiful mountains of the Sierra de Almijara, and is perched on a cliff above a succession of sandy coves. The main area for tourist activity in the resort centres around the promenade, running along a rocky promontory known as El Balcón de Europa (the Balcony of Europe). Spread along its length is a hotel and cafés with outdoor tables. There are sweeping views up and down the coast. On the edges of town, holiday villas and apartments proliferate.

Due east of the town are the **Cuevas de Nerja**, a series of vast caverns of considerable archaeological interest, which were discovered in 1959. Prehistoric wall paintings found in them are believed to be about 20,000 years old. Unfortunately most are closed to public view, but a few of the many cathedral-sized chambers are open to the public. One of these has

been turned into an impressive underground auditorium large enough to hold audiences of several hundred. Concerts are held there in the summer.

Cuevas de Nerja
♿ 🏠 Carretera Maro s/n ⏰ 9:30am–4:30pm daily 🚫 1 Jan, 15 May 🌐 cueva denerja.es

---

27

Axarquia

🅰E4 🏠 Málaga 🛈 Avenida de la Constitución 1; www. competa.es

The hills behind Torre del Mar and Nerja make up the pretty upland region of Axarquia, whose main town, Vélez-Málaga, has a few old streets and the remains of a castle to explore. A better base for excursions

> ## Did You Know?
>
> "Nerja" is derived from the word *narixa*, an Arabic term which translates as "bountiful spring".

is the attractive, sweet-wine-producing town of Cómpeta, 20 km (12 miles) from the coast by winding mountain roads. From here, there is an interesting "Mudéjar route" down the hill and up the valley to Archez and Salares, villages whose church towers are clearly undisguised brick minarets dating, respectively, from the 15th and 13th centuries.

Two other villages worth visiting are Frigiliana, close to the coast and easily accessible from Nerja; and Comares (northeast of Vélez-Málaga), perched on top of an impressive outcrop of rock from which there are superb views.

28
Montes de Málaga

▲D4 **▲Málaga** **▦To Colmenar** **🖫Lagar de Torrijos, on C345 at km 544; 600 62 00 54**

To the north and east of Málaga are the beautiful hills of Montes de Málaga. A wide area is undergoing reforestation and forms the Parque Natural de Montes de Málaga. Wildlife thrives in the strongly scented

↑ Hiking along well-maintained trails in the Montes de Málaga hills

undergrowth of lavender and wild herbs. Occasionally, there are glimpses of wild cats, stone martens, wild boars, eagles and other birds of prey.

The C35 road connects Málaga (p186) and the park and there are sensational views down to the sea en route. Once you reach the park, walkers can follow the well-marked trails, taking in the mountain panoramas.

29
Benalmádena

▲D4 **▲Málaga** **▦▦** **🖫Avenida Antonio Machado 10; 952 44 24 94**

Benalmádena hosts an array of great attractions, including the impressive **Castillo de Colomares**, built between 1987 and 1994 as a homage to Christopher Columbus. The Castillo de Colomares draws on the many architectural styles that have influenced Spanish culture over the centuries, including Byzantine, Romanesque and Arabic, and carved into the structure are representations of Spain's history.

Europe's largest Buddhist monument, the **Benalmádena Stupa**, is also located here.

Castillo de Colomares
♿ 🅿Carretera Costa del Sol (Finca la Carraca) 🕐Apr-Jun: 10am-1:30pm & 4-7pm Wed-Sun; Jul-Aug: 10am-1:30pm & 5-9pm Wed-Sun; Sep-Mar: 10am-1:30pm & 4-6pm Wed-Sun 🆆castillomonumento colomares.com

Benalmádena Stupa
♿ 🅿Avenida del Retamar 📞606 27 53 75 🕐10am-2pm & 4:30-8pm Tue-Sun (afternoon hours may vary in mid- and low season; call ahead to check)

> **The Castillo de Colomares draws on the many architectural styles that have influenced Spanish culture over the centuries.**

↓ The fanciful Castillo de Colomares, Benalmádena

> Marbella is one of Europe's most exclusive holiday resorts. Royalty, film stars and other members of the jet set spend their summers here.

③⓪ Marbella

🅐D5 🅐Málaga 🚌
🛈 Glorieta de la Fontanilla s/n, Paseo Maritímo; www.turismo.marbella.es

Marbella is one of Europe's most exclusive holiday resorts. Royalty, film stars and other members of the jet set spend their summers here, in smart villas or at one of Marbella's luxury hotels. In winter, the major attraction is the golf.

As well as extensive modern developments, Marbella boasts a well-preserved, charming Old Town. A number of streets lead from the main road, Avenida Ramón y Cajal, to Plaza de los Naranjos, the main square, surrounded by orange trees (hence its name).

The remains of the town's Arab walls loom over adjacent Calle Carmen, which leads to the 17th-century Iglesia de Nuestra Señora de la Encarnación. Nearby is the **Museo del Grabado Español Contemporáneo** (Museum of Contemporary Engravings), which contains works by big-name Spanish artists, including Miró and Picasso.

On the other side of Avenida Ramón y Cajal is the Paseo de la Alameda, a park with benches decorated with colourful ceramics. From here, the road to the seafront, Avenida del Mar, is lined with sculptures made from designs by famous Spanish artist Salvador Dalí.

Heading west, Avenida Ramón y Cajal becomes the A7/N340. The first stretch is known as the "Golden Mile" because of its real-estate value. At the other end of the Golden Mile is Puerto Banús, the most exclusive marina in Spain.

Beyond Puerto Banús is San Pedro de Alcántara, really a separate town but officially part of Marbella. It has a sleepy atmosphere, especially in the Plaza de la Iglesia, the town square. Most of the smart holiday developments are on the town's fringes, set amid a number of golf courses.

Museo del Grabado Español Contemporáneo

◈ 🅐Calle Hospital Bazán s/n 📞952 76 57 41 🕘9am-2pm Mon & Sat; 9am-7pm Tue-Fri 🚫Public hols

③① Fuengirola

🅐D4 🅐Málaga 🚉🚌
🛈 Paseo Jesús Santos Rein 6; www.turismo.fuengirola.es

Once a quiet fishing port, the town of Fuengirola is today a popular package-holiday resort, with a largely British clientele. Although some of its wilder visitors have moved on to newer pastures.

Nowadays Fuengirola attracts mainly families,

Orange trees in full fruit on a mild day in Marbella's Old Town

TOP 5 LOCAL BEACHES

Playa de Bolonia
One of the few truly virgin beaches in Cádiz.

Playa Cabo Trafalgar
Beautiful white-sand beach at Caños de Meca.

Playa de Valdevaqueros
The strong winds here at Tarifa make this a perfect surf-spot.

Playa Bil-Bil
Benalmádena's lovely dark-sand beach.

Playa de Puerto Banús
Deluxe Marbella sunning spot, with a marina and high-end hotels.

while during the mild winter months, retired people from the UK take advantage of the low-season prices and come to stroll along the promenade, meet friends in English bars, and waltz the afternoons away at hotel tea dances.

32 Torremolinos

D4 **Málaga** 🚃 💺
ℹ️ Plaza de Andalucía s/n; www.turismo torremolinos.es

Torremolinos grew from a village in the 1950s into one of the busiest resorts on the Costa del Sol, where British and, to a lesser extent, German holidaymakers enjoyed cheap package holidays. It also developed its red-light district and a raffish nightlife to offer "recreation" for sailors of the US navy in port at Málaga.

The town was revamped as part of a scheme that spent huge sums on new squares, a promenade, green spaces and enlarging the beach with tonnes of golden sand.

Although Torremolinos still has scores of English bars run by expatriates, the atmosphere is now decidedly less downmarket, especially at Carihuela beach, towards the adjoining resort of Benalmádena *(p203)*.

33 Estepona

C5 **Málaga** 💺
ℹ️ Plaza de las Flores; www.estepona.es

This former fishing village, midway between Marbella and Gibraltar, has been altered, but not totally overwhelmed, by tourist developments. Now a popular resort, it is not particularly attractive at first

↑ Quaint narrow streets away from the main tourist drag at Estepona

sight, with big hotels and apartment blocks fronting the town's busy main tourist area. Behind, however, there are endearing pockets of all that is quintessentially Spanish: orange trees lining the streets, and the lovely Plaza Arce and Plaza de las Flores – peaceful squares where old men sit reading newspapers while around them children kick footballs about. There are also a few good-value fish restaurants and tapas bars serving traditional delicacies. The beach is pleasant enough and evenings in the town tend to be quiet, which makes the resort popular with families with young children.

Not far away from Estepona is a popular nudist beach called the Costa Natura.

LIFE IN THE SUN

The idealized image of the Costa del Sol before tourism is of idyllic fishing villages where life was always at an easy pace. It is true to say that local economies have turned away from fishing and agriculture, and that the natural beauty of this coast has been marred by development. Any measured view, however, should consider the situation described by Laurie Lee, the author who in 1936 wrote of "... salt-fish villages, thin-ribbed, sea-hating, cursing their place in the sun". Today, few Andalucíans curse their new-found prosperity.

34
Ceuta

🅰 C5 🚢 From Algeciras
ℹ Calle Edrissis, Baluarte
de los Mallorquines; www.
ceuta.si

The closer of Spain's two North African enclaves is worth visiting if you want to dip your toe into North Africa without leaving Spain (although you will need to show an identity card or passport on entering). Ceuta, only 19 km (12 miles) from mainland Spain, is dominated by a hill called Monte Hacho, on which there is a fort occupied by the Spanish army. The city has Phoenician and Arab remains, and churches dating from the 17th to the 19th centuries; museums include the **Museo de la Legión**, dedicated to the Spanish Foreign Legion.

You will notice that both Ceuta and Melilla are surrounded by high fences to deter illegal migrants from all parts of Africa.

Museo de la Legión
🅰 Avenida Deán Navarro
Acuña 6 ☎ 956 52 62 19
🕙 10am–1pm Mon–Sat
☒ 1st Sat of month

💬 **INSIDER TIP**
Heli-Hurry

To get to Ceuta fast, take a helicopter instead of a ferry. For around €50 (single trip), you can fly there in about 10 minutes from Algeciras. Find out more at www.helity.es.

35
Melilla

🅰 F6 🚢 From Málaga or
Almería ℹ Plaza de las
Cuatro Culturas s/n; www.
melillaturismo.com

Spain's second North African enclave, settled by Spain in 1497, is located on the Moroccan coast, 150 km (90 miles) due south of Adra in Almería. It's a six-hour ferry ride from mainland Spain, but it is worth it as there is plenty to see, including the only Gothic architecture in Africa and samples of Modernisme, the Catalan version of Art Nouveau architecture.

Modern-day Melilla prides itself on being a place of peaceful co-existence between its main four component cultures: Christian, Muslim, Jewish and Hindu.

All the principal sights are located in Melilla La Vieja (Old Melilla), a cluster of four fortified areas separated by moats or walls, built in the 14th century on a hammer-head promontory jutting out into the sea. But the 19th- and 20th-century parts of the city are equally worth strolling around, since it is here that you'll find splendid Modernista and Art Deco buildings. There is also a small beach.

36
Tangier

🅰 B6 🏛 Morocco 🚢 From
Gibraltar, Tarifa and
Algeciras ℹ 29 Avenue
Pasteur; (212) 539 94 80 50

Tangier is only 45 minutes by fast ferry from Tarifa (p192), making it a perfect day trip. Despite its proximity, this ancient Moroccan port, founded by the Berbers before 1000 BC, will be a sharp culture shock for those used to life in Europe. Tangier is vibrant with colour, and the vast, labyrinthine Medina, the market quarter, pulsates with noise. From their workshops in back alleys, craftsmen make traditional goods for busy shops and stalls in the crowded streets.

Rue es Siaghin, "Silversmith's Street", was Tangier's main thoroughfare in the 1930s and still offers a staggering array of merchandise; shop owners will offer you mint tea in a bid to get you to buy. At the end of the street, a gateway in the walls leads to the Grand Socco, a busy square

← *Pillars of Hercules* statue on Ceuta's dock

↑ Looking over the Kasbah to Tangier's new town

where traders from the Rif mountains come to barter their goods.

The Kasbah or citadel, where the sultans once held court, is at the Medina's highest point. It is separated from its alleys by sturdy walls and four massive stone gateways. From the battlements there are views over the Strait of Gibraltar.

The Kasbah encloses the **Dar El Makhzen**, a palace built by Sultan Moulay Ismail, who unified Morocco in the 17th century. The sultans lived here until 1912. It is now a museum of crafts such as ceramics, embroidery and ironwork. The exhibits are arranged round a central courtyard and in cool rooms with tiled ceilings. There are illuminated Qur'ans in the Fez Room and a courtyard in the style of Andalucían Moorish gardens. The treasury house, the old prison and the law courts, and villas once owned by Americans and Europeans, such as Paul Bowles, the author of *The Sheltering Sky*, are also within the Kasbah walls.

Bowles was a central figure in the cosmopolitan, rather louche expatriate scene in Tangier, especially during the 1950s and '60s, when visitors included authors Truman Capote, Tennessee Williams and William S Burroughs. A museum inside the **American Legation**, itself housed in a former palace, has an exhibit devoted to Bowles' life and work. Scenes from Bernardo Bertolucci's film version of *The Sheltering Sky* were filmed at the **Hotel Continental**, which has seen numerous intrigues played out within its walls.

Dar El Makhzen
♿ ⌂ Place de la Kasbah
☎ (212) 539 93 20 97
🕐 8:30am-6pm Wed-Mon

American Legation
⌂ Rue d'Amerique 8
🕐 10am-5pm Mon-Fri, 10am-3pm Sat ⓦ legation.org

Hotel Continental
⌂ Rue Dar El Baroud ☎ (212) 539 93 10 24 🕐 Daily

↑ A dining room in the Hotel Continental, Tangier's most famous hotel

A DRIVING TOUR
AROUND THE
PUEBLOS BLANCOS

Length 205 km (127 miles) **Stopping-off points** Ubrique;
Zahara de la Sierra; Ronda; Gaucín **Terrain** Well-maintained
mountainous roads

Instead of settling on Andalucía's plains, where they would have
fallen prey to bandits, some Andalucíans chose to live in
fortified hilltop towns and villages. These are
known as *pueblos blancos* (white towns)
because they are whitewashed in the
Moorish tradition. Touring these
charming settlements
will reveal a host of
references to the
region's past.

*Embalse de
Bornos*

Prado del Rey

A384

Arcos de la
Frontera

START

El Bosque

Majaceite

Las Abiertas

A372

A373

After exploring
**Arcos de la
Frontera**'s
*beautiful Old Town
(p196), embark on
your tour of the
region's* peublos
blancos.

*Logo de los
Hurones*

Algar

A2034

↑ The white houses of Arcos de la Frontera,
spilling down the hillside

| 0 kilometres | 5 |
| 0 miles | 5 |

N
↑

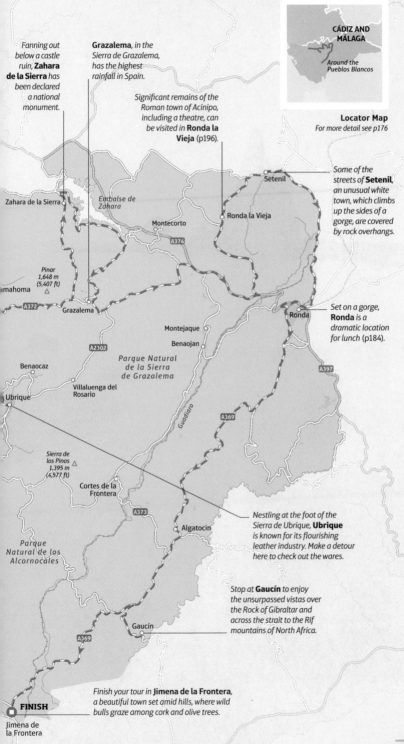

Fanning out below a castle ruin, **Zahara de la Sierra** has been declared a national monument.

Grazalema, in the Sierra de Grazalema, has the highest rainfall in Spain.

Significant remains of the Roman town of Acinipo, including a theatre, can be visited in **Ronda la Vieja** (p196).

CÁDIZ AND MÁLAGA

Around the Pueblos Blancos

Locator Map
For more detail see p176

Some of the streets of **Setenil**, an unusual white town, which climbs up the sides of a gorge, are covered by rock overhangs.

Set on a gorge, **Ronda** is a dramatic location for lunch (p184).

Nestling at the foot of the Sierra de Ubrique, **Ubrique** is known for its flourishing leather industry. Make a detour here to check out the wares.

Stop at **Gaucín** to enjoy the unsurpassed vistas over the Rock of Gibraltar and across the strait to the Rif mountains of North Africa.

Finish your tour in **Jimena de la Frontera**, a beautiful town set amid hills, where wild bulls graze among cork and olive trees.

Zahara de la Sierra

Embalse de Zahara

Montecorto

Ronda la Vieja

Setenil

Pinar 1,648 m (5,407 ft)

mahoma

A372

Grazalema

A374

Ronda

Montejaque

Benaojan

A2302

Parque Natural de la Sierra de Grazalema

A397

Benaocaz

Villaluenga del Rosario

Ubrique

Guadiaro

A369

Sierra de los Pinos 1,395 m (4,577 ft)

Cortes de la Frontera

Parque Natural de los Alcornocales

A373

Algatocin

Gaucín

A369

FINISH

Jimena de la Frontera

GRANADA AND ALMERÍA

The Christian *reconquista* worked its way steadily southwards over hundreds of years and by 1248 had reclaimed almost the entire peninsula, apart from the Emirate of Granada, which then included Almería and Málaga. Ruled by the Nasrid dynasty from 1230, this last remaining Moorish stronghold paid tribute – mostly in the form of African gold – to the Crown of Castile to be left to its own devices. This peaceful coexistence continued until 1482, when the Catholic Monarchs wrestled Alhama de Granada from the Emirate. Over the next ten years, the Christian foces pushed further into the territory and in 1492 Granada became part of Fernando and Isabel's kingdom.

Shortly after the conquest, spurred on by their victory, the Catholic Monarchs issued the Alhambra Decree, which ordered Jews and Muslims across Spain to either convert to Christianity or be exiled. This accelerated the Christianization of what had been a Muslim region for almost 800 years, but Granada and Almería still retain an indelible Moorish feel today, partly due to the proliferation of Mudéjar architecture in this area.

While the city of Granada, in particular, thrives off a tourism industry built on its Islamic history, Almería's economy has been revitalized by a new form of agriculture. Plastic greenhouses now cover hectares of the province, producing fruit and vegetables all year round.

GRANADA AND ALMERÍA

Must Sees
1. Granada
2. Almería

Experience More
3. Montefrío
4. Almuñécar
5. Salobreña
6. Santa Fé
7. Loja
8. Alhama de Granada
9. La Calahorra
10. Sierra Nevada
11. Lanjarón
12. Guadix
13. Poqueira Valley
14. Baza
15. Parque Natural de Cabo de Gata
16. Vélez Blanco
17. Tabernas
18. Sorbas
19. San José
20. Níjar
21. Mojácar
22. Roquetas de Mar

Martos

Baena

Alcaudete

Priego de Córdoba

Valdepeñas de Jaén

Huelma

Alcalá la Real

Benalúa de las Villas

Algarinejo

MONTEFRÍO **3**

Embalse de Iznájar

Huétor Tájar

Genil

Pinos-Puente

GRANADA

SANTA FÉ **6**

GRANADA **1**

Peligros

Guadahortuna

Moreda   Huélago

Iznalloz

Diezma

GUADIX **12**

Villanueva de las Torres

CORDOBA AND JAEN
p148

LA CALAHORRA **9**

Riofrío

LOJA **7**

Federico García Lorca Granada Airport

La Zubia

Mulhacén 3,482 m (11,424 ft)

Pico Veleta 3,398 m (11,148 ft)

SIERRA NEVADA **10**

Puerto de la Ragua

ALHAMA DE GRANADA **8**

Padul

Dúrcal

Embalse de los Bermejales

Trevélez

Va

POQUEIRA VALLEY **13**

Las   Alpujarras

Cádiar

CADIZ AND MALAGA
p174

Sierra de Almijara

LANJARÓN **11**

Órgiva

A348

Vélez Malaga

Nerja

Vélez de Benaudalla

Albuñol

Torre del Mar

ALMUÑÉCAR **4**

SALOBREÑA **5**

Motril

La Rábita

Á

Costa Tropical

Mediterranean Sea

Puente de Génave

N322

Beas de Segura

A317

Cortijos Nuevos

Embalse del Taibilla

GRANADA AND ALMERIA

A319

Embalse de Tranco de Beas

Santiago de la Espada

A317

Sagra 2,382 m (7,815 ft) △

Puebla de Don Fadrique

RM711

La Paca

Lorca

Sierra de Segura

A330

A317

Embalse de Puentes

A326

Huéscar

María

Castillejar

Galera

VÉLEZ BLANCO **16** Vélez Rubio

A7

Embalse de Negratín

A330

Cúllar

Chirivel

A92N

Puerto Lumbreras

RM11

Guardal

Benamaurel

A327

Zújar

Oria

Santa María de Nieva

14 BAZA

Pulpí

A92N

Caniles

A334

Almanzora

Albox

Huércal-Overa

AP7

Sierra de Baza

Serón

Purchena

Macael

N340

Cuevas del Almanzora

A7

Fiñana

A92

ALMERÍA

Tetica de Bacares △ 2,088 m (6,850 ft)

Vera

Abla

Sierra de los Filabres

Uleila del Campo

Garrucha

Gérgal

A349

21 MOJÁCAR

Laujar de Andarax

Canjáyar

A348

18 SORBAS

Sierra Cabrera

17 TABERNAS

Sierra Alhamilla

A92

Carboneras

Sierra de Gádor

Gádor

NÍJAR **20**

Benahadux

A341

Punta de los Muertos

rja

Dalías

A7

N340a

ALMERÍA **2**

Almería Airport

Rodalquilar

Punta de la Polacra

El Ejído

22 ROQUETAS DE MAR

El Cabo de Gata

15 PARQUE NATURAL DE CABO DE GATA

19 SAN JOSÉ

Cabo de Gata

0 kilometres   20

0 miles   20

N

The close-packed houses of Granada, with the Alhambra on the hill above them ↑

GRANADA

🅐E4 🅐Granada 🚇🚃🚌 𝒊Santa Ana 4; www.granadatur.com

The guitarist Andres Segovia (1893–1987) described Granada as a "place of dreams, where the Lord put the seed of music in my soul". It's not hard to see why as you explore the city's Moorish buildings – reminders of Granada's golden period during the rule of the Nasrid dynasty from 1238 until 1492. The most impressive of these monuments are the Alhambra *(p216)* and Generalife *(p218)*, which sit on the hill above the city.

① Cathedral

🅐Calle Gran Vía 5 📞958 22 29 59 🕐10am-6:30pm Mon-Sat, 3-5:45pm Sun

On the orders of the Catholic Monarchs, work on Granada's cathedral began in 1523, with Enrique de Egas as the architect. The building works continued for over 180 years, with the Renaissance maestro, Diego de Siloé, taking on the job in 1529. De Siloé also designed the façade and the magnificent Capilla Mayor. Under its dome, 16th-century windows depict Juan del Campo's *The Passion*. The west front was designed by Alonso Cano, who was born in the city and whose tomb lies in the cathedral.

② Capilla Real

🅐Calle Oficios 3 🕐10:15am-6:30pm Mon-Sat, 11am-6pm Sun 🚫1 Jan, Good Fri, 25 Dec 🌐capillareal granada.com

The Royal Chapel was built for the Catholic Monarchs between 1506 and 1521 by Enrique de Egas , although both monarchs died before it could be completed. A magnificent *reja* (grille) by Maestro Bartolomé de Jaén encloses the high altar and the Carrara marble figures of Fernando and Isabel, of their daughter Juana la Loca (the Mad) and her husband Felipe el Hermoso (the Handsome). Their lead-lined coffins are in the crypt. Don't miss the sacristy, which is full of a host of artistic treasures, including 15th-century paintings by Van der Weyden and Botticelli.

③ Monasterio de la Cartuja

🅐Paseo de la Cartuja 📞958 16 19 32 🕐Summer: 10am-8pm Sun-Fri, 10am-1pm & 3-8pm Sat; winter: 10am-6pm Sun-Fri, 10am-1pm & 3-6pm Sat

Founded in 1516 by Christian warrior El Gran Capitán, this monastery has a dazzling cupola by Antonio Palomino, and a Churrigueresque sacristy by mason Luis de Arévalo and sculptor Luis Cabello.

↑ Visitors admiring the sacristy within the Monasterio de la Cartuja

④
Corral del Carbón

🏛 Calle Mariana Pineda s/n
📞 958 57 51 31 🕐 10:30am-
1:30pm & 5-8pm Mon-Fri,
10:30am-2pm Sat

A relic of the Moorish era, this galleried courtyard was a theatre in Christian times. Today it houses a cultural centre.

---

⑤
Casa de los Tiros

🏛 Calle Pavaneras 19 📞 600
14 31 76 🕐 Sep-May: 9am-
9pm Tue-Sat, 9am-3pm Sun
& public hols; Jun-Aug: 9am-
3pm Tue-Sat, 10am-5pm
Sun & public hols

Built in Mudéjar style in the 1500s, this palace owes its name to the muskets projecting from its battlements (*tiro* means "shot"). It originally belonged to the family that was awarded the Generalife (*p218*) after the fall of Granada. Muhammad XII's sword is carved on the façade.

⑥ ⚒ 🍽
Centro Cultural Caja Granada

🏛 Avenida de la Ciencia
🕐 Hours vary, check
website 🚫 Aug 🌐 caja
granadafundacion.es

Set in a stark, white modern building, with a sweeping external staircase, this cultural centre is home to the superb Memoria de Andalucía Museum, which hosts temporary exhibitions, and a theatre and restaurant.

---

⑦
Palacio de la Madraza

🏛 Calle Oficios 14 📞 958 99
63 50 🕐 9am-2pm & 5-8pm
Mon-Fri

Originally an Arab university, this building later became the city hall (the façade dates from the 18th century) and today is a part of Granada University. The Moorish hall has a finely decorated *mihrab* (prayer niche).

EAT

Damasqueros
Order the tasty *guiso* (stew) at this tapas bar.

🏛 Calle de Damasqueros
3 🌐 damasqueros.com

€€€

Mirador de Morayma
A delightful patio restaurant, offering spectacular views.

🏛 Calle de Pianista Gracia
Carrillo 2 🌐 mirador
demorayma.com

€€€

Tragaluz
This eatery is lit by a huge skylight.

🏛 Calle Pintor López
Mezquita 13
📞 958 20 46 81

€€€

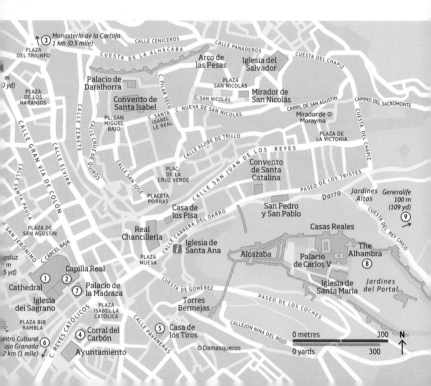

(8) 🚲 Ⓜ️ 🍴

THE ALHAMBRA

📍 Calle Real de la Alhambra 🚍 C3, C4 🕐 Mid-Mar-mid-Oct: 8:30am-8pm daily; mid-Oct-mid-Mar: 8:30am-6pm daily (arrive 1 hour before scheduled visit; allow 3 hours for visit) 🌐 alhambradegranada.org

A visit to the Alhambra – arguably the pinnacle of Europe's Moorish palaces – is a truly special experience. A magical use of space, light, water and decoration characterizes this most sensual piece of architecture.

This palace was built under Ismail I, Yusuf I and Muhammad V caliphs when the Nasrid dynasty ruled Granada. Seeking to belie an image of waning power, they created their idea of paradise on Earth. Modest materials were used (plaster, timber and tiles), but they were superbly worked. The Alhambra complex includes the Palacios Nazaríes, the 13th-century Alcazaba, the 16th-century Palace of Carlos I and the Generalife (p218). Although the Alhambra suffered pillage and decay, including an attempt by Napoleon's troops to blow it up, in recent times it has undergone extensive restoration and its delicate craftsmanship still dazzles the eye.

💬 INSIDER TIP
Night Vision

For a more unusual trip, book a visit to the Alhambra after dark, when the honey-coloured walls are lit with a warm glow (Mar-Oct: 10-11:30pm Tue & Sat; Nov-Feb: 8-9:30pm Fri & Sat).

→
The Palacios Nazaríes, just part of the vast Alhambra complex

Sala de la Barca

Washington Irving's apartments

Patio de Arrayanes, with a pool set amid myrtle hedges and graceful arcades

Salón de Embajadores, a sumptuous throne room

Patio del Mexuar, a council chamber, completed in 1365

Patio de Machuca

The spectacular Alhambra and *(inset)* a fountain in one of its ornate patios ↑

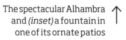

Jardín de Lindaraja

Palacio del Partal, the oldest building in the Alhambra

Sala de los Reyes, a great banqueting hall

Puerta de la Rawda

Sala de los Abencerrajes, with a geometrical ceiling pattern inspired by Pythagoras' theorem

Patio de los Leones

Baños Reales

Sala de las Dos Hermanas, regarded as the ultimate example of Spanish Islamic architecture

The Palace of Carlos I (1526), home to a collection of Spanish Islamic art

↑ Gorgeously intricate Moorish embellishments around a palace window

⑨ 🏛️ 🏛️

GENERALIFE

🏠 Calle Real de la Alhambra 🚌 C3, C4 🕐 Mid-Mar-mid-Oct: 8:30am-8pm daily; mid-Oct-mid-Mar: 8:30am-6pm daily (arrive one hour before scheduled visit; allow three hours for visit) 🌐 alhambradegranada.org

From the Alhambra's northern side, a footpath leads to the Generalife, the country estate of the Nasrid kings. Here, they could escape from palace intrigues and enjoy tranquillity high above the city, a little closer to heaven.

The name Generalife, or Yannat al Arif, has various interpretations, perhaps the most pleasing being "the garden of lofty paradise". The gardens, begun in the 13th century, originally contained orchards and pastures but have been modified over the years. In contrast to the spectacular architecture and wealth of detail that permeates the Alhambra, the buildings of the Generalife are largely simple, solid structures. Once an idyllic place of respite for kings, today the Generalife provides a magical setting for Granada's annual music and dance festival in late June and July.

💬 **INSIDER TIP**
Be an Early Bird

Book the earliest possible morning slot and scoot rapidly through the first couple of rooms – that way you will have the entire palace to yourself and can really appreciate just how tranquil a setting it once was.

Sala Regia

The Patio de la Acequia, an enclosed Persian garden built round a long central pool.

The Patio de Polo, a courtyard where visitors arriving on horseback would tether their steeds

Entrance

↑ The Patio de la Acequia, with its central water feature

Visitors wandering the carefully tended gardens of the Generalife

The Patio de los Cipreses, once a secret meeting place for Zoraya, wife of the Sultan Abu-I-Hasan, and her lover

The Escalera del Agua, a staircase with water flowing gently down it

Jardines Altos (Upper Gardens)

Did You Know?

The Generalife sits atop the Cerro del Sol (the Hill of the Sun).

The buildings and extensive gardens of the Generalife

A SHORT WALK
THE ALBAICÍN

Distance 1 km (0.5 miles) **Nearest train station** Estación Central **Time** 15 minutes

This corner of the city, on the hillside opposite the Alhambra, is where one feels closest to Granada's Moorish ancestry. Now mostly pedestrianized, this was the site of the first fortress, built in the 13th century, along with more than 30 mosques. Most of the city's churches replaced the latter. Along the cobbled alleys stand *cármenes*, villas with Moorish decoration and gardens, secluded from the world by high walls. In the jasmine-scented air of evening, stroll up to the Mirador de San Nicolás for a magical view over the rooftops of the Alhambra, glowing in the sunset.

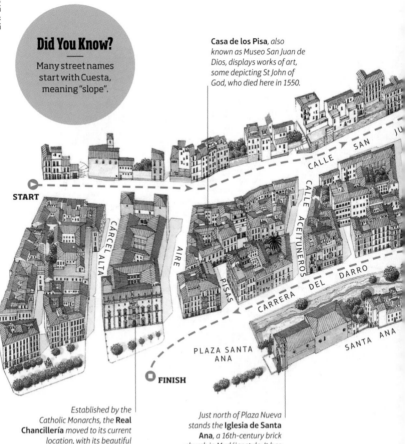

Did You Know?

Many street names start with Cuesta, meaning "slope".

Casa de los Pisa, *also known as Museo San Juan de Dios, displays works of art, some depicting St John of God, who died here in 1550.*

START

FINISH

Established by the Catholic Monarchs, the **Real Chancillería** *moved to its current location, with its beautiful Renaissance façade, in 1530.*

Just north of Plaza Nueva stands the **Iglesia de Santa Ana**, *a 16th-century brick church in Mudéjar style. It has an elegant Plateresque portal and, inside, a coffered ceiling.*

PLAZA SANTA ANA

CALLE SAN JU

CALLE ACEITUNEROS

CARRERA DEL DARRO

CÁRCEL ALTA

AIRE

PISAS

SANTA ANA

0 metres 50
0 yards 50

N

↑ Walking between the arches in the atmospheric El Bañuelo

Star-shaped openings in the vaults let light into **El Bañuelo**. *These well-preserved Moorish baths were built in the 11th century.*

DE LOS REYES

PLAZA CONCEPCIÓN

CARNERO

BAÑUELO

CONCEPCIÓN

CALLE ZAFRA

CALLE GLORIA

CARRETERA DEL SANTÍSIMO

CARRERA DEL DARRO

RÍO DARRO

The **Convento de Santa Catalina** *was founded in 1521.*

The Plateresque carvings on the **Museo Arqueológico** *depict the heraldic devices of the Nasrid kings, who were defeated by the Catholic Monarchs in 1492.*

The **Carrera del Darro** *runs along the Río Darro, past crumbling bridges and the fine façades of ancient buildings, now all restored.*

→ The Carrera del Darro, one of Granada's prettiest streets

②

ALMERÍA

△F4 **△Almería** 🚌🚕 🚢 **ℹ️Parque Nicolás Salmerón s/n;**
www.turismodealmeria.org

A colossal fortress bears witness to Almería's golden age, when it was an important port for the Caliphate of Córdoba. Known as al Mariyat (the Mirror of the Sea), the city was a centre for trade and textile industries. Today a North African air still pervades the city, with its flat-roofed houses, desert-like environs and palm trees, and regular ferry services still link the city with Morocco.

① ⊗

Catedral

△Plaza de la Catedral 8
☎950 23 48 48 **🕙10am-6pm Mon-Fri, 10am-2pm Sat**

Berber pirates from North Africa would often raid Almería. Consequently, the cathedral looks more like a fortress than a place of worship, with four towers, thick walls and small windows. It was designed by Spanish architect Diego de Siloé and work on it began in 1524.

②

Museo de Almería

△Carretera de Ronda 91
☎950 01 62 56 **🕙Mid-Jun-mid-Sep: 9am-3pm Tue-Sat, 9am-3pm Sun & public hols; mid-Sep-mid-Jun: 9am-9pm Tue-Sat, 9am-3pm Sun**

Almería's two main prehistoric civilizations, Los Millares and El Algar, are explained in this archaeological museum that displays 900 exhibits from its collection of 80,000 pieces at any one time.

←

El Buen Pastor de Gador (The Good Shepherd of Gádor) in the Museo de Almería

③

Iglesia San Juan

△Calle San Juan & Calle Gen Luque **☎950 23 30 07**
🕙Apr-Sep: 7-7:30pm daily; Oct-Mar: 6-6:30pm Sat-Thu

Traces of Almería's most important mosque can still be seen at the Iglesia San Juan – one wall of the present church is Moorish. Inside is a 12th-century *mihrab*, a prayer niche with cupola. Damaged in the Spanish Civil War, the church has since been restored.

④

Alcazaba

△Calle Almanzor s/n **☎950 80 10 08** **🕙9am-8:30pm Tue-Sat, 9am-3:30pm Sun & public hols** **🕙1 Jan, 25 Dec**

This was the largest fortress built by the Moors and once covered an area of more than

A panoramic view of Almería and its port, crowned by the imposing Alcazaba

←

A panoramic view of Almería and its port, crowned by the imposing Alcazaba

its walls are pleasant gardens and a Mudéjar chapel. Fine views are offered from the top of the fortress. In the past, a bell in the Alcazaba was rung to advise the farmers in the surrounding countryside when irrigation was allowed. Bells were also heard when pirates had been sighted off the coast.

25,000 sq m (269,000 sq ft), with the walls extending for 430 m (1,410 ft). Construction started in AD 955, under Abd al Rahman III, but there were considerable additions later. The fort withstood two major sieges but fell to the Catholic Monarchs in 1489. Their coat of arms can be seen on the exterior of the Torre del Homenaje, which was built during the monarchs' reign. The 1,000-year-old Alcazaba has been restored and within

⑤
Puerta de Purchena
🏠 Paseo de Almería

Located at the heart of the city, the Puerta de Purchena was once one of the main gateways in the city walls. From it run a number of shopping streets, including the wide Paseo de Almería. A tree-lined thoroughfare, this is the focus of city life, with its cafés, Teatro Cervantes and nearby food market.

Must See

EAT

Jovellanos 16

This unassuming tapas bar serves an exquisite selection of traditional and innovative dishes.

🏠 Calle Jovellanos 16
🕐 Sun L, Mon
ⓦ barjovellanos16.es

€€€

Taberna Entrevinos

Excellent wine. Quality food. Good vibes. What more could you ask for? This highly acclaimed eatery is always busy so advance booking is recommended.

🏠 Calle Francisco García Góngora 11 🕐 Mon
ⓦ tabernaentre vinos.net

€€€

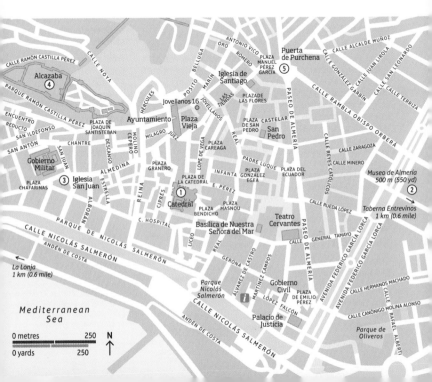

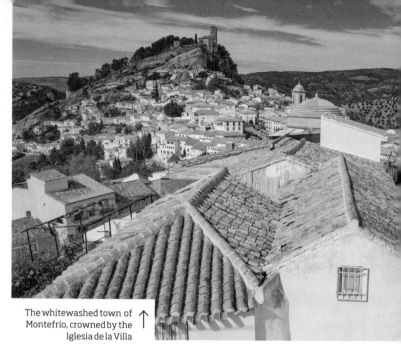

The whitewashed town of Montefrío, crowned by the Iglesia de la Villa ↑

EXPERIENCE MORE

❸ Montefrío

🅰E3 🏠Granada 🚌 𝒊Plaza de España 1; 958 33 60 04

Seen from the approach road to the south, this archetypal Andalucían town, famed for its pork products, is a tapestry of tiled rooftops and white-washed houses spilling down from a steep crag. This hill is topped by the remains of Moorish fortifications and the Gothic Iglesia de la Villa, which is attributed to Diego de Siloé. In the centre of town is the Iglesia de la Encarnación.

❹ Almuñécar

🅰E4 🏠Granada 🚌 𝒊Avenida Europa s/n; www.turismoalmunecar.es

Almuñécar lies on the Costa Tropical, where mountains rise to over 2,000 m (6,560 ft) from the Mediterranean shore. The Phoenicians founded the earliest settlement here, and the Romans later built an aqueduct. When the English writer Laurie Lee made his long trek across Spain in 1936, he described Almuñécar as "a tumbling little village fronted by a strip of grey sand, which some hoped would be an attraction for tourists", and Almuñécar is indeed now a holiday resort. Above the old town is the **Castillo de San Miguel**. Phoenician artifacts are displayed in the **Museo Arqueológico Cueva de Siete Palacios**.

Castillo de San Miguel

⊛ 🕽650 02 75 84 🕘10am–1:30pm & 6:30–9pm Tue–Sat, 10am–1pm Sun

Museo Arqueológico Cueva de Siete Palacios

⊛ 🏠Calle Cueva de Siete Palacios s/n 🕽958 83 86 23 🕘10am–1:30pm & 6:30–9pm Tue–Sat, 10am–1pm Sun

❺ Salobreña

🅰E4 🏠Granada 🚌 𝒊Plaza de Goya s/n; www.ayto-salobrena.org

From across the coastal plain, Salobreña looks like a white liner sailing above a sea of waving sugar cane. Narrow streets wend their way up a hill first fortified by the Phoenicians. The hill later became the site of the now-restored **Castillo Arabe**, which gives fine views of the Sierra Nevada (p226). Modern developments, bars and

Did You Know?

Salobreña's Castillo Arabe features in Washington Irving's *Tales of the Alhambra*.

restaurants line part of this resort's lengthy beach.

Castillo Arabe

Ⓢ ⊗ 🏛 Falda del Castillo, Calle Andrés Segovia ℂ 958 61 03 14 🕐 10am–2pm & 5–7pm daily

---

6

Santa Fé

🅐 E4 🚇 Granada 🚌 🛈 Arco de Sevilla, Calle Isabel la Católica 7; 958 44 00 00

This town was built on the site where the army of the Catholic Monarchs camped as it lay siege to Granada *(p214)*. When the camp burned down, after a maid placed a candle too close to a curtain in Queen Isabel's tent, the king ordered a model town to be built and the devout queen named it "holy faith". In 1492 the Moors made a formal surrender at Santa Fé. Look for the severed head, carved in stone, which decorates the spire of the parish church. It was here, too, that the Catholic Monarchs met with Columbus in 1492.

7

Loja

🅐 E4 🚇 Granada 🚍 🚌 🛈 Edificio Espacio Joven, Calle Comedias 2; www. lojaturismo.com

A ruined Moorish fort rises above the crooked streets of the old town of Loja on the Río Genil. Known as "the city of water", Loja also has some beautiful fountains. East of the town, the fast-flowing Río Genil cuts through Los Infiernos gorge. Sample local trout in Riofrío, to the west.

8

Alhama de Granada

🅐 E4 🚇 Granada 🚌 🛈 Carrera de Francisco Toledo 10; 958 36 06 86

Alhama is a charming small town balanced above a gorge. It was known as *Al hamma* (hot springs) to the Arabs and their baths can still be seen in **Hotel Balneario** on the edge of town.

The town is home to some interesting churches. The 16th-century Iglesia de Carmen has fine paintings inside its dome, restored after being damaged in the Spanish Civil War. Narrow, whitewashed streets lead to the Iglesia de la Encarnación, founded by the Catholic Monarchs in the 16th century. Some of the vestments worn by the priests today are said to have been embroidered by Queen Isabel herself. Nearby is the 16th-century Hospital de la Reina, which now houses the **Centro de Exposición de Artesanal**, displaying the works of local artists.

Hotel Balneario

🏛 Calle Balneario 🕐 Mar–Nov 🌐 balnearioalhamade granada.com

Centro de Exposición de Artesanal

🏛 Calle Vendederas s/n 🕐 9am–2pm Mon–Fri

SHOP

Centro de Alfarería Municipal

Workshop where the art of traditional pottery thrives. Pick up a unique piece to take home.

🅐 E4 🏛 Calle San Crescencio 10, Almuñécar ℂ 620 26 12 17

Ánforas de Mar

This innovative company makes replicas of ancient amphoras then ages them in the sea, creating a phenomenal patina of fossilized sea life.

🅐 G4 🏛 Avenida de Garrucha 78, Carboneras 🌐 anforasdemar.com

Abuela ili Chocolate

Chocolate factory where you can sample over 60 artisan blends, with additions such as chilli.

🅐 E4 🏛 Plaza de la Libertad 1, Pampaneira 🌐 abuelaili chocolates.com

↑ An old mill wheel outside a ruined flour mill in Alhama de Granada

⑨

La Calahorra

🅰F4 🅰Granada 🚇Guadix
🅸Plaza Ayuntamiento 1;
958 67 70 40

This village is crowned by a castle, perched on a hillock and encircled by immensely thick walls. Rodrigo de Mendoza, son of Cardinal Mendoza, ordered the **Castillo de La Calahorra** to be built for his bride between 1509 and 1512, using architects and craftsmen from Italy. Inside is a Renaissance courtyard with Carrara marble pillars.

Castillo de La Calahorra

🅰Calle San Sebastián
☎958 67 70 98 🕙10am–1pm & 4–6pm Wed

⑩

Sierra Nevada

🅰E4 🅰Granada 🚌From Granada 🅸Carretera de Sierra Nevada, km 23, Güéjar Sierra; www.sierranevada.es

Fourteen peaks more than 3,000 m (9,800 ft) high crown the heights of the Sierra Nevada. Surprisingly, these mountains are often covered in powder and the snow lingers until July and begins falling again in late autumn.

Europe's highest road (closed to traffic) runs past a ski resort at 2,100 m (6,890 ft), and skirts the two highest peaks, Pico Veleta at 3,398 m (11,145 ft) and Mulhacén at 3,482 m (11,420 ft). The altitude and closeness to the Mediterranean of this mountain range account for its array of fauna and flora, including golden eagles, rare butterflies and over 60 species of flowers unique to the area.

The park authorities run minibus excursions to the high slopes from checkpoints on the two sides of the Sierra Nevada: Hoya de la Mora (above the ski station on the Granada side) and Hoya del Portillo (above Capileira in the Alpujarras).

⑪

Lanjarón

🅰E4 🅰Granada 🚌
🅸Avenida de Madrid s/n;
www.lanjaron.es

Scores of snow-fed springs bubble from the slopes below the Sierra Nevada, and the town of Lanjarón has a long history as a spa. From June to October visitors flock to the **Balneario de Lanjarón** to

take the waters and enjoy water treatments for a variety of ailments. Lanjarón bottled water is sold all over Spain. On the 23 June, the eve of the festival of San Juan, a water battle takes place. Anybody who dares venture into the streets gets liberally doused.

Balneario de Lanjarón

 🅰Avenida de Madrid 2
🕙Daily 🕙Mid-Dec–mid-Jan
🌐balneariodelanjaron.es

⑫

Guadix

🅰F3 🅰Granada 🚍🚌
🅸Avenida de la Constitución 15-18; www.guadix.es

The most fascinating feature of the town of Guadix is its

troglodyte quarter, with 2,000 cave houses carved out of the rock. Cool in summer and cosy in winter, these homes are not only popular but also have all the mod cons, including Wi-Fi. Several operate as hotels and rental apartments. Both the **Museo de Alfarería** and **Centro de Interpretación Cuevas de Guadix** have fine displays on daily life underground.

Around 2,000 years ago Guadix had iron, copper and silver mines. The town thrived under the Moors and after the *reconquista*, but declined in the 18th century. Check out the cathedral, begun in 1594 and finished between 1701 and 1796, the 9th-century Alcazaba, the Mudéjar Iglesia de Santiago and the Palacio de Peñaflor, dating from the 16th century.

Museo de Alfarería

⊛ ⌂ Calle San Miguel 56
☎ 958 66 47 67 🕒 10:30am-2pm & 4:30-8pm daily

Centro de Interpretación Cuevas de Guadix

⊛ ⌂ Ermita Nueva s/n
☎ 958 66 55 69 🕒 Summer: 10am-2pm & 5-7pm Mon-Fri, 10am-2pm Sat; winter: 10am-2pm & 4-6pm Mon-Fri, 10am-2pm Sat

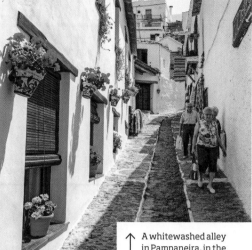

↑ A whitewashed alley in Pampaneira, in the Poqueira Valley

↑ Hiking down from Mulhacén, a peak in the Sierra Nevada

13

Poqueira Valley

🅰 E4 ⌂ Barranco de Poqueira, Granada
🚆 Plaza de la Libertad 7, Pampaneira; 958 76 31 27

Many visitors to the Alpujarras (*p234*) get no further than this deep, steep-sided valley above Órgiva, and it is certainly the best place to head for on a short visit. It contains three pretty, well-kept villages climbing the slope. In ascending order, they are Pampaneira, Bubión and Capileira. All these villages are perfect examples of the singular architectural style of the Alpujarras, which has its closest relation in the Atlas Mountains of Morocco. The whitewashed houses of each village huddle together seemingly randomly ("a confused agglomeration of boxes" as the writer Gerald Brenan described them), with flat grey gravel roofs sprouting a variety of eccentrically tall chimneys. The streets between the houses are rarely straight, often stepped and tapering, and they sometimes disappear into short tunnels.

Skiers taking advantage of the Sierra Nevada's pristine snow

↑ Scenic views and cooling coastal breezes at the Parque Natural de Cabo de Gata

DRINK

La Goleta

Quench your thirst with a flavourful cocktail, or cool off with an ice cream sundae, at this Roquetas de Mar bar.

F4 🏠 Avenida de Playa Serena 28, Roquetas de Mar 📞 950 33 47 18

La Cochera

Eclectic beach-bar in Almuñécar, with quirky decor and a large terrace. You can chill out to live music during the summer nights.

E4 🏠 Paseo Andrés Segovia 44, Almuñécar 📞 692 03 78 23

El Sitio

This bar in Mojácar has an extensive wine list, refreshing cocktails and live music. It's perfect for a romantic night out.

G4 🏠 Paseo del Mediterráneo 137, Mojácar 📞 950 61 54 11 🗓 Sun

⓮ Baza

F3 🏠 Granada 🚌 🛈 Calle Alhóndiga 1, under museum; 958 86 13 25

Impressive evidence of ancient cultures based around Baza came to light in 1971, when a large, seated, female figure was found in a necropolis. She is the Dama de Baza, believed to represent an Iberian goddess, and estimated to be 2,400 years old. She was removed to the Museo Arqueológico in Madrid but a replica can be seen in the **Museo Arqueológico** in Baza. The Renaissance Colegiata de Santa María, nearby, has a fine 18th-century tower.

During the first few days of September a riotous fiesta takes place. An emissary, El Cascamorras, is despatched from the neighbouring town of Guadix to try to bring back a coveted image of the Virgin from Baza's Convento de la Merced. He is covered in oil and chased back to Guadix by youths, also covered in oil. There, he is taunted again for returning empty-handed.

Museo Arqueológico

🏠 Plaza Mayor s/n 📞 958 86 13 25 🕐 11am–2pm Tue–Sun (also 6:30–8pm Thu–Sat)

⓯ Parque Natural de Cabo de Gata

G4 🏠 Almería 🚌 To San José 🛈 Carretera Cabo de Gata, km 6; 950 16 04 35

Towering cliffs of volcanic rock, rolling sand dunes, endless salt flats and secluded coves can be found in the 290-sq-km (112-sq-mile) Parque Natural de Cabo de Gata.

Within its confines are a few fishing villages and the small resort of San José. The end of the cape, near the Arrecife de las Sirenas (Sirens' Reef), is marked by a lighthouse. The park includes a stretch of sea-bed about 2 km (1.2 miles) wide, which allows protection of the marine flora and fauna, and the clear waters attract divers and snorkellers. Attempts to reintroduce the monk seal, which died out in the 1970s, however, have now ceased.

The area of dunes and saltpans between the cape and the Playa de San Miguel is a habitat for thorny jujube trees. Thousands of migrating birds stop here en route to and from Africa. Among the 170 or so bird species recorded in the park there are avocets, flamingos, Dupont's larks and griffon vultures. At the northern end of the park, where there is a cormorants' fishing area, is Punta de los Muertos ("dead man's point"); this takes its name from the bodies of shipwrecked sailors that are said to have washed ashore there.

16

Vélez Blanco

G3 **Almería** Vélez Rubio *Marqués de los Vélez s/n; 950 41 95 85*

Dominating this pleasant little village is the mighty **Castillo de Vélez Blanco**. It was built from 1506 to 1513 by the first Marquis de Los Vélez, and its interior was richly adorned by Italian craftsmen. Unfortunately for the visitor, its Renaissance splendour has since been ripped out and shipped to the Metropolitan Museum of New York. There is, however, a reconstruction of one of the original patios. A blend of Gothic, Renaissance and Mudéjar styles can be seen in the Iglesia de Santiago, in the village's main street.

Just outside Vélez Blanco is the **Cueva de los Letreros**, which contains paintings from

around 4000 BC. One image depicts the Indalo, a figure believed to be a deity with magical powers, still used as a symbol of Almería.

Castillo de Vélez Blanco

Calle Castillo s/n 607 41 50 55 Apr-Sep: 10am-2pm & 5-8pm Wed-Sun; Oct-Mar: 10am-2pm & 4-6pm Wed-Sun

Cueva de los Letreros

Camino de la Cueva de los Letreros 694 46 71 36 Wed, Sat, Sun & public hols by appointment

The view from the Castillo de Vélez Blanco, and *(inset)* its imposing exterior

---

17

Tabernas

G4 **Almería** *N340, km 464; 950 52 50 30*

A Moorish hilltop fortress presides over the town of Tabernas and the surrounding dusty, cactus-dotted landscape of eroded hills and dried-out riverbeds. The harsh, rugged scenery has figured in many so-called spaghetti westerns.

Not far from Tabernas is a solar energy research centre, where hundreds of mirrored heliostats follow the course of the powerful Andalucían sun, reflecting its rays onto a tulip-shaped solar receiver.

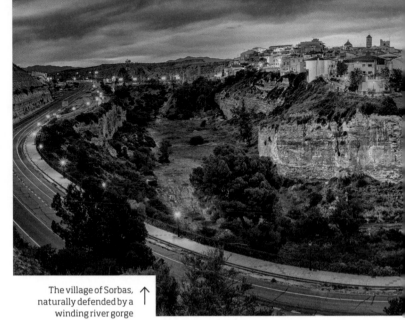

The village of Sorbas, naturally defended by a winding river gorge ↑

⑱
Sorbas

🗺️G4 **🏠Almería** **🚌** **ℹ️Calle Terraplen 9 ;950 36 45 63**

Balanced on the edge of a deep chasm, Sorbas overlooks the Río de Aguas. There are two buildings in this village worth a look: the 16th-century Iglesia de Santa María and a 17th-century mansion said to have once been a summer retreat for the Duke of Alba. Another point of interest for visitors is the traditional, rustic earthenware turned out and sold by the local potters.

Near Sorbas is the peculiar Yesos de Sorbas nature reserve. This is an unusual region of karst, where water action has carved out hundreds of underground galleries and chambers in the limestone and gypsum strata. Speleologists are allowed to explore the caves, but only if they are granted permission in writing by Andalucía's environmental department. On the surface, the green, fertile valley of the Río de Aguas cuts through dry, eroded hills. Look out for tortoises, peregrine falcons and the other wildlife that lies in this reserve.

BLOOD WEDDING AT NÍJAR

Bodas de Sangre (Blood Wedding), a play by Federico García Lorca*(p53)*, is based on a tragic event that occurred in 1928 near Níjar. A woman named Paquita la Coja agreed, under pressure, to marry her sister's husband's brother, Casimiro. Hours before the ceremony, however, she fled with her cousin. Casimiro felt humiliated and Paquita's sister, who had hoped to benefit from the dowry, was furious. The cousin was found shot dead and Paquita half-strangled. Paquita's sister and her husband were found guilty of the crime. Shamed by this horrific incident, Paquita hid from the world until her death in 1987. Lorca never visited Níjar, basing his play on newspaper reports.

---

⑲
San José

🗺️G4 **🏠Almería** **🚌** **ℹ️Avenida de San José 27; 950 38 02 99**

Located on a fine, sandy bay, San José is a small but fast-growing sea resort. Rising behind it is the arid Sierra de Cabo de Gata, a range of bleak grandeur. Nearby are fine beaches, including Playa de los Genoveses. Along the coast are Rodalquilar, a town once important for gold-mining, and La Isleta, a fishing hamlet.

---

⑳
Níjar

🗺️G4 **🏠Almería** **🚌** **ℹ️Fundición s/n, Rodalquilar; 671 59 44 19**

Set amid a lush oasis of citrus trees on the edge of the Sierra Alhamilla, Níjar is famous for its colourful pottery and *jarapas*, handwoven rugs and blankets. The town's historic quarter is typical of Andalucía, with narrow streets and wrought-iron balconies. The

16th-century Iglesia de Nuestra Señora de la Anunciación has a coffered Mudéjar ceiling.

In Spanish minds, the name of Níjar is closely associated with a violent incident that occurred here in the 1920s, which became the subject of a play by Federico García Lorca.

㉑
Mojácar

🅰G4 🅰Almería 🚌 🅸Plaza del Frontón 1; 950 61 50 25

From a distance, the village of Mojácar shimmers like the mirage of a Moorish citadel, its white houses cascading over a lofty ridge near to the sea. The village was taken by the Christians in 1488 and the Moors were later expelled. In the years after the Spanish Civil War the village fell into ruin, as much of its population emigrated. In the 1960s Mojácar was discovered by tourists, giving rise to a new era of prosperity. The old gateway in the walls is still here, but otherwise the village has been completely rebuilt.

㉒
Roquetas de Mar

🅰F4 🅰Almería 🅸Avenida del Mediterráneo 2; 950 33 32 03

Much of Almería's southern coastal plain is given over to massive plastic greenhouses in which vegetables and flowers are raised for export. Interrupting the

←
Traditional pottery jar from Níjar, glazed in the rich blue of *azulejo* tiles, with a floral motif

greenhouses is the resort of Roquetas de Mar, which has a 17th-century castle and a squat lighthouse, both used for exhibitions. There's also a good **aquarium**.

Aquarium
♿ 🅰Avenida Reino de España 🕐Jun-Aug: 10am-9pm daily; Sep-May: 10am-6pm Wed-Fri, 10am-7pm Sat & Sun 🆆aquarium roquetas.com

A DRIVING TOUR

LAS ALPUJARRAS

Length 85 km (56 miles) **Stopping-off points** There are bars and restaurants in Órgiva and Trevélez **Terrain** Twisting, narrow mountain roads

The fertile, upland valleys of Las Alpujarras, clothed with chestnut, walnut and poplar trees, lie on the southern slopes of the Sierra Nevada and make for a scenic drive. The architecture of the quaint white villages which cling to the hillsides – compact clusters of irregularly shaped houses with tall chimneys sprouting from flat, grey roofs – is unique in Spain. Be sure to try the local speciality – ham cured in the cold, dry air of Trevélez.

*In the shadow of Mulhacén, mainland Spain's highest mountain, **Trevélez** is famous for its cured ham, so stop here for lunch.*

*Capileira, Bubión and Pampaneira are three villages typical of Las Alpujarras in the pretty **Poqueira Valley** (p227).*

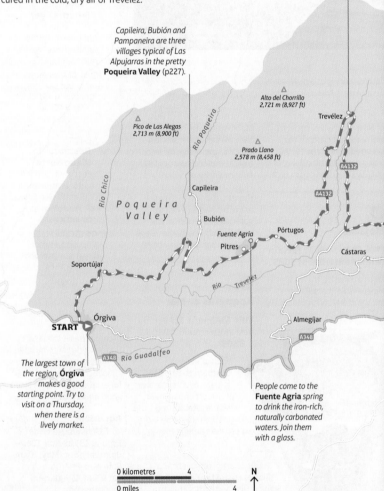

*The largest town of the region, **Órgiva** makes a good starting point. Try to visit on a Thursday, when there is a lively market.*

*People come to the **Fuente Agria** spring to drink the iron-rich, naturally carbonated waters. Join them with a glass.*

0 kilometres 4

0 miles 4

N ↑

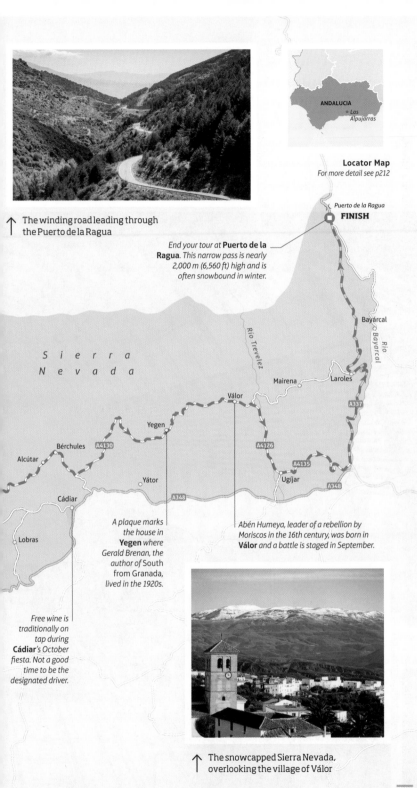

↑ The winding road leading through the Puerto de la Ragua

Puerto de la Ragua
FINISH

End your tour at **Puerto de la Ragua**. *This narrow pass is nearly 2,000 m (6,560 ft) high and is often snowbound in winter.*

Bayárcal

Río Bayárcal

S i e r r a   N e v a d a

Río Trevelez

Mairena

Laroles

A337

Válor

Yegen

A4130

Bérchules

A4126

Alcútar

A4135

Yátor

Ugíjar

A348

Cádiar

A348

Lobras

A plaque marks the house in **Yegen** *where Gerald Brenan, the author of* South from Granada, *lived in the 1920s.*

Abén Humeya, leader of a rebellion by Moriscos in the 16th century, was born in **Válor** *and a battle is staged in September.*

Free wine is traditionally on tap during **Cádiar**'s *October fiesta. Not a good time to be the designated driver.*

↑ The snowcapped Sierra Nevada, overlooking the village of Válor

NEED TO KNOW

The cavernous Santa Justa station, Seville

Before You Go...238

Getting Around..240

Practical Information..............................244

BEFORE
YOU GO

Forward planning is essential to any successful trip. Be prepared for all eventualities by considering the following points before you travel.

AT A GLANCE

CURRENCY
Euro

AVERAGE DAILY SPEND

SAVE	SPEND	SPLURGE
€35	€75	€150+

BOTTLED WATER	COFFEE	BEER	DINNER FOR TWO
€0.80	€1	€3	€40

ESSENTIAL PHRASES

Hello	Hola
Goodbye	Adiós
Please	Por favor
Thank you	Gracias
Do you speak English	¿Hablas inglés?
I don't understand	No comprendo

ELECTRICITY SUPPLY

Power sockets are type F, fitting a two-prong, round-pin plug. Standard voltage is 230 volts.

Passports and Visas

EU nationals may visit for an unlimited period, registering with local authorities after three months. Citizens of the US, Canada, Australia and New Zealand can reside without a visa for up to 90 days. For those arriving from other countries, check with your local Spanish embassy or on the **Exteriores** website.
Exteriores
w exteriores.gob.es

Travel Safety Advice

Visitors can get up-to-date travel safety information from the **UK Foreign and Commonwealth Office**, the **US Department of State** and the **Australian Department of Foreign Affairs and Trade**.
Australia
w smartraveller.gov.au
UK
w gov.uk/foreign-travel-advice
US
w travel.state.gov

Customs Information

An individual is permitted to carry the following within the EU for personal use:
Tobacco products 800 cigarettes, 400 cigarillos, 200 cigars or 1 kg of smoking tobacco.
Alcohol 10 litres of alcoholic beverages above 22 per cent strength, 20 litres of alcoholic beverages below 22 per cent strength, 90 litres of wine (60 litres of which can be sparkling wine) and 110 litres of beer.
Cash If you plan to enter or leave the EU with €10,000 or more in cash (or the equivalent in other currencies) you must declare it to the customs authorities.
Limits vary if travelling outside the EU, so always check restrictions before travelling.

Insurance

It is advisable to take out an insurance policy covering theft, loss of belongings, medical

problems, cancellations and delays. EU citizens are eligible for free emergency medical care in Spain provided they have a valid **EHIC** (European Health Insurance Card).

EHIC
🅦 ec.europa.eu

Vaccinations

No inoculations are necessary for Spain.

Money

Most establishments accept major credit, debit and prepaid currency cards. Contactless payments are common in cities, but it's always a good idea to carry cash for smaller items. ATMs are widely available throughout Andalucía, although many charge for cash withdrawals.

Booking Accommodation

Andalucía offers everything from boutique hotels and villas to guesthouses, hostels and campsites. Spain also offers government-run hotels called *paradors*, many of which are in Andaluciá. A useful list of accommodation can be found on the **Turespaña** website.

Throughout peak season (June to August), room rates are high and hotels are soon fully booked, so reserve in advance where possible. Prices are also higher during major fiestas.

Most hotels quote their prices without including tax (IVA), which is 10 per cent.

Turespaña
🅦 spain.info

Travellers with Specific Needs

COCEMFE (Confederación Española de Personas con Discapacidad Física y Orgánica) and **Accessible Spain** provide information and tailored itineraries, and companies such as **Tourism For All** offer specialist tours, for those with reduced mobility, sight and hearing.

Spain's public transport system generally caters for all passengers, providing wheelchairs, adapted toilets and ramps. All public transport in Seville, including the metro and bus services, can accommodate wheelchair users. Airports offer reserved car parking, as well as other facilities. Metro maps in Braille are available from **ONCE** (Organización Nacional de Ciegos).

Accessible Spain
🅦 accessiblespaintravel.com
COCEMFE
🅦 cocemfe.es
ONCE
🅦 once.es
Tourism For All
🅦 tourismforall.org.uk

Language

Castellano (Castilian) is Spain's primary language and is spoken in Andalucía. English is widely spoken in the cities and other tourist spots, but the same cannot always be said for rural areas. Mastering a few phrases in *Castellano* will go down well with many locals, who will appreciate the effort.

Closures

Lunchtime Many shops and some museums and public buildings may close for the siesta between 1pm and 5pm.
Monday Many museums, public buildings and monuments are closed all day.
Sunday While most points of interest are open on Sunday, churches and cathedrals are closed to the public during Mass. Some public transport runs less frequently.
Public holidays Most museums, public buildings and many shops either close early or do not open at all.

PUBLIC HOLIDAYS	
1 Jan	New Year's Day
6 Jan	Epiphany
28 Feb	Andalucía Day
Mar/ Apr	Good Friday
1 May	Labour Day
15 Aug	Assumption Day
12 Oct	Spain's National Day
1 Nov	All Saints' Day
6 Dec	Spanish Constitution Day
8 Dec	Feast of the Immaculate Conception
25 Dec	Christmas Day

GETTING AROUND

Whether you are visiting for a short city break or rural country retreat, discover how best to reach your destination and travel like a pro.

AT A GLANCE

PUBLIC TRANSPORT COSTS

SEVILLE

€5.00

Day ticket
Buses and tram

CÓRDOBA

€1.30

Single journey
Bus

MÁLAGA

€1.30

Single journey
Bus

TOP TIP
Buses are the best way to get around Seville, so don't just get a metro pass.

SPEED LIMIT

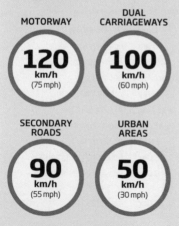

MOTORWAY

120 km/h
(75 mph)

DUAL CARRIAGEWAYS

100 km/h
(60 mph)

SECONDARY ROADS

90 km/h
(55 mph)

URBAN AREAS

50 km/h
(30 mph)

Arriving by Air

The three main airports in Andalucía are Jerez, Málaga–Costa del Sol and Seville, which all offer frequent European and internal flights. Some long-haul flights land at Málaga airport, but to travel elsewhere in Andalucía, a connection in Madrid or Barcelona is likely.

Almería, Gibraltar and Granada have small airports operating primarily domestic flights, as well as a handful of international services.

For information on getting to and from Andalucía's main airports, see the table opposite.

Train Travel

International Train Travel

Spain's international and domestic rail services are operated by state-run **Renfe** (Red Nacional de Ferrocarriles Españoles). For international train trips, it is advisable to purchase your ticket well in advance. **Eurail** and **Interrail** sell passes (to European non-residents and residents respectively), which are valid on Renfe trains.

International train services terminate in either Madrid or Barcelona, from where you can catch a domestic service to Andalucía (p242). Trains from Paris, London, Brussels, Amsterdam, Geneva, Zürich and Milan reach Barcelona via Cerbère. At Cerbère, you can connect to the TALGO (Tren Articulado Ligero Goicoechea Oriol), a high-speed luxury train service (operated by Renfe). There are also direct TALGO trains to Madrid and Barcelona from Paris, and to Barcelona from Milan, Geneva and Zürich.

There are two main rail routes from Portugal to Spain. The Sud Express departs daily from Lisbon and terminates in the French town of Hendaye, from where you can catch one of the regular services to Madrid. Alternatively, Lusitania is a sleeper train from Lisbon, which will take you to Madrid in around nine hours.

Eurail
W eurail.com
Interrail
W interrail.eu
Renfe
W renfe.com

GETTING TO AND FROM THE AIRPORT

Airport	Distance to City	Taxi Fare	Public Transport
Almería	10 km (6 miles)	€30	Bus: 35 mins
Gibraltar	1.5 km (1 mile)	€10	Bus: 10 mins
Granada	15 km (10 miles)	€25–30	Bus: 45 mins
Jerez	9 km (5.5 miles)	€25	Rail: 10 mins
			Bus: 30 mins
Málaga	8 km (5 miles)	€20	Rail 15 mins
			Bus: 20 mins
Seville	10 km (6 miles)	€25	Bus: 25–30 mins

CAR JOURNEY PLANNER

Plotting the main driving routes according to journey time, this map is a handy reference for travelling between Andalucía's main cities by car. The times given reflect the fastest and most direct routes available. Tolls apply on *autopista* motorways (AP roads), but not on *autovías* (A roads).

Jerez to Cádiz	0.5 hrs	**Madrid to Málaga**	5.5 hrs
Málaga to Granada	1.5 hrs	**Madrid to Seville**	5.5 hrs
Málaga to Murcia	4.5 hrs	**Seville to Cádiz**	1.5 hrs
Málaga to Seville	2.5 hrs	**Seville to Granada**	2.75 hrs

Domestic Train Travel

Renfe, along with some regional companies, operate a good train service throughout Andalucía. You can buy tickets online on the individual operators' websites or at stations. The fastest intercity services are the TALGO and AVE (operated by Renfe), which link Madrid with Seville in two and a half hours. AVE routes also link Barcelona with Seville and Málaga – both trips take five and a half hours.

The *largo recorrido* (long-distance) trains are much cheaper than the high-speed trains, but they are so slow that you usually need to travel overnight. Book at least a month in advance. *Regionales y cercanías* (the regional and local services) are frequent and cheap.

Long-Distance Bus Travel

Often the cheapest and easiest way to reach and travel around Andalucía is by coach. Coaches run frequently between major cities and towns in Andalucía, and connect the region to the rest of Spain. The major coach stations in Andalucía are in Seville, Córdoba, Granada, Málaga and Almería. Buses may provide the only public transport to and from small villages. **Eurolines** links Andalucía to Portugal and there are also international links to France, the Netherlands, Belgium, Switzerland and Austria.

Spain has no national coach company, but private regional companies operate routes around the country. The largest of these is **Alsa**, which runs in all regions and has routes and services that cover most of Spain. Other companies operate in particular regions – Alsina Graells, for instance, covers most of the south and east of Spain.

For short journeys, tickets can be bought from the driver when boarding the bus. For medium- to long-distance travel, you can make reservations at bus stations, or online via **Movelia**, as well as from individual bus companies. Tickets and information for long-distance travel are available at all main coach stations as well as on company websites, but note that it is not always possible to book tickets in advance.

Alsa
w alsa.es
Eurolines
w eurolines.com
Movelia
w movelia.es

Public Transport

Sightseeing and getting around Andalucía is best done on foot and by public transport. In most towns and cities, bus services suffice as the sole means of public transport. However,

Seville and Granada also have tram and metro systems. Jaén has the infrastructure for a tram system, but it is currently out of use. Municipal or tourism websites in **Córdoba**, **Seville**, **Granada**, **Málaga**, **Almería** and **Cádiz** offer up-to-date information about their public transport options.

Almería
w almeriaciudad.es
Cádiz
w cadizturismo.com
Córdoba
w cordoba.es
Granada
w granada.org
Málaga
w malaga.eu
Seville
w visitasevilla.es

Tickets

The best place to purchase public transport tickets is at stations themselves, either from windows or automatic machines. They are also available at newsagents. They come either in the form of a physical ticket or as a smart card which can either hold a season ticket or be topped up with cash and used pay-as-you-go.

Metro

The **Metro de Sevilla** was designed to aid transport between the outer areas of Seville and the city centre. Line 1 is useful for getting from the historical centre (Puerta Jerez) to shopping centres (Nervión or Ciudad Expo's MetroMar). The system will eventually consist of four metro lines, which will provide easy access to bus and train stations and include a line to the airport (Line 4).

The **Metropolitano de Granada** connects central Granada with the towns Armilla, Albolote and Maracena.

Metropolitano de Granada
w metropolitanogranada.es
Metro de Sevilla
w metro-sevilla.es

Trams

Seville's city centre operates a tram system called the MetroCentro. It provides air-conditioned, rapid transport between San Bernardo station and Plaza Nueva in an otherwise pedestrian-only zone. Other lines are due to be completed in 2020, which will extend the network to Puerta Osario and Santa Justa train station.

Pay at the machine at tram stops (or pass your smart card over the reader on board) and press the green button to open the door. Stops are announced on overhead monitors. MetroCentro trams run every 3 to 5 minutes and stop briefly at all stops.

Bus

Buses remain the most common mode of public transport throughout Andalucía and the rest of Spain, but they can sometimes follow an erratic timetable. Be aware that many services do not run after 10pm, although there are some night buses in the cities.

Buses are the easiest and cheapest way to get around Seville's main sights. The routes can be found on the **TUSSAM** website but, generally speaking, the most useful lines for visitors are the *circulares*, numbered C1 to C6, which run around the city centre.

In Granada, Nos 31, 32 and 34 run from the centre to the Albaicín, Alhambra and Sacramonte.

TUSSAM
w tussam.es

Cycling

There are cycle lanes in most Andalucían cities. Seville has pedestrianized a main thoroughfare in the centre, creating a wide promenade, which allows for bikes.

SEVICI is a self-service bike rental programme in Seville, with 2,500 bikes available 24 hours a day. Bikes can be hired free for 30 minutes and are charged per hour after that. A €150 credit card deposit is paid and refunded upon return of the bike.

Motorists tend to treat cyclists as a nuisance and city traffic can be dangerous for cyclists. Helmets are recommended.

SEVICI
w en.sevici.es

Taxis

Throughout Andalucía, particularly in cities and towns, taxis are a reasonably priced way to get around if public transport isn't an option. Generally speaking, the journey starts with a flat fee and then increases depending on the distance travelled. Fares tend to be higher at night and also during the weekend and public holidays. Surcharges usually apply for trips to airports and bus and train stations.

Driving

If you drive to Spain in your own car, you must carry the vehicle's registration document, a valid insurance certificate, a passport or a national identity card, and your driving licence at all times. You must also display a sticker on the back of the car showing its country of registration and you risk on-the-spot fines if you do not carry a red warning triangle and a reflective jacket with you at all times.

Spain has two types of motorway: *autopistas*, which are toll roads, and *autovías*, which are toll-free. You can establish whether a motorway is toll-free by the letters that prefix the number of the road: A = free; AP = toll motorway.

Carreteras nacionales, Spain's main roads, have black-and-white signs and are designated by the letter N (Nacional) plus a number. Those with Roman numerals start at the Puerta del Sol in Madrid, and those with ordinary numbers have kilometre markers giving the distance from the provincial capital.

Carreteras comarcales, secondary roads, have a number preceded by the letter C. Other minor roads have numbers preceded by letters representing the name of the province, such as the LE1313 in Lleida.

Car Hire

The most popular car-hire companies in Spain are **Europcar**, **Avis** and **Hertz**. All have offices at airports and major train stations, as well as in the larger cities. Fly-drive, an option for two or more travellers where car hire is included in the cost of your airfare, can be arranged by travel agents and tour operators. If you wish to hire a car locally for around a week or less, you will be able to arrange it with a local travel agent. A car for hire is called a *coche de alquiler*.

Avis
w avis.com
Europcar
w europcar.com
Hertz
w hertz-europe.com

Rules of the Road

When using a car in Spain, drive on the right and use the left lane only for passing other vehicles.

Most traffic regulations and warnings to motorists are represented on signs by easily recognized symbols. However, a few road rules and signs may be unfamiliar to some drivers from other countries.

If you have taken the wrong road, and it has a solid white line, turn round as indicated by a *cambio de sentido* sign. At crossings, give way to all on-coming traffic, unless a sign indicates otherwise.

The blood-alcohol concentration (BAC) limit is 0.5 mg/ml and is strictly enforced.

Boats and Ferries

Ferries connect the Spanish mainland to the Balearic and Canary Islands, and to North Africa, Italy and the UK. All the important routes are served by car ferries. **Acciona Trasmediterránea** operates a weekly service from Cádiz to the main ports of the Canary Islands. Always make an advance booking, especially in summer.

Acciona Trasmediterránea
w trasmediterranea.es

PRACTICAL
INFORMATION

A little local know-how goes a long way in Seville and Andalucía. Here is all the essential advice and information you will need during your stay.

AT A GLANCE

EMERGENCY NUMBERS

GENERAL
EMERGENCY

112

TIME ZONE

CET/CEST: Central European Summer time (CEST) runs last Sunday in March to last Sunday in October.

TAP WATER
Tap water in Andalucía is safe to drink unless stated otherwise.

TIPPING

Spain does not have a big tipping culture, but it is appreciated and it's common to round-up the bill.

Waiter	5-10%
Hotel Porter	€1-2 per bag
Housekeeping	Not expected
Bar Staff	Not expected
Taxi Driver	Round up to nearest euro

Personal Security

Violent crime is rare in Andalucía, but pickpocketing is common in the major cities. Take particular care on crowded transport, at stations, markets and the big-name sights, and wear bags and cameras across your body. Contact your embassy if you have your passport stolen, or in the event of a serious crime.

Health

Seek medicinal supplies and advice for minor ailments from a pharmacy *(farmacia)*, identifiable by a green or red cross. Each pharmacy displays a card in the window showing the address of the nearest all-night pharmacy.

Emergency medical care in Spain is free for all EU citizens. If you have an EHIC *(p239)*, present this as soon as possible. You may have to pay after treatment and reclaim the money later.

For visitors coming from outside the EU, payment of medical expenses is the patient's responsibility, so it is important to arrange comprehensive insurance before travelling.

Smoking, Alcohol and Drugs

Smoking is banned in enclosed public spaces and is a fineable offence, although you can still smoke on the terraces of bars and restaurants.

Spain has a relaxed attitude towards alcohol consumption, but it is frowned upon to be openly drunk. In cities it is common to drink on the street outside the bar of purchase.

Recreational drugs are illegal, and possession of even a very small quantity can lead to an extremely hefty fine. Amounts that suggest an intent to supply drugs to other people can lead to custodial sentences.

ID

By law you must carry identification with you at all times in Spain. A photocopy of your passport should suffice. If stopped by the police you may be asked to report to a police station with the original document.

Local Customs

A famous Spanish tradition is the siesta, which sees many shops closing between 1pm and 5pm. This is not always observed by large stores or in very touristy areas.

Bullfighting

Corridas (bullfights) are widely held in Andalucía. Supporters argue that the bulls are bred for the industry and would be killed as calves were it not for bullfighting, while organizations such as the **ADDA** (Asociación Defensa Derechos Animal) say that it's cruel and organize protests throughout the country. If you do decide to attend a *corrida*, bear in mind that it's better to see a big-name matador because they are more likely to make a clean and quick kill. The audience will make their disapproval evident if they don't.
ADDA
w addaong.org

Visiting Churches and Cathedrals

Spain retains a strong Catholic identity. Most churches and cathedrals will not permit visitors during Sunday Mass. Generally, entrance to churches is free, however a fee may apply to enter special areas, like cloisters. When visiting religious buildings ensure that you are dressed modestly, with knees and shoulders covered.

Mobile Phones and Wi-Fi

Free Wi-Fi is reasonably common in Spain, particularly in large public spaces, restaurants and bars. Some places, such as airports and hotels, may charge for you to use their Wi-Fi.
Visitors travelling to Spain with EU tariffs are able to use their devices abroad without being affected by roaming charges. Users will be charged the same rates for data, calls and texts as at home.

Post

Correos is Spain's postal service. Postal rates fall into three price bands: Spain; Europe and North Africa; and the rest of the world. Parcels must be weighed and stamped at Correos offices, which are open 8:30am–9:30pm Monday to Friday (outside the cities they close by 1–2pm on weekdays) and 9:30am–1pm on Saturday.
Letters sent from a post office usually arrive more quickly than if posted in a *buzón* (postbox). In cities, *buzóns* are yellow pillar boxes; elsewhere they are small, wall-mounted postboxes.
Correos
w correos.es

Taxes and Refunds

IVA (value added tax) in mainland Spain is normally 21 per cent, but with lower rates for certain goods and services.
Under certain conditions, non-EU citizens can claim a rebate of these taxes. Retailers can give you a form to fill out, which you can then present to a customs officer at your point of departure. If the shop offers DIVA, you can fill that form out instead and validate it automatically at one of the self-service machines found at Spain's main ports and airports.

Discount Cards

Some cities offer a visitor's pass or discount card, such as the Sevilla Card. This can be used for free or reduced-price entry to exhibitions, events and museums, and even discounts at participating restaurants. These are not free, so consider carefully how many of the offers you are likely to take advantage of before purchasing a card.

WEBSITES AND APPS

Andalucía
Offers infomation from Andalucía's tourism board (*www.andalucia.org*).
España
Spain's official tourism website (*www.spain.info*).
Moovit
A route-planning app.
WiFi Map
Finds free Wi-Fi hotspots near you (*www.wifimap.io*).

INDEX

Page numbers in **bold** refer to main entries

A

Accommodation
  booking 239
  see also Hotels
Aguilar de la Frontera **165**
Airports 241
Air travel 240
Alameda Apodaca (Cádiz) 182
Alameda de Hércules (Seville) **98**
Albaicín (Granada)
  walk **220–21**
Alcalá la Real **167**
Alcazaba (Almería) **222–3**
Alcazaba (Málaga) **189**
Alcázar (Jerez de la Frontera) **179**
Alcázar de los Reyes Cristianos (Córdoba) **152**, 156
Alcohol 244
Alhama de Granada **225**
Alhambra (Granada) 12, **216–17**
Almería **222–3**
  map 223
  see also Granada and Almería
Almuñécar **224**
Álora **200**
Álvarez-Ossorio, Aníbal González 28
Ambulances 244
Andalucía **127–235**
  bars 35
  Cádiz and Málaga 130, **175–209**
  Córdoba and Jaén 129, **149–73**
  Granada and Almería 131, **211–35**
  Huelva and Sevilla 128, **133–47**
  itineraries 21–5
  restaurants 33
Andújar **169**
Añora 173
Antequera **200–201**
Antigua Universidad (Baeza) 163
Apes' Den (Gibraltar) 194, 195
Apoteosis de Santo Aquino Zurbarán) 67
Apps 245
Aquariums
  Roqueosis de Mar 233
Arches, Moorish **155**
Archidona **200**
Architecture **28–9**
  architects **28**
  Moorish **30–31**
  Moorish arches **155**
Archivo de Indias (Seville) **86**, 90
Arcos de la Frontera **196**, 208
Art see Museums and galleries

Artists **26**
Axarquia **202–3**
Ayamonte **141**
Ayuntamiento (Baeza) 163
Ayuntamiento (Cádiz) 183
Ayuntamiento (Seville) **80**, 93
Azulejos (tiles) **88**

B

Baelo Claudia **192**
Baena **167**
Baeza **162–3**
  map 163
Baluarte de la Candelaria (Cádiz) 182
Baños Arabes (Jaén) **158**
Baños de la Encina **168**
Baños del Alcázar Califal (Córdoba) **153**
Barbate **193**
Bars **36–7**
  Andalucía 35
  beach bars 41
  Cádiz and Málaga 179, 201
  Córdoba and Jaén 165
  Granada and Almería 230
  Seville 35, 98
Basílica de la Macarena (Seville) **99**
Baths see Spas and baths
Baza **230**
Beaches 11, **40–41**
  Cádiz and Málaga **205**
  Matalascañas **147**
  Mazagón **140**
  Punta Umbría **138–9**
Beer **34**
Belalcázar 172
Bell towers, Seville **100**
Bélmez 172
Benalmádena **203**
Bicycles **43**, 243
Birds
  Fuente de Piedra **201**
  see also Wildlife
Blood Wedding at Níjar **232**
Boats and ferries 243
Bowles, Paul 207
Bridges
  Puente de Isabel II (Seville) 121
  Puente Nuevo (Ronda) 185
  Puente Romano (Córdoba) 157
Buddhism
  Benalmádena Stupa 203
Bullfighting 245
  Plaza de Toros (El Puerto de Santa María) 191
  Plaza de Toros de la Maestranza (Seville) **69**, 70
  Ronda **184**
Buses 242, 243

C

Cabra **167**
Cádiz **180–83**
  map 181
  walk **182–3**
Cádiz and Málaga 130, **175–209**
  bars 179, 201
  beaches **205**
  hotels 197
  map 176–7
  restaurants 181, 202
  shopping 186, 192
  tour **208–9**
  windfarms **192**
CaixaForum (Seville) **123**
Calle Betis (Seville) 121
Calle de la Feria (Seville) 104
Calle Honduras (Cádiz) 183
Callejón del Agua (Seville) 91
Callejón de las Flores (Córdoba) 157
Calle Nueva (Cádiz) 183
Calle Pelay Correa (Seville) 121
Calle Rodrigo de Triana (Seville) 121
Calle Sierpes (Seville) **81**, 93
Cámara Oscura (Seville) **99**
Caminito del Rey (Garganta del Chorro) 197
Campo del Sur (Cádiz) 182
Capilla de los Marineros (Seville) 121
Capilla del Salvador (Úbeda) **161**
Capilla de San Andrés (Jaén) **158**
Capilla de San Bartolome (Córdoba) 156
Capilla Real (Granada) **214**
Capillita del Carmen (Seville) 121
Carmen **114**
Carmona **147**
Carnival 39
Carrera del Darro (Granada) 221
Cars 243
  journey planner 241
  Museo Automovilístico y de la Moda (Málaga) **186–7**
  speed limits 240
  see also Tours
Casa de los Pisa (Granada) 220
Casa de los Tiros (Granada) **215**
Casa del Rey Moro (Ronda) 185
Casa de Pilatos (Seville) **89**
Casa de Sefarad (Córdoba) 156
Casa Natal de Picasso (Málaga) **188**
Castles and fortresses **30**
  Alcazaba (Almería) **222–3**
  Alcázar (Jerez de la Frontera) **179**
  Alcázar de los Reyes Cristianos (Córdoba) **152**, 156
  Castillo Árabe (Álora) 200
  Castillo Arabe (Salobreña) 224–5

Castles and fortresses (cont.)
Castillo de Almodóvar del Río **164–5**
Castillo de Colomares (Benalmádena) 203
Castillo de Gibralfaro (Málaga) **189**
Castillo de Guzmán el Bueno (Tarifa) 192
Castillo de La Calahorra 226
Castillo de San Miguel (Almuñécar) 224
Castillo de Santa Catalina (Jaén) **159**
Castillo de Segura de la Sierra 170
Castillo de Vélez Blanco 231
Castillo San Marcos (El Puerto de Santa María) 191
Keep, The (Gibraltar) 194, 195
Murallas (Seville) **100**
Cástulo **168**
Cathedrals *see* Churches and cathedrals
Caves
Cueva de los Letreros (Vélez Blanco) 231
Cuevas de la Pileta (Ronda la Vieja) 196
Cuevas de Nerja 202
Flamenco caves 45
Gruta de las Maravillas 138
Guadix 227
Cazorla **168**
wildlife **171**
Centre Pompidou Málaga **188**
Centro Andaluz de Flamenco (Jerez de la Frontera) **179**
Centro Cerámica Triana (Seville) 121
Centro Condado de Huelva (El Condado) 145
Centro Cultural Caja Granada **215**
Ceramics **27**
azulejos (tiles) **88**
Ceuta **206**
Chapels
Capilla de los Marineros (Seville) 121
Capilla del Salvador (Úbeda) **161**
Capilla de San Andrés (Jaén) **158**
Capilla de San Bartolome (Córdoba) 156
Capilla Real (Granada) **214**
see also Churches and cathedrals
Children **38–9**
Chipiona **190**
Churches and cathedrals 245
Basílica de la Macarena (Seville) **99**
Catedral (Almería) **222**
Catedral (Cádiz) **180**, 183
Catedral (Jaén) **158**
Catedral del Salvador (Jerez de la Frontera) **178–9**

Churches and cathedrals (cont.)
Cathedral (Baeza) 163
Cathedral (Granada) **214**
Cathedral and La Giralda (Seville) **76–7**, 90
Iglesia de la Magdalena (Seville) **68**
Iglesia del Salvador (Seville) **80–81**
Iglesia de Nuestra Señora de la O (Seville) **125**
Iglesia de San Marcos (Seville) **100**, 105
Iglesia de San Pablo (Úbeda) **160**
Iglesia de San Pedro (Seville) **100–101**, 104
Iglesia de Santa Ana (Granada) 220
Iglesia de Santa Ana (Seville) 121, **124–5**
Iglesia de Santa Catalina (Seville) **103**, 105
Iglesia de Santa Cruz (Seville) 93
Iglesia San Ildefonso (Jaén) **159**
Iglesia San Juan (Almería) **222**
Iglesia San Juan de la Palma (Seville) 104
Iglesia San Luís de los Franceses (Seville) **101**
Iglesia Santa Ana (Seville) 92
Oratorio de San Felipe Neri (Cádiz) **181**, 182
San Román (Seville) 105
Santa María de los Reales Alcázares (Úbeda) **161**
Santa María la Mayor (Ronda) 185
Seville's bell towers **100**
Cinema
Spaghetti Westerns **231**
City halls *see* Town halls
Closures 239
Clubs **36**
Columbus, Christopher **139**
Convento de Santa Catalina (Granada) 221
Convento de Santa Iñes (Seville) 104
Convento de Santa Paula (Seville) **102–3**, 105
Convento de Santo Domingo (Ronda) 185
Convento San José del Carmen (Seville) 93
Cookery courses 33
Córdoba **152–7**
map 153
walk **156–7**
Córdoba and Jaén 129, **149–73**
hotels 170
map 150–51
restaurants 153, 166
shopping 159, 169
tour **172–3**
Wildlife in Cazorla, Segura and Las Villas **171**

Corral del Carbón (Granada) **215**
Costa del Sol **205**
Costurero de la Reina (Seville) 116
Craft markets **27**
Credit cards 239
Crime 244
Currency 238, 239
Customs information 238
Cycling **43**, 243

D

Dance *see* Flamenco
Desfiladero de Despeñaperros **169**
Día de los Royes 39
Disabled travellers 239
Discount cards 245
Diving **42**
Doctors 244
Drinks *see* Food and drink
Driving *see* Cars
Drugs 244

E

Écija **146**
El Arenal (Seville) 58, **63–71**
map 64–5
walk **70–71**
El Bañuelo (Granada) 221
El Cano, Monument to (Seville) 116
El Condado **145**
Electricity supply 238
El Puerto de Santa María **191**
El Rinconcillo (Seville) 105
El Rocío **144**
Emergency numbers 244
Esquivel, Antonio María 121
Estepa **146**
Estepona **205**
Events *see* Festivals and events

F

Families, Seville and Andalucía for **38–9**
Ferries 243
Festivals and events 11, **37**, **46–7**
family-friendly festivals **39**
flamenco **44**
Fiesta de San Juan 39
Films
Spaghetti Westerns **231**
Fire services 244
Flamenco 13, **44–5**, **85**
Centro Andaluz de Flamenco (Jerez de la Frontera) **179**
Museo del Baile Flamenco (Seville) **84**
Food and drink **32–3**
drinks **34–5**
olive oil **158**
oranges 10, **33**
sherry 13
tapas 10, **32**
see also Restaurants; Wines

Fuengirola **204-5**
Fuente Agria 234
Fuente de Piedra **201**
Fuente de Santa María (Baeza) 163
Fuente Obejuna 172

G

Galleries see Museums and galleries
Gardens see Parks and gardens
Garganta del Chorro **197**
Gaucín 209
Generalife (Granada) **218-19**
Gibraltar **194-5**
  Gibraltar Controversy **194**
Gothic architecture **28**
Granada **214-21**
  map 215
  walk **220-21**
Granada and Almería 131, **211-35**
  bars 230
  hotels 227
  map 212-13
  restaurants 215, 223, 233
  shopping 225
Gran Teatro Falla (Cádiz) 182
Grazalema 209
Gruta de las Maravillas 138
Guadix **226-7**

H

Health care 244
Hiking see Walks
Hinojosa del Duque 172
Historic buildings
  Baños del Alcázar Califal (Córdoba) **153**
  Casa del Rey Moro (Ronda) 185
  Corral del Carbón (Granada) **215**
  Hospital de la Caridad (Seville) **68**, 71
  Hospital de los Venerables (Seville) **86-7**, 91
  Hospital de Santiago (Úbeda) **160**
  Hotel Alfonso XIII (Seville) **114**, 117
  La Alhóndiga (Baeza) 163
  Palacio de la Madraza (Granada) **215**
  Palacio de Lebrija (Seville) **80**
  Palacio de Viana (Córdoba) **153**
  Parlamento de Andalucía (Seville) **99**
  Puerta de Purchena (Almería) **223**
  Real Chancillería (Granada) 220
  see also Castles and fortresses; Chapels; Churches and cathedrals; Libraries; Monasteries and convents; Palaces; Towers
History **48-53**

Horses
  Real Escuela Andaluza de Arte Ecuestre (Jerez de la Frontera) **178**
Hospital de la Caridad (Seville) **68**, 71
Hospital de los Venerables (Seville) **86-7**, 91
Hospital de Santiago (Úbeda) **160**
Hospitals 244
Hotels
  booking 239
  Cádiz and Málaga 197
  Córdoba and Jaén 170
  Granada and Almería 227
  Hotel Alfonso XIII (Seville) **114**, 117
  Hotel Continental (Tangier) 207
  Huelva and Sevilla 141
  Seville 81, 125
  Úbeda 161
Huelva **139**
Huelva and Sevilla 128, **133-47**
  hotels 141
  map 134-5
  restaurants 138, 147
  shopping 145

I

ID 244
Iglesia de la Magdalena (Seville) **68**, 92
Iglesia del Salvador (Seville) **80-81**
Iglesia de Nuestra Señora de la O (Seville) **125**
Iglesia de San Marcos (Seville) **100**, 105
Iglesia de San Pablo (Úbeda) **160**
Iglesia de San Pedro (Seville) **100-101**, 104
Iglesia de Santa Ana (Granada) 220
Iglesia de Santa Ana (Seville) 92, 121, **124-5**
Iglesia de Santa Catalina (Seville) **103**, 105
Iglesia de Santa Cruz (Seville) 93
Iglesia San Ildefonso (Jaén) **159**
Iglesia San Juan (Almería) **222**
Iglesia San Juan de la Palma (Seville) 104
Iglesia San Luís de los Franceses (Seville) **101**
Insurance 238-9
Internet access 245
Isla, Camón de la 44
Isla Cristina **138**
Islam see Mosques
Isla Mágica (Seville) **122**
Itálica **144**
Itineraries
  2 days in Seville 19
  5 days in Andalucía 21
  10 days in Andalucía 23-5
  24 hours in Seville 17

J

Jaén **158-9**
  map 159
  see also Córdoba and Jaén
Jardines de Cristina (Seville) 93
Jardines de Murillo (Seville) **87**, 93
Jerez de la Frontera **178-9**
  map 179
Jews
  Sinagoga (Córdoba) **152**, 156
Jimena de la Frontera 209
Justa, Santa 121

L

La Alhóndiga (Baeza) 163
La Calahorra **226**
La Carolina **168**
La Giralda (Seville) **76-7**, 90
La Inmaculada (Valdés Leal) 67
La Línea de la Concepción **195**
La Macarena (Seville) 60, **95-105**
  map 96-7
  walk **104-5**
La Mezquita (Seville) 10
Language 238, 239
Lanjarón **226**
Las Alpujarras tour **234-5**
La Servilleta (Murillo) 67
Las Villas
  wildlife **171**
Lebrija **144**
Libraries
  Archivo de Indias (Seville) **86**, 90
Linares, Carmen 44
Local customs 245
Loja **225**
López de Rojas, Eufrasio 28
Lorca, Federico García, Bodas de Sangre **232**
Lucena **167**
Lucía, Paco de 44
Lynx **137**

M

Málaga 27, **186-9**
  map 187
  see also Cádiz and Málaga
Maps
  Almería 223
  Baeza 163
  Cádiz 181, 182-3
  Cádiz and Málaga 176-7
  car journey planner 241
  Córdoba 153, 156-7
  Córdoba and Jaén 150-51
  Granada 215, 220-21
  Granada: Albaicín 220-21
  Granada and Almería 212-13
  Huelva and Sevilla 134-5
  Jaén 159
  Jerez de la Frontera 179
  Las Alpujarras 234-5
  Málaga 187
  Pueblos Blancos 208-9

Maps (cont.)
Ronda 185
Seville 56-7, 92-3
Seville: Across the river 119
Seville: El Arenal 64-5, 70-71
Seville: La Macarena 96-7, 104-5
Seville: Parque María Luisa 108-9
Seville: Santa Cruz 74-5, 90-91
Seville: Triana 121
Seville: Universidad 116-17
Seville and Andalucía 14-15
Sierra Morena 172-3
Spain 56
Úbeda 161
Marbella **204**
Markets
arts and crafts **27**
Calle de la Feria (Seville) 104
Metropol Parasol (Seville) **103**
Matalascañas 41, **147**
Mazagón 41, **140**
Medina Azahara **164**
Medina Sidonia **190**
Melilla **206**
Mérimée, Prosper **114**
Metro 242
Metropol Parasol (Seville) 29, **103**
Mezquita (Córdoba) **154-5**, 157
Minarete San Sebastiano (Ronda) 185
Minas de Riotinto **138**
Mobile phones 245
Moguer **140**
Mojácar **233**
Monasteries and convents
Convento de Santa Catalina (Granada) 221
Convento de Santa Iñes (Seville) 104
Convento de Santa Paula (Seville) **102-3**, 105
Convento San José del Carmen (Seville) 93
Monasterio de la Cartuja (Granada) **214**
Monasterio de la Rábida **140-41**
Monasterio de San Clemente (Seville) **98**
Monasterio de Santa Clara (Moguer) 140
Monasterio de Santa María de las Cuevas (Seville) **124**
Real Monasterio de Santa Clara (Jaén) **158-9**
Money 238, 239
Montefrío **224**
Montes de Málaga **203**
Montilla **164**
Montoro **165**
Monument to El Cano (Seville) 116
Moorish architecture **30-31**
arches **155**
Morocco
Tangier **206-7**

Mosques **30**
La Mezquita (Seville) 10
Mezquita (Córdoba) **154-5**, 157
Minarete San Sebastiano (Ronda) 185
Mountains 13
Mudéjar architecture **29**
Murallas (Seville) **100**
Murallas de San Carlos (Cádiz) 183
Murillo, Bartolomé Esteban 26
La Servilleta 67
Museums and galleries **26-7**, 39
American Legation (Tangier) 207
CaixaForum (Seville) **123**
Casa de los Pisa (Granada) 220
Casa de Sefarad (Córdoba) 156
Casa Museo de Martín Alonso Pinzón (Palos de la Frontera) 141
Casa Natal de Picasso (Málaga) **188**
Castillo de la Yedra (Cazorla) 168
Centre Pompidou Málaga **188**
Centro Cultural Caja Granada **215**
Centro de Exposición de Artesanal (Alhama de Granada) 225
Centro de Interpretación Cuevas de Guadix 227
Gibraltar Museum 194
Metropol Parasol (Seville) **103**
Museo Arqueológico (Baza) 230
Museo Arqueológico (Córdoba) **152**
Museo Arqueológico (Granada) 221
Museo Arqueológico (Seville) **113**
Museo Arqueológico (Úbeda) **160**
Museo Arqueológico Cueva de Siete Palacios (Almuñécar) 224
Museo Automovilístico y de la Moda (Málaga) **186-7**
Museo Carmen Thyssen Málaga **186**
Museo de Alfarería (Guadix) 227
Museo de Almería **222**
Museo de Artes y Costumbres Populares (Seville) **111**
Museo de Bellas Artes (Córdoba) **153**
Museo de Bellas Artes (Seville) **66-7**
Museo de Cádiz **181**
Museo de la Inquisición (Seville) 121, 125
Museo de la Legión (Ceuta) 206
Museo del Baile Flamenco (Seville) **84**

Museums and galleries (cont.)
Museo del Grabado Español Contemporáneo (Marbella) 204
Museo de Málaga **187**
Museo de Zenobia y Juan Ramón Jiménez (Moguer) 140
Museo Minero (Minas de Riotinto) 138
Museo Picasso Málaga **188**
Museo Provincial (Huelva) 139
Museo Provincial (Jaén) **159**
Museos de la Atalaya (Jerez de la Frontera) **178**
Necrópolis Romana (Carmona) 147
Palacio de Nájera (Antequera) 201
Music *see* Flamenco

N

National parks
Parque Nacional de Doñana 12, **136-7**
Nature reserves
Parque Natural de Cabo de Gata **230**
Parque Natural de Cazorla, Segura y Las Villas **170**
Parque Natural de Los Alcornocales **193**
Parque Natural del Torcal **200**
Parque Natural Sierra de las Nieves **196-7**
see also Wildlife
Necrópolis Romana (Carmona) 147
Nerja **202**
Nightlife **36-7**
Níjar **232-3**
Blood Wedding at Níjar **232**

O

Olive oil **158**
Oranges 10, **33**
Oratorio de San Felipe Neri (Cádiz) **181**, 182
Osuna **146**
Outdoor activities *see* Sports and outdoor activities

P

Pabellón de Chile (Seville) 116
Pabellón de Perú (Seville) 117
Palaces
Alcazaba **189**
Alhambra (Granada) **216-17**
Casa de los Tiros (Granada) **215**
Casa de Pilatos (Seville) **89**
Dar El Makhzen (Tangier) 207
Generalife (Granada) **218-19**
Medina Azahara **164**
Moorish palaces **31**

Palaces (cont.)
  Palacio Arzobispal (Seville) 90, 93
  Palacio de Jabalquinto (Baeza) 163
  Palacio de la Madraza (Granada) **215**
  Palacio de las Cadenas (Úbeda) **161**
  Palacio de las Dueñas (Seville) **102**, 104
  Palacio de Lebrija (Seville) **80**
  Palacio del Marqués de Salvatierra (Ronda) 185
  Palacio del Mayorazgo 196
  Palacio de Peñaflor (Écija) 146
  Palacio de San Telmo (Seville) **115**, 117
  Palacio de Viana (Córdoba) **153**
  Parador de Úbeda **161**
  Real Alcázar (Seville) 12, **78-9**, 91
Palma del Río (Baeza) **165**
Palos de la Frontera **141**
Parador de Úbeda **161**
Parks and gardens
  Alameda Apodaca (Cádiz) 182
  Generalife (Granada) **218-19**
  Jardines de Cristina (Seville) 93
  Jardines de Murillo (Seville) **87**, 93
  Parque Genovés (Cádiz) 182
  Parque María Luisa (Seville) **110-11**
  PCT Cartuja (Seville) **122-3**
Parlamento de Andalucía (Seville) **99**
Parque Genovés (Cádiz) 182
Parque María Luisa (Seville) 60, **107-17**
  map 108-9
Parque Nacional de Doñana **136-7**
Parque Natural de Cabo de Gata 41, **230**
Parque Natural de Cazorla, Segura y Las Villas **170**
Parque Natural de Los Alcornocales **193**
Parque Natural del Torcal **200**
Parque Natural Sierra de las Nieves **196-7**
Paseo de las Delicias (Seville) 116
Passports 238, 244
Pastori, Nina 44
PCT Cartuja (Seville) **122-3**
Pedroche 173
Peñarroya-Pueblonuevo 172
Personal security 244
Pharmacies 244
Phones 245
Picasso, Pablo 26
  Casa Natal de Picasso (Málaga) **188**
  Museo Picasso Málaga **188**

Pinzón, Martín Alonso
  Casa Museo de Martín Alonso Pinzón (Palos de la Frontera) 141
Playa Bil-Bil (Benalmádena) 205
Playa Cabo Trafalgar (Caños de Meca) 205
Playa de Barrosa 41
Playa de Bolonia 205
Playa de Caleta (Cádiz) 41, 182
Playa de Puerto Banús (Marbella) 205
Playa de Valdevaqueros (Tarifa) 205
Plaza de España (Cádiz) 183
Plaza de España (Seville) **112-13**
Plaza de la Cruz Verde (Cádiz) 182
Plaza del Altozano (Seville) 121
Plaza del Pópulo (Baeza) 163
Plaza del Triunfo (Seville) **87**, 90
Plaza de San Francisco (Cádiz) 183
Plaza de Toros de la Maestranza (Seville) **69**, 70
Plaza Santa Cruz (Seville) 91
Plaza Virgen de los Reyes (Seville) **84**, 90
Police 244
Poqueira Valley **227**, 234
Postal services 245
Pozoblanco 173
Prehistoric sites
  Cueva de los Letreros (Vélez Blanco) 231
  Cuevas de la Pileta (Ronda la Vieja) 196
  Cuevas de Nerja 202
  dolmens (Antequera) 201
Priego de Córdoba **166-7**
Public holidays 239
Public transport 240, 242-3
Pueblos blancos ("white towns") 11
  tour **208-9**
Puente de Isabel II (Seville) 92, 121
Puente Nuevo (Ronda) 185
Puente Romano (Córdoba) 157
Puerta de Jaén y Arco de Villalae (Baeza) 163
Puerta de Purchena (Almería) **223**
Puerto de la Ragua 235
Punta Umbría 41, **138-9**

R

Railways *see* Train travel
Real Alcázar (Seville) 12, **78-9**, 91
Real Chancillería (Granada) 220
Real Escuela Andaluza de Arte Ecuestre (Jerez de la Frontera) **178**
Real Monasterio de Santa Clara (Jaén) **158-9**
Renaissance architecture **28**
Restaurants
  Andalucía 33
  Cádiz and Málaga 181, 202

Restaurants (cont.)
  Córdoba and Jaén 153, 166
  Granada and Almería 215, 223, 233
  Huelva and Sevilla 138, 147
  Seville 69, 86, 101, 112, 115, 123
  see also Food and drink
Roldan, Luisa 26
Romans 49
  Itálica 144
  Necrópolis Romana (Carmona) 147
Ronda **184-5**, 209
  bullfighting **184**
  map 185
Ronda la Vieja **196**, 209
Roquetas de Mar **233**
Rufina, Santa 121
Ruiz, Hernán the Younger 28
Rules of the road 243

S

Safety
  personal security 244
  travel safety advice 238
Salobreña **224-5**
San Hugo en el Refectorio (Zurbarán) 67
San Jerónimo (Torrigiano) 67
San José **232**
Sanlúcar de Barrameda **190-91**
San Román (Seville) 105
Santa Cruz (Seville) 59, **73-93**
  map 74-5
  walk **90-91**, **92-3**
Santa Fé **225**
Santa Justa 121
Santa María de los Reales Alcázares (Úbeda) **161**
Santa María la Mayor (Ronda) 185
Santa Rufina 121
Santuario Virgen de la Cabeza **169**
Scuba diving **42**
Segura de la Sierra **170**
  wildlife **171**
Setenil 209
Sevilla *see* Huelva and Sevilla
Seville **58-125**
  Across the river 61, **119-25**
  bars 35, 98
  El Arenal 58, **63-71**
  hotels 81, 125
  itineraries 17-19
  La Macarena 60, **95-105**
  map 56-7
  Parque María Luisa 60, **107-17**
  restaurants 69, 86, 101, 112, 115, 123
  Santa Cruz 59, **73-93**
  shopping 102
Sherry 13, **35**
  Bodegas Barbadillo (Sanlúcar de Barrameda) 190-91
  Bodegas Osborne (El Puerto de Santa María) 191
  Bodegas Terry (El Puerto de Santa María) 191

Shopping
   Cádiz and Málaga 186, 192
   Córdoba and Jaén 159, 169
   Granada and Almería 225
   Huelva and Sevilla 145
   Seville 102
   taxes and refunds 245
Siege Tunnels (Gibraltar) 194, 195
Sierra de Aracena **138**
Sierra Morena tour **172-3**
Sierra Nevada **226**
Sierra Norte **145**
Sign of Seville **80**
Sinagoga (Córdoba) **152**, 156
Skiing **43**
   Sierra Nevada 226
Smoking 244
Sorbas **232**
Sotogrande **195**
Spaghetti Westerns **231**
Spas and baths
   Balneario de Lanjarón 226
   Baños Arabes (Jaén) **158**
   Baños del Alcázar Califal (Córdoba) **153**
   El Bañuelo (Granada) 221
   Hotel Balneario (Alhama de Granada) 225
Specific needs, travellers with 239
Speed limits 240
Sports and outdoor activities **42-3**
St Michael's Cave (Gibraltar) 194, 195

T

Tabernas **231**
Tangier **206-7**
Tapas 10, **32**
Tap water 244
Tarifa **192**
Taxes 245
Taxis 243
Theatre
   Gran Teatro Falla (Cádiz) 182
   Teatro de la Maestranza (Seville) **69**, 70
   Teatro Lope de Vega (Seville) **115**, 117
Theme parks **38**
   Isla Mágica (Seville) **122**
Tiles (*azulejos*) **88**
Time zone 244
Tipping 244
Torre de Don Fadrique (Seville) **99**
Torre de la Calahorra (Córdoba) **153**
Torre del Oro (Seville) **69**, 71, 92
Torre de los Aliatares (Baeza) 163
Torremolinos **205**
Torre Sevilla (Seville) 29, **125**
Torre Tavira (Cádiz) **181**, 182
Torrigiano, Pietro
   San Jerónimo 67

Tours
   Las Alpujarras **234-5**
   Pueblos Blancos **208-9**
   Sierra Morena **172-3**
Towers
   Belalcázar 172
   La Giralda (Seville) **76**, 90
   Moorish **31**
   Seville's bell towers **100**
   Torre de Don Fadrique (Seville) **99**
   Torre de la Calahorra (Córdoba) **153**
   Torre del Oro (Seville) **69**, 71, 92
   Torre de los Aliatares (Baeza) 163
   Torre Sevilla (Seville) **125**
   Torre Tavira (Cádiz) **181**, 182
Town halls
   Ayuntamiento (Baeza) 163
   Ayuntamiento (Cádiz) 183
   Palacio de las Cadenas (Úbeda) **161**
Train travel 240, 242
Trams 242
Travel **240-43**
Travel safety advice 238
Trevélez 234
Triana (Seville) 92, **120-21**
   map 121

U

Úbeda **160-61**
   hotels 161
   map 161
Ubrique 209
Universidad (Seville) 93, **114**
   walk **116-17**

V

Vaccinations 239
Valdés Leal, Juan de
   La Inmaculada 67
Válor 235
Vega, Lope Félix de
   Teatro Lope de Vega (Seville) 115
Vejer de la Frontera **192**
Velázquez, Diego 26
Vélez Blanco **231**
Virgen de la Macarena **99**
Visas 238

W

Walks
   Cádiz **182-3**
   Córdoba **156-7**
   Granada **220-21**
   hiking **42**
   Parque Nacional de Doñana 137
   Seville **92-3**
   Seville: El Arenal **70-71**
   Seville: La Macarena **104-5**
   Seville: Santa Cruz **90-91**
   Seville: Universidad **116-17**

Water, drinking 244
Websites 245
Wheelchair access 239
Wi-Fi 245
Wildlife **43**
   Cazorla, Segura and Las Villas **171**
   lynx **137**
   Montes de Málaga **203**
   see also Aquariums; National parks; Nature reserves; Zoos
Windfarms
   Cádiz and Málaga **192**
Windsurfing 40
Wines
   Centro Condado de Huelva (El Condado) 145
Winter sports **43**
World War II bunkers (La Línea de la Concepción) 195

Y

Yegen 235

Z

Zahara de la Sierra 209
Zoos
   Apes' Den (Gibraltar) 194, 195
   see also Aquariums; Wildlife
Zurbarán, Francisco
   San Hugo en el Refectorio 67
Zurbarán, Tomás de Aquino
   Apoteosis de Santo 67

PHRASE BOOK

IN AN EMERGENCY

Help!	¡Socorro!	soh-**koh**-roh
Stop!	¡Pare!	**pah**-reh
Call a doctor!	¡Llame a un médico!	**yah**-meh ah **oon meh**-dee-koh
Call an ambulance!	¡Llame a una ambulancia!	**yah**-meh ah oonah ahm-boo-**lahn**-a thee-ah
Call the police!	¡Llame a la policía!	**yah**-meh ah lah poh-lee-**thee**-ah
Call the fire brigade!	¡Llame a los bomberos!	**yah**-meh ah lohs bohm-**beh**-rohs
Where is the nearest telephone?	¿Dónde está el teléfono más próximo?	**dohn**-deh ehs-**tah** ehl teh-**leh**-foh-noh mahs **prohx**-ee-moh
Where is the nearest hospital?	¿Dónde está el hospital más próximo?	**dohn**-deh ehs-**tah** ehl ohs-pee-**tahl** mahs **prohx**-ee-moh

COMMUNICATION ESSENTIALS

Yes	Sí	see
No	No	noh
Please	Por favor	pohr fah-**vohr**
Thank you	Gracias	**grah**-thee-ahs
Excuse me	Perdone	pehr-**doh**-neh
Hello	Hola	**oh**-lah
Goodbye	Adiós	ah-dee-**ohs**
Goodnight	Buenas noches	**bweh**-nahs **noh** chehs
Morning	La mañana	lah mah-**nyah**-nah
Afternoon	La tarde	lah **tahr**-deh
Evening	La tarde	lah **tahr**-deh
Yesterday	Ayer	ah-**yehr**
Today	Hoy	oy
Tomorrow	Mañana	mah-**nyah**-nah
Here	Aquí	ah-**kee**
There	Allí	ah-**yee**
What?	¿Qué?	keh
When?	¿Cuándo?	**kwahn**-doh
Why?	¿Por qué?	pohr-**keh**
Where?	¿Dónde?	**dohn**-deh

USEFUL PHRASES

How are you?	¿Cómo está usted?	**koh**-moh ehs-**tah** oos-**tehd**
Very well, thank you.	Muy bien, gracias.	mwee bee-**ehn grah**-thee-ahs
Pleased to meet you.	Encantado de conocerle.	ehn-kahn-**tah**-doh deh koh-noh-**thehr**-leh
See you soon.	Hasta pronto.	ahs-tah **prohn**-toh
That's fine.	Está bien.	ehs-**tah** bee-**ehn**
Where is/are ...?	¿Dónde está/están ...?	**dohn**-deh ehs-**tah**/ehs-**tahn**
How far is it to ...?	Cuántos metros/ kilómetros hay de aquí a ...?	**kwahn**-tohs meh-trohs/kee-**loh**-meh-trohs **eye** deh ah-**kee** ah
Which way to ...?	¿Por dónde se va a ...?	pohr dohn-deh seh **bah** ah
Do you speak English?	¿Habla inglés?	ah-blah een-**glehs**
I don't understand	No comprendo	noh kohm-**prehn**-doh
Could you speak more slowly, please?	¿Puede hablar más despacio, por favor?	pweh-deh ah-**blahr mahs** dehs-pah-thee-oh pohr fah-**vohr**
I'm sorry.	Lo siento.	loh see-**ehn**-toh

USEFUL WORDS

big	grande	**grahn**-deh
small	pequeño	peh-**keh**-nyoh
hot	caliente	kah-lee-**ehn**-teh
cold	frío	**free**-oh
good	bueno	**bweh**-noh
bad	malo	**mah**-loh
enough	bastante	bahs-**tahn**-the
well	bien	bee-**ehn**
open	abierto	ah-bee-**ehr**-toh
closed	cerrado	thehr-**rah**-doh
left	izquierda	eeth-key-**ehr**-dah
right	derecha	deh-**reh**-chah
straight on	todo recto	toh-doh **rehk**-toh
near	cerca	**thehr**-kah
far	lejos	**leh**-hohs
up	arriba	ah-**ree**-bah
down	abajo	ah-**bah**-hoh

early	temprano	tehm-**prah**-noh
late	tarde	**tahr**-deh
entrance	entrada	ehn-**trah**-dah
exit	salida	sah-**lee**-dah
toilet	lavabos, servicios	lah-**vah**-bohs sehr-**bee**-thee-ohs
more	más	mahs
less	menos	**meh**-nohs

SHOPPING

How much does this cost?	¿Cuánto cuesta esto?	**kwahn**-toh kwehs-tah ehs-toh
I would like ...	Me gustaría ...	meh goos-ta-**ree**-ah
Do you have...?	¿Tienen...?	tee-**yeh**-nehn
I'm just looking, thank you.	Sólo estoy mirando, gracias.	soh-loh ehs-**toy** mee-rahn-doh **grah**-thee-ahs
Do you take credit cards?	¿Aceptan tarjetas de crédito?	ah-**thehp**-tahn tahr-**heh**-tahs deh **kreh**-dee-toh
What time do you open?	¿A qué hora abren?	ah **keh** oh-rah **ah**-brehn
What time do you close?	¿A qué hora cierran?	ah keh oh-rah thee-**ehr**-rahn
This one.	Este.	**ehs**-the
That one.	Ese.	**eh**-she
expensive	caro	**kahr**-oh
cheap	barato	bah-**rah**-toh
size, clothes	talla	**tah**-yah
size, shoes	número	**noo**-mehr-oh
white	blanco	**blahn**-koh
black	negro	**neh**-groh
red	rojo	**roh**-hoh
yellow	amarillo	ah-mah-**ree**-yoh
green	verde	**behr**-deh
blue	azul	ah-**thool**
antiques shop	la tienda de antigüedades	lah tee-**ehn**-dah deh ahn-tee-gweh-**dah**-dehs
bakery	la panadería	lah pah-nah-deh-**ree**-ah
bank	el banco	ehl **bahn**-koh
book shop	la librería	lah lee-breh-**ree**-ah
butcher's	la carnicería	lah kahr-nee-theh-**ree**-ah
cake shop	la pastelería	lah pahs-teh-leh-**ree**-ah
chemist's	la farmacia	lah fahr-**mah**-thee-ah
fishmonger's	la pescadería	lah pehs-kah-deh-**ree**-ah
greengrocer's	la frutería	lah froo-teh-**ree**-ah
grocer's	la tienda de comestibles	lah tee-**yehn**-dah deh koh-mehs-**tee**-blehs
hairdresser's	la peluquería	lah peh-loo-keh-**ree**-ah
market	el mercado	ehl mehr-**kah**-doh
newsagent's	el kiosko de prensa	ehl kee-**ohs**-koh deh **prehn**-sah
post office	la oficina de correos	lah oh-fee-**thee**-nah deh kohr-**reh**-ohs
shoe shop	la zapatería	lah thah-pah-teh-**ree**-ah
supermarket	el supermercado	ehl soo-pehr-mehr-**kah**-doh
tobacconist	el estanco	ehl ehs-**tahn**-koh
travel agency	la agencia de viajes	lah ah-**hehn**-thee-ah deh bee-**ah**-hehs

SIGHTSEEING

art gallery	el museo de arte	ehl moo-**seh**-oh deh **ahr**-the
cathedral	la catedral	lah kah-teh-**drahl**
church	la iglesia la basílica	lah ee-**gleh**-see-ah lah bah-**see**-lee-kah
garden	el jardín	ehl hahr-**deen**
library	la biblioteca	lah bee-blee-oh-**teh**-kah
museum	el museo	ehl moo-**seh**-oh
tourist information office	la oficina de turismo	lah oh-fee-**thee**-nah deh too-**rees**-moh
town hall	el ayuntamiento	ehl ah-yoon-tah-mee-**ehn**-toh
closed for holiday	cerrado por vacaciones	thehr-**rah**-doh pohr bah-kah-cee-**oh**-nehs
bus station	la estación de autobuses	lah ehs-tah-ee-**ohn** deh owtoh-**boo**-sehs
railway station	la estación de trenes	lah ehs-tah-thee-**ohn** deh **treh**-nehs

STAYING IN A HOTEL

Do you have a vacant room?	¿Tienen una habitación libre?	tee-**eh**-nehn **oo**-nah ah-bee-tah-**thee-ohn lee**-breh
double room	habitación doble	ah-bee-tah-**thee-ohn doh**-bleh
with double bed	con cama de matrimonio	kohn **kah**-mah deh mah-tree-**moh**-nee-oh
twin room	habitación con dos camas	ah-bee-tah-**thee-ohn** kohn dohs **kah**-mahs
single room	habitación individual	ah-bee-tah-**thee-ohn** een-dee-vee-doo-**ahl**
room with a bath	habitación con baño	ah-bee-tah-**thee-ohn** kohn **bah**-nyoh
shower	ducha	**doo**-chah
porter	el botones	ehl boh-**toh**-nehs
key	la llave	lah **yah**-veh
I have a reservation.	Tengo una habitación reservada.	**tehn**-goh oo-na ah-bee-tah-**thee-ohn** reh-sehr-**bah**-dah

EATING OUT

Have you got a table for ...?	¿Tienen mesa para ...?	tee-**eh**-nehn meh-sah pah-**rah**
I want to reserve a table.	Quiero reservar una mesa.	kee-eh-roh reh-sehr-**bahr** oo-nah meh-**sah**
The bill, please.	La cuenta, por favor.	lah **kwehn**-tah pohr fah-**vohr**
I am a vegetarian	Soy vegetariano/a	soy beh-heh-tah-ree-**ah**-no/na
waitress/ waiter	camarera/ camarero	kah-mah-**reh**-rah/ kah-mah-**reh**-roh
menu	la carta	lah **kahr**-tah
fixed-price menu	menú del día	meh-**noo** dehl **dee**-ah
wine list	la carta de vinos	lah **kahr**-tah deh **bee**-nohs
glass	un vaso	oon **bah**-soh
bottle	una botella	oo-nah boh-**teh**-yah
knife	un cuchillo	oon koo-**chee**-yoh
fork	un tenedor	oon teh-neh-**dohr**
spoon	una cuchara	oo-nah koo-**chah**-rah
breakfast	el desayuno	ehl deh-sah-**yoo**-noh
lunch	la comida/ el almuerzo	lah koh-**mee**-dah/ ehl ahl-**mwehr**-thoh
dinner	la cena	lah **theh**-nah
main course	el primer plato	ehl pree-**mehr plah**-toh
starters	los entrantes	lohs ehn-tran **tehs**
dish of the day	el plato del día	ehl **plah**-toh dehl **dee**-ah
coffee	el café	ehl kah-**feh**
rare	poco hecho	**poh**-koh eh-choh
medium	medio hecho	**meh**-dee-oh eh-choh
well done	muy hecho	mwee **eh**-choh

MENU DECODER

asado	ah-**sah**-doh	roast
el aceite	ah-**thee-eh**-teh	oil
las aceitunas	ah-theh-**toon**-ahs	olives
el agua mineral	**ah**-gwa mee-neh-**rahl**	mineral water
sin gas/con gas	seen gas/kohn gas	still/sparkling
el ajo	**ah**-hoh	garlic
el arroz	ahr-**rohth**	rice
el azúcar	ah-**thoo**-kahr	sugar
la carne	**kahr**-neh	meat
la cebolla	theh-**boh**-yah	onion
la cerveza	thehr-**beh**-thah	beer
el cerdo	**therh**-doh	pork
el chocolate	choh-koh-**lah**-teh	chocolate
el chorizo	choh-**ree**-thoh	chorizo
el cordero	kohr-**deh**-roh	lamb
el fiambre	fee-**ahm**-breh	cold meat
frito	**free**-toh	fried
la fruta	**froo**-tah	fruit
los frutos secos	froo-tohs seh-kohs	nuts
las gambas	**gahm**-bahs	prawns
el helado	eh-**lah**-doh	ice cream
el horno	ahl **ohr**-noh	baked
el huevo	oo-**eh**-voh	egg
el jamón serrano	hah-**mohn** sehr-**rah**-noh	cured ham

el jerez	heh-**rehz**	sherry
la langosta	lahn-**gohs**-tah	lobster
la leche	**leh**-cheh	milk
el limón	lee-**mohn**	lemon
la limonada	lee-moh-**nah**-dah	lemonade
la mantequilla	mahn-teh-**kee**-yah	butter
la manzana	mahn-**thah**-nah	apple
los mariscos	mah-**rees**-kohs	seafood
la menestra	meh-**nehs**-trah	vegetable stew
la naranja	nah-**rahn**-hah	orange
el pan	**pahn**	bread
el pastel	pahs-**tehl**	cake
las patatas	pah-**tah**-tahs	potatoes
el pescado	pehs-**kah**-doh	fish
la pimienta	pee-mee-**yehn**-tah	pepper
el plátano	**plah**-tah-noh	banana
el pollo	**poh**-yoh	chicken
el postre	**pohs**-treh	dessert
el queso	**keh**-soh	cheese
la sal	sahl	salt
las salchichas	sahl-**chee**-chahs	sausages
la salsa	**sahl**-sah	sauce
seco	**seh**-koh	dry
el solomillo	soh-loh-**mee**-yoh	sirloin
la sopa	**soh**-pah	soup
la tarta	**tahr**-tah	pie/cake
el té	teh	tea
la ternera	tehr-**neh**-rah	beef
las tostadas	tohs-**tah**-dahs	toast
el vinagre	bee-**nah**-greh	vinegar
el vino blanco	**bee**-noh **blahn**-koh	white wine
el vino rosado	**bee**-noh roh-**sah**-doh	rosé wine
el vino tinto	**bee**-noh **teen**-toh	red wine

NUMBERS

0	cero	**theh**-roh
1	uno	**oo**-noh
2	dos	dohs
3	tres	trehs
4	cuatro	**kwa**-troh
5	cinco	**theen**-koh
6	seis	says
7	siete	**see**-eh-the
8	ocho	**oh**-choh
9	nueve	**nweh**-veh
10	diez	dee-**ehth**
11	once	**ohn**-theh
12	doce	**doh**-theh
13	trece	**treh**-theh
14	catorce	kah-**tohr**-theh
15	quince	**keen**-theh
16	dieciséis	dee-eh-thee-**seh-ees**
17	diecisiete	dee-eh-thee-see-**eh**-the
18	dieciocho	dee-eh-thee-**oh**-choh
19	diecinueve	dee-eh-thee-**nweh**-veh
20	veinte	**beh**-een-the
21	veintiuno	beh-een-tee-**oo**-noh
22	veintidós	beh-een-tee-**dohs**
30	treinta	**treh**-een-tah
31	treinta y uno	treh-een-tah ee **oo**-noh
40	cuarenta	kwah-**rehn**-tah
50	cincuenta	theen-**kwehn**-tah
60	sesenta	seh-**sehn**-tah
70	setenta	seh-**tehn**-tah
80	ochenta	oh-**chehn**-tah
90	noventa	noh-**vehn**-tah
100	cien	thee-**ehn**
101	ciento uno	thee-**ehn**-toh **oo**-noh
102	ciento dos	thee-**ehn**-toh dohs
200	doscientos	dohs-thee-**ehn**-tohs
500	quinientos	khee-nee-**ehn**-tohs
700	setecientos	seh-teh-thee-**ehn**-tohs
900	novecientos	noh-veh-thee-**ehn**-tohs
1,000	mil	meel
1,001	mil uno	meel **oo**-noh

TIME

one minute	un minuto	oon mee-**noo**-toh
one hour	una hora	oo-na oh-rah
half an hour	media hora	meh-dee-a oh-rah
Monday	lunes	**loo**-nehs
Tuesday	martes	**mahr**-tehs
Wednesday	miércoles	mee-**ehr**-koh-lehs
Thursday	jueves	hoo-**weh**-vehs
Friday	viernes	bee-**ehr**-nehs
Saturday	sábado	**sah**-bah-doh
Sunday	domingo	doh-**meen**-goh

ACKNOWLEDGMENTS

The publisher would like to thank the following for their kind permission to reproduce their photographs

Key: a-above; b-below/bottom; c-centre; f-far; l-left; r-right; t-top

123RF.com: akulamatiau 30-1b; Francisco de Casa Gonzalez 227t; Inacio Pires 11br; Aleksandrs Tihonovs 8clb; Anibal Trejo 61t, 118-9, 120-1b.

4Corners: Francesco Carovillano 194-5t; Jan Wlodarczyk 112-3t.

akg-images: Album / Oronoz 222bl.

Alamy Stock Photo: age fotostock / Juanma Aparicio 98-9t, 221tl, / José Antonio Moreno 166b, / Douglas Williams 178t; Agencja Fotograficzna Caro / Rodriguez 16t; Jerónimo Alba 47tr, 167tr, 173tr, 173br, 193br, 200br, 203tc, 221br; Mark Alexander 214br; All Canada Photos 165br; Alpineguide 157tr; Antiqua Print Gallery 48t; Juanma Aparicio 18crb, 79cra; Arco Images GmbH / K. Loos 45cla; Artokoloro Quint Lox Limited / liszt collection 49bl; Gonzalo Azumendi 130t, 174-5, 193t; David Bagnall 160t; Darren Baker 85tr; Ben Welsh Premium 41br; Bildagentur-online / Moreno 34bl; Biosphoto / Oscar Diez Martinez 171tr; Tibor Bognar 93tr; Piere Bonbon 87t; Katharina Brandt 99br; Michael Brooks 67bl, 70bl, 116cl; Nano Calvo 32-3t; Michelle Chaplow 235br; Chronicle 52tl, 52cb; Sorin Colac 154clb; Colin Palmer Photography 13cr; Neil Cooper 22crb; Luis Dafos 69bc; Ian Dagnall 66-7t, 77tl; dbimages / Allen Brown 206bl; Debu55y 192bl; dleiva 232-3t; downunder 50-1t; EFE News Agency / Raul Caro 44-5t; Greg Balfour Evans 207bl; Peter van Evert 86br, 113cr; Juan Manuel Pelegrín Franco 190-1b; Brian Gadsby 171crb; Maria Galan 128c, 132-3; Saturnino Perez Garrido 168-9t; geogphotos 88cr, 184br; hemis.fr / René Mattes 124cra; Heritage Image Partnership Ltd 51tr, / Index 49cb, / Index / Image 50bc; Kate Hockenhull 146tr; Peter Horree 85bl; HP Canada 124t; IanDagnall Computing 139cr; imageBROKER / Thomas Dressler 47tl, / Moritz Wolf 16bl, 22clb, 29t, 89tr, 138-9b; itdarbs 42-3b; Jam World Images 164-5t, 171cra, 224-5t; Kiko Jimenez 46clb; Jon Arnold Images Ltd 196t; John Kellerman 91t; Chris Knapton 226-7b; Juanca Lagares 123tl; Lanmas 48crb, 50cla, 113bl; Lebrecht Music & Arts 51bl; Jose Lucas 49tl, 122-3b, 140bl, 158br, 191tl; mauritius images GmbH / Walter Bibikow 71tr; Perry Van Munster 35cla, 187tr; The Natural History Museum; London 48bl;

Nature Photographers Ltd / Lee Morgan 171cr; Nature Picture Library / Jose B. Ruiz 137cr; North Wind Picture Archives 50tl; Sean Pavone 18t, 152t; carlos sanchez pereyra 170bl; Will Perrett 91br; peterforsberg 111cra; Pictorial Press Ltd 52bl; The Picture Art Collection 121br; M Ramírez 46cl; Right Perspective Images 101tl; robertharding 2-3, / Stuart Black 24-5ca, / Neil Farrin 206-7t, / Melissa Kuhnell 67clb; Felipe Rodriguez 26tr; Anders Ryman 46crb; Miguel Ángel Fernández Sáinz 171br; Maurice Savage 114bc; Alfredo Garcia Saz 139tl; SCFotos - Stuart Crump Photography 46cla; Alex Segre 105br; Stefan Lange on Alamy 231bl; travelib europe 183tr; Lucas Vallecillos 44-5b, 162b; VWPics / Felipe Rodriguez 101tr; Ross Warner 114tl; Sebastian Wasek 202t; Monica Wells 188b; Ken Welsh 205tr; Hugh Williamson 233bl; Wim Wiskerke 80tl; Xinhua / Xie Haining 53crb.

Barro Azul Cultural Management: 27clb.

Depositphotos Inc: mmedp 208bl.

Dreamstime.com: Christian Bertrand 45crb; Christine Bird 142-3; Artur Bogacki 115b; Rimma Bondarenko 35br; Brasilnut 29br, 54-5; Boris Breytman 10ca; Ryhor Bruyeu 40-1t, 40-1b; Francisco Jose Martín Cabrera 230tl; Carpaumar 146bl; Ramon Carretero 12clb; Sorin Colac 10-1b, 214t; Felipe Caparros Cruz 28br, 129t, 148-9; Tomasz Czajkowski 219t; Dwnld777 29clb; Sergey Dzyuba 158t; Fosterss 33cla; Antonio Francisco Alvarez Gimenez 222-3t; Nataliia Gr 20cr; Olivier Guiberteau 154bl; Csaba Henriksen 231clb; Silvia Blaszczyszyn Jakiello 47cra; Joserpizarro 8cla, 49tr, 88cra; García Juan 172bl; Rami Katzav 13t; Karol Kozlowski 100tl; Lachris77 203b; Leonovo 18cr; Lifestyle27 10clb; Nikolai Link 49cra; Lunamarina 58c, 62-3; Marazem 26-7b; Minnystock 20bl; Mistervlad 31cla; Juan Moyano 47clb; Aitor Muñoz Muñoz 145br; Irina Paley 28tl; Sean Pavone 8-9b, 82-3, 186t, 236-7; Lamberto Jesus Luque Perez 30-1t; William Perry 50clb; Photogolfer 60t, 67crb, 68t, 94-5,102tl; Radiokafka 22br; Rui Santos 31crb, 218bl; Sborisov 16cr; Sjors737 22t; Opreanu Roberto Sorin 20crb; Ivan Soto 12ct; Alena Stalmashonak 18bl; Steveheap 235tl; Aleksandar Todorovic 156bl; Typhoonski 13br; Stefano Valeri 11crb; Cezary Wojtkowski 217cra.

Elio Studio: Emilio Simon 16crb.

EME Catedral Mercer Hotel: 37tr.

Festival de Jerez: Javier Fergo 37cr, 37cb.

Foodie & Experiences, Cordoba: Luis Muñoz Photography 24tl.

Getty Images: 500Px Plus / Jgarciad 25tl; AFP / Jose Luis Roca 46cr; age fotostock / Eduardo Grund 147b; Corbis Documentary / Laurie Chamberlain 93crb; De Agostini Picture Library / G. Dagli Orti 51crb; Hulton Archive / Michael Putland 53bl; The Image Bank / Silvestre Garcia - IntuitivoFilms 200-1t; Lonely Planet Images / Dan Herrick 81b; Moment / Luis Dafos 216-7t, / fhm 184-5t, / John Harper 41cla, / Angel Villalba 197br; Moment Unreleased / Ventura Carmona 84b; Redferns / Jordi Vidal 47cla; Sygma / Christine Spengler 52-3t; Universal Images Group / VW Pics / Pascal Saez 46cra.

Isla Magica: 38tc, 38-9t.

iStockphoto.com: benedek 126-7; Lux Blue 140-1t; Chalffy 60bl, 106-7; Javier Conejero 144cra; Costamundo 228-9; E+ / Imgorthand 42tl, / Saro17 25tr, 43br, / WillSelarep 131t, 210-1; Elijah-Lovkoff 88b; FrankCornfield 53tr; Jiann Ho 32bl; horstgerlach 183br; jacquesvandinteren 144t; JohnnyGreig 33crb; juanorihuela 24cra; Marcus Lindstrom 36-7t; m-martinez 43clb; Jon Chica Parada 92bl; Ruhey 111t; SeanPavonePhoto 102-3b; Sloot 11t, 38bl, 204-5b; stefanopolitimarkovina 180-1t; titoslack 77tr; Worledit 43tr.

Museum Picasso Malaga: Eduardo Grund 27tr.

naturepl.com: Wild Wonders of Europe / Oxford 137clb, 137br.

Ocio Aventura Cerro Gordo: 24tr.

Museo Parque de las Ciencias: 39b.

Planta Baja: Javier Martin Ruiz 36bl.

Río Azul Beers: Diego Gallego 34-5t.

Robert Harding Picture Library: Kav Dadfar 20t; Luis Davilla 6-7; Eduardo Grund 47crb; Roberto Moiola 79t; Ramon Navarro 136-7t; Lucas Vallecillos 217br.

Shutterstock: Jose Ignacio Soto 198-9.

SuperStock: age fotostock / George Munday 225br.

Torre Sevilla: 125br.

Unsplash: Akshay Nanavati / @anphotos 12-3b; Joan Oger / @joanoger 59t, 72-3; Okwaeze Otusi / @oo7ab 8cl; Mateusz Plinta / @matplinta 4.

We Love Granada Market : 27br.

Front flap images
4Corners: Jan Wlodarczyk t; **Alamy Stock Photo:** robertharding / Stuart Black cb, Ross Warner cla; **Dreamstime.com:** Sean Pavone bl, Stefano Valeri cra; **Unsplash:** Akshay Nanavati / @anphotos br.

Sheet map cover
Dreamstime.com: Ionut David.

Cover images
Front and Spine: **Dreamstime.com:** Ionut David.
Back: **Alamy Stock Photo:** M Ramírez c, Lucas Vallecillos cla; **Dreamstime.com:** Sorin Colac tr, Ionut David b.

For further information see: www.dkimages.com

Penguin
Random
House

Main Contributers Lynnette McCurdy Bastida,
Ben Ffrancon Davies, Daniel Stables, David Baird,
Martin Symington, Nigel Tisdall

Senior Editor Ankita Awasthi Tröger

Senior Designer Bess Daly

Project Editor Rebecca Flynn

Designers Van Anh Le, Ankita Sharma,
Vinita Venugopal, Priyanka Thakur

Factchecker Lynnette McCurdy Bastida

Editor Louise Abbott

Proofreader Kathryn Glendenning

Indexer Hilary Bird

Senior Picture Researcher Ellen Root

Picture Research Marta Bescos,
Sumita Khatwani, Rituraj Singh,
Manpreet Kaur, Vagisha Pushp

Illustrators Richard Draper,
Isidoro González-Adalid Cabezas
(Acanto Arquitectura y Urbanismo S.L.),
Steven Gyapay, Claire Littlejohn, Maltings,
Chris Orr, John Woodcock

Cartographic Editor James Macdonald

Cartography Subhashree Bharati,
Mohammad Hassan

Jacket Designers Van Anh Le, Bess Daly,
Maxine Pedliham

Jacket Picture Research Susie Watters

Senior DTP Designer Jason Little

DTP Designer Rohit Rojal

Producer Kariss Ainsworth

Managing Editor Hollie Teague

Art Director Maxine Pedliham

Publishing Director Georgina Dee

MIX
Paper from
responsible sources
FSC™ C018179
www.fsc.org

**The information in this
DK Eyewitness Travel Guide is checked regularly.**
Every effort has been made to ensure that this book
is as up-to-date as possible at the time of going to
press. Some details, however, such as telephone
numbers, opening hours, prices, gallery hanging
arrangements and travel information, are liable to
change. The publishers cannot accept responsibility
for any consequences arising from the use of this
book, nor for any material on third party websites,
and cannot guarantee that any website address
in this book will be a suitable source of travel
information. We value the views and suggestions
of our readers very highly. Please write to: Publisher,
DK Eyewitness Travel Guides, Dorling Kindersley,
80 Strand, London, WC2R 0RL, UK, or email:
travelguides@dk.com

First edition 1996

Published in Great Britain by Dorling Kindersley Limited,
80 Strand, London, WC2R 0RL

Published in the United States by DK Publishing,
1450 Broadway, Suite 801, New York, NY 10018

Copyright © 1996, 2020 Dorling Kindersley Limited
A Penguin Random House Company
19 20 21 22 10 9 8 7 6 5 4 3 2 1

A CIP catalog record for this book
is available from the British Library.

A catalog record for this book is available
from the Library of Congress.

ISSN: 1542 1554
ISBN: 978 0 2414 0 8308

Printed and bound in China.

www.dk.com